Practicing Organization Development

**The Change Agent Series
for Groups and Organizations**

MISSION STATEMENT

The books in this series are intended to be cutting-edge, state-of-the-art, innovative approaches to organization change and development. They are written for and by practitioners interested in new approaches to facilitating effective organization change. They are geared to providing both theory and advice on practical applications.

SERIES EDITORS

**William J. Rothwell
Roland Sullivan
Kristine Quade**

EDITORIAL BOARD

**David Bradford
W. Warner Burke
Edith Whitfield Seashore
Robert Tannenbaum
Christopher G. Worley
Shaolin Zhang**

Other Practicing Organization Development Titles

Organization Development
and Consulting

With Contributions by..

Dean Anderson
Norma Jean Anderson
Barbara Brewer
Cheryl Gitlin
Jerry B. Harvey
Ginger Lapid-Bogda
Joseph Luft
Robert Tannenbaum

Organization Development and Consulting

Perspectives and Foundations

Fred Massarik

Marissa Pei-Carpenter

Foreword by Richard Beckhard

JOSSEY-BASS/PFEIFFER
A Wiley Company
www.pfeiffer.com

Published by

JOSSEY-BASS/PFEIFFER

A Wiley Company
989 Market Street
San Francisco, CA 94103-1741
415.433.1740; Fax 415.433.0499
800.274.4434; Fax 800.569.0443

www.pfeiffer.com

Jossey-Bass/Pfeiffer is a registered trademark of Jossey-Bass Inc., A Wiley Company.

ISBN: 0-7879-4664-8

Library of Congress Cataloging-in-Publication Data

Massarik, Fred.
  Organization development and consulting: perspectives and
foundations / Fred Massarik, Marissa Pei-Carpenter.
    p. cm.—(The practicing organization development
series)
Includes bibliographical references and index.
  ISBN 0-7879-4664-8 (alk. paper)—
1. Organizational change. 2. Business consultants. 3.
Management. I. Pei-Carpenter, Marissa. II. Title. III. Series.
  HD58.8 .M323 2002
  658.4'06—dc21

2001005789

Printed in the United States of America

We at Jossey-Bass strive to use the most environmentally sensitive paper stocks available to us. Our publications are printed on acid-free recycled stock whenever possible, and our paper always meets or exceeds minimum GPO and EPA requirements.

Acquiring Editor: Josh Blatter

Director of Development: Kathleen Dolan Davies

Developmental Editor: Susan Rachmeler

Editor: Rebecca Taff

Senior Production Editor: Dawn Kilgore

Manufacturing Supervisor: Becky Carreño

Interior and Cover Design: Bruce Lundquist

Illustrations: Richard Sheppard

Printing 10 9 8 7 6 5 4 3 2 1

Contents

List of Tables
and Figures

Foreword
to the Series

ON 1967, Warren Bennis, Ed Schein, and I were faculty members of the Sloan School of Management at MIT. We decided to produce a series of paperback books that collectively would describe the state of the field of organization development (OD). Organization development as a field had been named by myself and several others from our pioneer change effort at General Mills in Minneapolis, Minnesota, some ten years earlier.

Today I define OD as "a systemic and systematic change effort, using behavioral science knowledge and skill, to transform the organization to a new state."

In any case, several books and many articles had been written, but there was no consensus on whether OD was a field of practice, an area of study, or a profession. We had not even established OD as a theory or even as a practice.

We decided that there was a need for something that would describe the state of OD. Our intention was to each write a book and also to recruit three other authors. After some searching, we found a young editor who had just joined the small publishing house of Addison-Wesley. We made contact, and the series was born. Our audience was to be human resource professionals who spent their time consulting with managers in their development through various small-group activities, such as team building. More than thirty books have been published in that series, and the series has had a life of its own. We just celebrated its thirtieth anniversary.

At last year's National OD Network Conference, I said that it was time for the OD profession to change and transform itself. Is that not what we change agents tell our clients to do? This new Jossey-Bass/Pfeiffer series will do just that. It can be seen as:

- A documentation of the re-invention of OD;

- An effort that will take us to the next level; and

- A practical effort to transfer to the world the theory and practice of leading-edge practitioners and theorists.

The books in this new series will thus prove to be valuable resources for change agents to keep current with the new and leading-edge ideas and practices.

May this very exciting change agent series be most creative and innovative. May it give our field a renewed burst of energy and awareness.

Richard Beckhard
Written on Labor Day weekend 1999 from my summer cabin near Bethel, Maine

Introduction
to the Series

THERE ARE WATERSHED MOMENTS—moments in history that change everything after them. The attack on Pearl Harbor was one of those. The bombing of Hiroshima was another. The terrorist attack on the World Trade Center in New York City was our most recent. All resulted in significant change that transformed many lives and organizations.

Practicing Organization Development: The Change Agent Series for Groups and Organizations is a series of books that was launched to help those who must cope with or create change. The series is designed for the authors to share what is working or not working, to provoke critical thinking about change, and to offer creative ways to deal with change, rather than the destructive ones noted above.

The Current State of Change Management and Organization Development

Almost as soon as the ink was dry on the first wave of books published in this series, we heard that its focus was too narrow. We heard that the need for theory and practice extended beyond OD into change management. More than one respected authority urged us to reconsider our focus, moving beyond OD to include books on change management generally.

Organization development is not the only way that change can be engineered or coped with in organizational settings. We always knew that, of course. And we remain grounded in the view that change management, however it is carried out, should be based on such values as respect for the individual, participation and involvement in change by those affected by it, and interest in the improvement of organizational settings on many levels—including productivity improvement, but also improvement in achieving work/life balance and in a values-based approach to management and to change.

A Brief History of the Genesis of the Series

A few years ago, and as a direct result of the success of *Practicing Organization Development: A Guide for Practitioners* by Rothwell, Sullivan, and McLean, the publisher—feeling that OD was experiencing a rebirth of interest in the United States and in other nations—wanted to launch a new OD series. The goal of this new series was not to replace, or even to compete directly with, the well-established Addison-Wesley OD Series (edited by Edgar Schein). Instead, as the editors saw it, the series would provide a means by which the most promising authors in OD whose voices had not previously been heard could share their ideas. The publisher enlisted the support of Bill Rothwell, Roland Sullivan, and Kristine Quade to turn the dream of a series into a reality.

This series was long in the making and has been steadily evolving since its inception. The original vision was an ambitious one—and involved no less than reinventing OD and re-energizing interest in the research and practice surrounding it. Sponsoring books was one means to that end.

There were to be others. Indeed, after nearly a year of planning, the editors are pleased to note that the series is hosting a website (pfeiffer.com/go/od). Far more than just a place to advertise the series, the site serves as a real-time learning community for OD practitioners. Additionally, the series is hosting a conference, entitled "Practicing Cutting-Edge OD," which is to be held at The Pennsylvania State University in University Park in April 2002 (see www.outreach.psu.edu/C&I/CuttingEdgeOD).

What Distinguishes the Books in this Series

The books in this series are meant to be challenging, cutting-edge, and state-of-the-art in their approach to OD and change management. The goal of the series is to provide an outlet for proven authorities in OD and change management who have not put their ideas into print or for up-and-coming writers in OD and change management who have new, sometimes unorthodox, approaches that are stimulating and exciting. Some books in this series describe inspirational concepts that can lead to actionable change and purvey ideas so new that they are not fully developed.

Unique to this series is the cutting-edge emphasis, the immediate applicability, and the ease of transferability of the concepts. The aim of this series is nothing less than to reinvent, re-energize, and reinvigorate OD and change management. In each book, we have also recommended that the author(s) provide:

- A research base of some kind, meaning new information derived from practice and/or systematic investigation and
- Practical tools, worksheets, case studies, and other ready-to-go approaches that help the authors drag "theory" to "practice" to make these new, cutting-edge approaches more concrete.

Subject Matter That Will (and Will Not) Be Covered

The books in this series are varied in their approach, but they are united by their focus. All share an emphasis on organization development (OD) and change management (CM). Hence, books in this series are about participative change efforts. They are not about such other popular topics as leadership, management development, consulting, or group dynamics—unless those topics are treated in new, cutting-edge ways and are geared to OD and change management practitioners.

This Book

In *Organization Development and Consulting: Perspectives and Foundations*, Fred Massarik and Marissa Pei-Carpenter explore the current condition and future prospects of the field of organization development. Acknowledging the rich and varied history of the field, the authors examine OD concepts in light of the rapidly changing environment in which organizations exist today. Massarik and Pei-Carpenter stress the importance of self-knowledge for the practitioner and of the relationship between practitioner and client. These elements then serve as the basis for an in-depth look at change and the consulting process.

William J. Rothwell
University Park, PA

Roland Sullivan
Deephaven, MN

Kristine Quade
Minnetonka, MN

Statement
of the Board

IT IS OUR PLEASURE TO PARTICIPATE in and influence the start up of *Practicing Organization Development: The Change Agent Series for Groups and Organizations.* The purpose of the series is to stimulate the profession and influence how organization change is defined and practiced. This statement is intended to set the context for the series by addressing three important questions: (1) What are the key issues facing organization change and development in the 21st Century? (2) Where does—and should—OD fit in the field of organization change and development? and (3) What is the purpose of this series?

What Are the Key Issues Facing Organization Change and Development in the 21st Century?

One of the questions is the extent to which leaders can control forces or can only be reactive. Will globalization and external forces be so powerful that they will prevent organizations from being able to "stay ahead of the change curve"? And what will be the role of technology, especially information technology, in the change process? To what extent can it be a carrier of change (as well as a source of change)?

What will the relationship be between imposed change and collaborative change? Will the increased education of the workforce demand the latter, or will the requirement of having to make fundamental changes demand leadership that sets goals that participants would not willingly set on their own? And what is the relationship between these two forms of change?

Who will be the change agent? Is this a separate profession, or will that increasingly be the responsibility of the organization's leaders? If the latter, how does that change the role of the change professional?

What will be the role of values for change in the 21st Century? Will the key values be performance—efficiency and effectiveness? And what role will the humanistic values of more traditional OD play? Or will the growth of knowledge (and human competence) as an organization's core competence make this a moot point in that performance can only occur if one takes account of humanistic values?

What is the relationship between other fields and the area of change? Can any change process that is not closely linked with strategy be truly effective? Can change agents focus only on process, or do they need to be knowledgeable and actively involved in the organization's products/services and understand the market niche in which the organization operates?

Where Does—or Should—OD Fit in the Field of Organization Change and Development?

We offer the following definition of OD to stimulate debate:

> Organization development is a system-wide and values-based collaborative process of applying behavioral science knowledge to the adaptive development, improvement, and reinforcement of such organizational features as the strategies, structures, processes, people, and cultures that lead to organization effectiveness.

The definition suggests that OD can be understood in terms of its several foci:

First, *OD is a system-wide process.* It works with whole systems. In the past, the bias has been toward working at the individual and group levels. More recently, the focus has shifted to organizations and multi-organization systems. We support that trend in general but honor and acknowledge the fact that the traditional focus on smaller systems is both legitimate and necessary.

Second, *OD is values-based.* Traditionally, OD has attempted to distinguish itself from other forms of planned change and applied behavioral science by promoting a set of humanistic values and by emphasizing the importance of personal growth as a key to its practice. Today, that focus is blurred and there is much debate about the value base underlying the practice of OD. We support a more formal and direct conversation about what these values are and how the field is related to them.

Third, *OD is collaborative.* Our first value commitment as OD practitioners is to bring about an inclusive, diverse workforce with a focus of integrating differences into a world-wide culture mentality.

Fourth, *OD is based on behavioral science knowledge.* Organization development should incorporate and apply knowledge from sociology, psychology, anthropology, technology, and economics toward the end of making systems more effective. We support the continued emphasis in OD on behavioral science knowledge and believe that OD practitioners should be widely read and comfortable with several of the disciplines.

Fifth, *OD is concerned with the adaptive development, improvement, and reinforcement of strategies, structures, processes, people, culture, and other features of organizational life.* This statement describes not only the organizational elements that are the target of change, but also describes the process by which effectiveness is increased. That is, OD works in a variety of areas, and it is focused on improving these areas. We believe that such a statement of process and content strongly implies that a key feature of OD is the transference of knowledge and skill to the system so that it is more able to handle and manage change in the future.

Sixth and finally, *OD is about improving organization effectiveness.* It is not just about making people happy; it is also concerned with meeting financial goals, improving productivity, and addressing stakeholder satisfaction. We believe that OD's future is closely tied to the incorporation of this value in its purpose and the demonstration of this objective in its practice.

This definition raises a host of questions:

- Are OD and organization change and development one and the same, or are these different?

- Has OD become just a collection of tools, methods, and techniques? Has it lost its values?

- Does it talk "systems," but ignore them in practice?

- Are consultants facilitators of change or activists of change?

- To what extent should consulting be driven by consultant value versus holding the value only of increasing the client's effectiveness?

- How can OD practitioners help formulate strategy, shape the strategy development process, contribute to the content of strategy, and drive how strategy will be implemented?

- How can OD focus on the drivers of change external to individuals, such as the external environment, business strategy, organization change, and culture change, as well as on the drivers of change internal to individuals, such as individual interpretations of culture, behavior, style, and mindset?

- How much should OD be part of the competencies of all leaders? How much should it be the sole domain of professionally trained, career-oriented OD practitioners?

What Is the Purpose of this Series?

This series is intended to provide current thinking about organization change and development as a field and to provide practical approaches based on sound theory and research. It is targeted for full-time external or internal change practitioners; top executives in charge of enterprise-wide change; and managers, HR practitioners, training and development professionals, and others who have responsibility for change in organizational and trans-organizational settings. At the same time, these books will be directed toward cutting-edge thinking and state-of-the-art approaches. In some cases, the ideas, approaches, or techniques described are still evolving, so the books are intended to open up dialogue.

We know that the books in this series will provide a leading forum for thought-provoking dialogue within the field.

About the Board Members

David Bradford is senior lecturer in organizational behavior at the Graduate School of Business, Stanford University, Palo Alto, California. He is co-author (with Allan R. Cohen) of *Managing for Excellence, Influence Without Authority,* and *POWER UP: Transforming Organizations Through Shared Leadership.*

W. Warner Burke is professor of psychology and education in the department of organization and leadership at Teachers College at Columbia University in New York. He also serves as a senior advisor to PricewaterhouseCoopers. His most recent publication is *Business Profiles of Climate Shifts: Profiles of Change Makers*, with William Trahant and Richard Koonce.

Edith Whitfield Seashore is an organization consultant and co-founder (with Morley Segal) of AUNTL Masters Program in Organization Development. She is co-author of *What Did You Say?* and *The Art of Giving and Receiving Feedback* and co-editor of *The Promise of Diversity*.

Robert Tannenbaum is emeritus professor of development of human systems, Graduate School of Management, University of California, Los Angeles, and recipient of the Lifetime Achievement Award by the National OD Network. He has published numerous books, including *Human Systems Development* (with Newton Margulies and Fred Massarik).

Christopher G. Worley is director, MSOD Program, Pepperdine University, Malibu, California. He is co-author of *Organization Development and Change* (7th ed.), with Tom Cummings, and of *Integrated Strategic Change*, with David Hitchin and Walter Ross.

Shaolin Zhang is senior manager of organization development for Motorola (China) Electronics Ltd. He received his master's degree in American Studies from Beijing Foreign Studies University, Beijing, China, and holds a Ph.D. in sociology from York University, Toronto, Ontario.

My work on this book is dedicated
to the memory of Irving R. Weschler,
who would have enjoyed its process
and completion.

—Fred Massarik

My work on this book is dedicated
to my father, who died of lymphoma
in the Spring of 2000. I miss your
wisdom and quiet strength, dad—
whatever I have, I owe to your spirit;
whoever I am, I am part of you. And
to my new quiet strength, Kevin, my
support beam and loving father of
my happy girls.

—Marissa Pei-Carpenter

Acknowledgments

THIS IS AN NTL BOOK, rooted directly and indirectly in the evolution of experiential learning, from NTL's beginnings, circa 1947, to the present. The first listed co-author (Fred Massarik) has been privileged to relate to this evolution over the years in various roles and capacities and expresses his appreciation for these opportunities.

More immediately, the co-authors wish to thank the NTL Board Members and Executives who have been associated with the development of this book. They include the following:

Lennox E. Joseph, Ph.D., President/CEO, 1996–1998

Diane Porter, M.A., President/CEO, 1998-present

Jacqueline S. Bearce

Racine Brown

Ian Bryden

Al Cooke

Kaye Craft

Richard P. Francisco

Barbara Greig

Anne Litwin

Margaret James Neill

Patricia Parham

Lindbergh Sata

Suzanne Stier

Ted Tschudy

Richard Weber

Edward L. Williams

Jane Lee Wolfe

Also, we wish to thank all reviewers who have provided their viewpoints at various stages of manuscript preparation; we gladly acknowledge their candid and helpful inputs.

A special "big thank you" goes to Susan Rachmeler, Jossey-Bass/Pfeiffer development editor, who enhanced and indeed saved the editorial process following a series of happenings and mis-happenings, including publisher mergers, acquisitions, and shifting policies that complicated the co-authors' writing efforts and challenged their respective equanimity.

Finally, the principal co-authors are delighted to include in this book the statements of a number of distinguished colleagues, highlighting their significant contributions to OD as practice and as discipline.

And, of course, the most important *dramatis personae* are yet to come: the readers of this volume. We thank all of you for what you may say to us in times ahead as the field of organization development affirms its commitment to the improvement of the human condition from individual to organization to society.

Fred Massarik
Marissa Pei-Carpenter

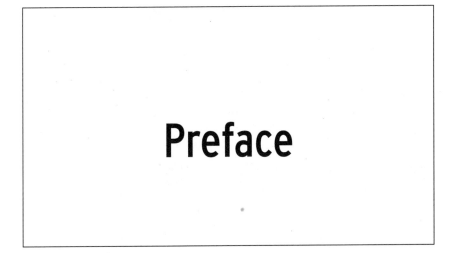

Preface

EVERY TIME IN HISTORY has its favorite phrases, slogans, and passwords. Sometimes these expressions of valued belief flash briefly across the horizon and then pass into oblivion. Other times they become more lasting parts of people's vocabulary and thinking. Often they prove to be the proverbial "old wine in new bottles." By this time, the term "organization development" (OD) has been around long enough so that we may consider it as a symbol or label for something of some substance. Just what "it" is, was, or is becoming is subject to some controversy. A few observers even note that OD is "dead." Yet, consultants in large numbers continue to practice a craft under this heading. Organization development networks continue in their meetings, and every once in a while the term surfaces in various training-and-development and human resources operations. Of course, over the years a number of books have been written under the OD heading (see the Bibliography at the end of the book). These books have varied widely in their approach, and some have had impact in defining the field in greater measure than others.

Now that we are in a new millennium, it is appropriate to get down to work with new perspectives and to re-examine the present status—as well as the future—of organization development. No matter what the fate of the term, there is no doubt that the concepts involved in OD relate to fields of inquiry that have their roots in a most distant past and that remain of paramount importance in contemporary practice, in management, and in coping with a world in continuing rapid change. However the current definition may suggest the field's contours, questions such as, "Why do people in organizations and elsewhere behave as they do?" and "How can we constructively influence organizations by purposeful action?" have been asked throughout the ages, in varied vocabularies. Organization development today needs to address these questions in highly dynamic situations—often under extreme and unpredictable conditions. The central focus on the OD consultant and client(s) as *persons* and on *the self* existing and coping within complex systems constitutes an important cornerstone in this quest.

We regard this volume primarily as a *foundations book.* We present positions that we consider to be basic regardless of vintage or source, whether old or new, drawn from whatever discipline. In this sense, this book is essentially unconfined by conventional academic boundaries. It is not a "psychology book," nor even a "management book." The source discipline list—if it were subject to Internet search—would be a long one, including both traditional areas of inquiry as well as broad study fields: human sciences, human systems, psychology, sociology, anthropology, political science, human engineering, mental health, psychotherapy, psychiatry, history, religion, and philosophy, among others. Some aspects of philosophy themselves cut across a range of fields (for example, parts of psychology, governance in political science, the nature of human existence, and so forth) and thus some philosophic overlay is reflected in our concepts.

Yet focus is required within this challenging territory. No doubt some would prefer one or another source discipline (social psychology? industrial/organizational psychology? organizational behavior?). However, our purpose here is to provide eclectic resources and guidelines that may assist the reader, including the OD consultant and those who teach and study organization development in universities and elsewhere, to find their ways within OD's wide parameters. "Feel" and intuitive insight are viewed as welcome companions in this context, importantly linked to asserted "fact," to procedure, and to intervention technique. In fact, we have seen instances where technique and tools were overemphasized to the detriment of the intervention.

This is not to suggest that techniques or tools are less important than intuition. To clarify, tools themselves *are* indeed useful for practitioners in so far as they enhance skills and abilities for work with clients, in appropriate joint effort. What is being cautioned against is a strictly tool-driven approach, which is unfortunately very common in recent OD practice. The touting of any tools as "magic potions" not only hurts the OD field as responsible endeavor but also contributes to non-systemic, linear, short-term thinking, which we discourage to assure sound growth and development by all concerned.

Whether a book becomes a "textbook" depends on many factors. Many a textbook is written with a specific course format in mind, to entice a set of instructors in academic institutions who happen to offer particular courses under certain rubrics. We would expect that some institutions teaching OD would include faculty who may choose to use this book as a principal reading. However, course offerings include all kinds of titles and labels, for a variety of reasons both intellectual and procedural. Thus the book may also prove of some use in courses in organizational behavior, industrial psychology, industrial sociology, training and development, human resources, and the like and in practical workshops and retreats. On the other hand, it is our experience that many such learning events go beyond use of a single text, reaching out to a variety of differentiated reading, cases, videos, and all kinds of supplementary materials.

Guiding Viewpoints

We have already alluded to some core positions:

- Emphasis on the *OD consultant and client as persons,* and on the self in complex systems;
- The relevance of *"feel" and intuition* together with fact and technique;
- The primary importance of *real people* doing real things in real time holistically—not high-level abstractions in rarified conceptual space, nor techniques recited by rote;
- *Broad scope and wide range of disciplinary sources;*
- Especially in the conceptual sections *"theory"* and *"philosophic breadth"* seen as not antithetical to *"practice"* and *"application."* Indeed, we believe that sound theory and effective practice support each other, echoing Kurt Lewin's much cited proposition to the effect that there is nothing so practical as a good theory[1].

Additional Viewpoints

In addition to our core premises, we find the following points to be particularly relevant in today's rapidly changing world.

Non-Linearity. Neat linear relationships prove elusive. It is our position that "quick fix" linear approaches (even if extensive), although preferred by some managers as well as occasionally by OD consultants, are not likely to bring substantial lasting results. Vogues rule only temporarily. Just feeling good after reciting a (usually numbered) set of rules or admonitions (for example, "7 Great Packages" or "30-Minute Ways of Doing Stuff") turns out to be simplistic.

No Guarantees: Complexity. Reassuringly firm answers cannot be guaranteed in OD practice, especially if such answers adduce overgeneralization or are based on superficial if pleasing rhetoric. It is our view that OD must be rooted in the considerable available knowledge about the human condition, recognizing real-life complexity.

Values as Cornerstone. Further, we will emphasize that the issue of values is central and somehow inevitably hidden within the term "development." Value is the essential cornerstone. Just what is to be improved and how such improvement is to occur depends on values chosen. There is no value-free OD.

The Audience

This book is addressed to both practitioners and academics. The emphasis, however, is on practice. In this approach, we include theoretic positions that *underlie* practice often rooted in ideas that we believe should be understood by practitioners, regardless of their formal academic training. In turn, academics, many of whom are also practitioners in some sense or concerned with the nature of the consultative process, may want to explore what goes on explicitly and implicitly in the world of OD practice in action. Managers with special concern with the "people side" of organizations as well may find this book of interest.

The Structure of This Book

This is not intended to be a "cookbook"; this is not intended to be an "encyclopedia." That is to say that we are not presenting discrete "recipes" (as might be contained in a handbook of interventions), nor are we covering all nooks and crannies of an evolving field. Overall, we highlight certain aspects of the field as seen by co-authors and contributors, for the most part in generic and eclectic perspective, and provide selective examples of interventions as these play out in the spirit of proposed viewpoints. Finally, we provide some reflections and orientations to the future.

In Chapter 1, A Way In, we lay a general foundation for the work ahead. In this section we suggest three dimensions—words, values, and management—to guide our exposition, providing steps toward exploring the nature of OD as a field of thought and application.

Why Words? It is evident that words remain prime (but not sole) vehicles for communicating meaning. We cannot ignore this presumably obvious but compelling circumstance, and we cannot take for granted that words speak for themselves[2]. As it relates to the study of signs—and indeed words are necessarily signs and symbols representing something thought about by human beings—*the words of OD* carry meanings that ultimately guide what OD is all about.

To the extent that OD is concerned with change (more of this later), words necessarily establish a basis for value propositions that inevitably underlie any change effort. Mission statements and operational values come from constellations of words, ranging from benign emptiness to "fighting words" to admonitions intended to motivate certain ways of doing things. Thus, words are not to be taken lightly as we establish a substructure for organization development today. In the formulation of mission statements, as well as in more delimited instruments such as business plans, words and the meanings imputed create a framework within which value statements and eventually mandated task formulations necessarily grow. We urge, therefore, that words and their interpretations be carefully considered in our effort to understand and enhance OD's potential usefulness.

Why Values? As noted, "development" (as in organization *development*) and its closely allied relative, "change," imply values. For instance, if we are to develop, then in what direction with what desired outcomes? The concern with teleology— the study of goals and end states—cannot be avoided. Do we expect development to be totally random? Even that would not prove to be truly devoid of valuation. People try to make sense even in chaos. And change, if it is intended to deal with "change for the *better*," cannot escape the requirement to determine what is "better." And surely what is seen as better for some may appear to be worse for others. We must be cautious not to lay *our* definition of what is better on other people or systems[3].

Why Management? There is no OD unless there is management; OD exists in a "management-intensive" environment. Managers necessarily determine policy and operations and emerge as direct or implicit clients. Whatever the power distribution, including power emanating at the employee or "associates" level, the *managerial function* is pervasive.

We then proceed to exposition of some basic ideas that, we believe, "make a difference" at all points in the OD process. In Chapter 2, A Framework for OD Consultation, we consider an array of constructs at various levels of complexity that we believe need to be taken into account in virtually all OD engagements. This does not suggest that each must be given equal weight in comparison to all the others; indeed, their relative importance varies with the specifics of the engagement. But the OD consultant will do well to at least consider one and all, examining what is at stake in particular emphases within this panoply of nine Cs and an S-R: Consultants, Clients, Capabilities, Contacts, Contracts, Contexts, Cultures, Chaos, Change, Self, and Relationships. (As noted as well in actual use of the nine Cs, we're apprehensive about the potential danger of "numbering"; such 1-2-3 efforts run the risk of oversimplifying and of losing sight of interrelationships and holistic qualities in the OD process.)

It is immediately clear that these concepts do not line up in linear fashion. And so it was in determining the order of the subsequent parts of this book. But as a matter of priority, we urge prompt attention to the core: Chapter 3, The Self. In our view, OD in its essence is fundamentally involved with self and basic human interactions.

Within this frame, the contributions of Joseph Luft and of Barbara Brewer are instructive. Luft's "Johari Window," originally conceived with Harrington Ingham, is well-known but warrants reflection, concise restatement, and a contemporary revisitation. And Barbara Brewer's Disclosure Exercise points powerfully to the importance of the oft-unspoken that deeply influences how people—consultants, clients, and others—feel about themselves.

Yet there are more outward and operational role issues involved that relate directly to the kind of job the consultant holds. Here a practical task differentiation presents itself: The similarities and contrasts that are associated with *internal vs. external* consultant roles. We find a set of differences in degree, not kind, and a number of tradeoffs in how the work is done.

With the consultant's personal, interpersonal, and role dynamics considered, we next focus on clients and on the nature of client systems: Chapter 4, Working with the Client. We hold that, with rare exception, there are always multiple clients.

For instance, the "presenting" client at the outset of an engagement may fade and be superceded by a later "actual" client. A "client matrix" is provided to help our thinking on this, noting principal, shadow, and peripheral clients and stakeholders.

In OD, virtually since the field's inception, some notion of change has played a pivotal role, and our present definition of OD as well embodies this idea in more comprehensive context. In Chapter 5, Rethinking the Issue of Change, we proceed to make explicit some selected theoretic and practical precepts that animate the field's directions. Loud and clear are caveats (a) that change in various forms is inevitable and more than ever non-linear, and (b) that change occurs *simultaneously* in any number of interrelated systems (consultant, client, culture, and so forth). Organization development never faces a metaphoric pond of comforting tranquility, nor can we compare simple cause-and-effect from OD's activity to a particular ripple on the pond or outcome.

One encompassing concept that has received heightened attention in OD and organization theory in recent years is culture. Within its scope falls a most remarkably diverse range of subconcepts: culture in groups and organizations, beliefs, traditions, artifacts, heroes, ideologies, and so on. We regard culture as a highly significant but sometimes unwieldy variable in OD's quest, especially in light of asserted efforts to bring about "culture change." In Chapter 6, Changing Cultures: Concepts and Constraints, we deal with some of the underlying issues and discuss some salient cultural dimensions.

Having discussed the pervasive issues of self, client, and change, we then move on to the consulting process. In Chapter 7, Getting on with It: Entry, Contracting, and Engagement, we consider some of the vagaries of this process, identify several types of financial arrangements, and discuss informal as well as formal contracting. The nature of engagement plans is briefly noted, and then a main thrust of professional work begins. However, our sequencing again is somewhat artificial as we place Chapter 8, Diagnosis and Turbulence, following entry and engagement. After all, even the earliest stages of entry involve some rudimentary diagnostic effort. But going beyond these, we observe organizational and environmental volatility and disorder and the need to deal with ongoing "shifting ground" as diagnosis proceeds. We suggest some main dimensions to be addressed in any diagnostic effort and offer some suggestions on how diagnosis may be carried out under conditions of rapid change, ever-current, always impending.

The next chapter begins with the topic that perhaps is the most salient in OD: interventions and how they play out in recounted real-life situations. In Chapter 9,

Doing Something About It: The Intervention Concept, we address the meaning of the term "intervention" and the nature of intervention choice. We do not propose THE single classification scheme to this end, but instead propose some perspectives on how such classification may be viewed, particularly by means of Ginger Lapid-Bogda's paper and by citation of some other attempts to order interventions within one or another typology.

With this background, we provide a substantial number of intervention scenarios in various companies, reflecting differences in styles, complexities, and settings. Chapter 10, Intervention Scenarios, while not following a rigid format, typically include characterization of company (or other organization), usually followed by statements on "symptoms of distress," OD objectives, chosen intervention vehicles, and points of theory or further commentary. In discursive form, Cheryl Gitlin reports on the evolution of a strategic and participative process in a multifaceted military operation.

As the discourse winds down, there is a chance for reflection in Chapter 11, Reflections and Perspectives, as several contributors provide glimpses of past experience related to the field's evolution. Jerry Harvey remembers some spiritual moments at a meeting attended by a number of the field's pioneers. Norma Jean Anderson discusses the use of music in training. Dean Anderson explores the issue of the spiritual foundations of becoming an OD practitioner. And Robert Tannenbaum raises poignant issues and considers their implications for OD practice.

In the final chapter, Beyond the Horizon, the principal co-authors speculate on a continuing rediscovery of basic values and a deepened understanding of fundamental principles, in retrospect and by metaphor.

A Note on Boxed Text and Vignettes

Throughout this book, text will be boxed or separated in some manner, and vignettes will be used to raise issues and to provide examples of matters considered in the text itself. It is our purpose to present *lifelike* examples of various kinds and to point at issues.

Most examples are based on the author(s) experiences and/or are adapted from popular sources such as *Fortune*, *The Wall Street Journal*, *Forbes*, and *The New York Times*. These examples are shaped as vignettes—short and pointed—not as case studies. They do not pretend to follow either the Harvard case approach nor any other on what arguably "actually happened." It is our view that the latter phrase is always misleading, requiring interpretation and selectivity by the person(s) directly "living" the case, by the case writer, and by the reporter of a secondhand case. Such interpretational forces cannot be ruled out in vignettes either . . . the latter however are constructed here so as to make particular didactic points briefly within a template of recounted statements without much case-like detail.

Often the reader may guess at the companies described. However, for the most part we provide no actual names, *only* fictitious labels and pseudonyms when necessary, for purposes of readability.

Some vignettes are an amalgam from two or more sources. All are based directly, as noted, on real-world "stuff" and are presented as interpreted by the author(s), journalists, or managers, not as absolute fact but as *reflections of experiences*, presented succinctly in a learning context.

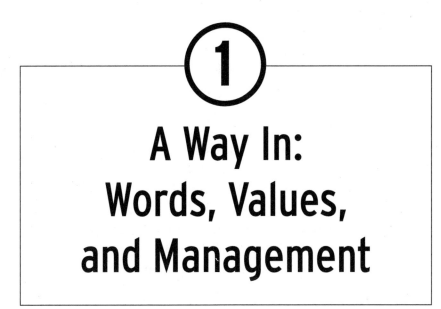

A Way In:
Words, Values,
and Management

EMPOWERMENT . . . enneagram . . . creative storytelling . . . crossing boundaries . . . people of color . . . new professional learning groups . . . OD "godparents" . . . consulting in nonprofit organizations . . . moving from internal to external "consulting" . . . transforming a middle-aged graduate school . . . transcultural environments . . . dialogue about OD values . . . organization culture . . . open space . . . integrating mind body work . . . strategies for changing personal and organizational mindset . . . criteria for international collaboration . . . career patterns . . . (OD) in relation to gay, lesbian, bisexual, transgender issues . . . Latinos . . . men . . . gender issues . . . virtual teaming . . . Appreciative Inquiry . . . "reasonable" conversation . . . heart and mind of the practitioner . . . creating networks . . . dissolving boundaries . . . scenario planning and thinking . . . fast cycle change . . . Tao of change . . . bounded or boundaryless organizations . . .

Words

The above snippets of session titles taken from an OD Network meeting program constitute a truly impressive yet dismaying array, apparently without pattern. Initially words; eventually actions. In this way, OD unfolds with the proverbial "thousand flowers blooming," in a vast variety of approaches and styles representing "what goes on in the field." These words characterize a range of conceptual and practice positions in exercising the craft of OD. Even at best, verbal descriptions within the OD profession constitute but one aspect. Words give rise to varied attributions of meaning or may just draw a blank! These struggles with words are not new, of course. *How* the words are expressed—vocal tone, body language, and emotional context—all contribute to their interpretation.

Organization development is no stranger to tag lines, "flavors of the month," and words in and out of vogue. We need to be aware that words that seemed clear at one time mean little to many at other times. Empowerment? M.B.O? Servant Leadership? Years ago who had heard of coaching or "virtual teaming"? In ten years, will people know what some of these words mean?

And then there is the question as to whether the words "organization development" connote a specific field of inquiry and/or practice. What about the many current organizational designations for actual *work* in this "field," however it may be bounded and defined? How about words such as "organization effectiveness," "leadership development," "diversity management," "change management," and just the generic "consulting" without any other label? Here too room remains for a variety of interpretations, depending on individual and professional preference.

Defining OD

Having said all this and stipulating to the manifest complexity of what words in this field denote, we present a working definition of OD.

> In the context of continuing natural change at all interrelated levels of environment, society, organization, group, and individual, with focus on specified client systems, OD engages people within and among human systems (organizations) in activities (interventions) intended to bring about positive change for specifiable clients and stakeholders and directed toward improvement of the human condition—guided by humane values—by means of significant application of knowledge rooted in the social and behavioral sciences.

Further examination of this definition follows.

Definition Excerpt	Comment
In the context of continuing natural change . . .	Change goes on all the time; there is only relative stability, with or without OD. And even planning of change interacts with the natural and unpredicted.
Interrelated levels of environment, society, organization, group, and individual . . .	In some sense OD needs to pay attention to *all* these levels, each changing at *all* times; but in practice, *strategic* delimitation is necessary.
With focus on specified client systems, engaging people within and among human systems . . .	In every instance, *emphasis* is placed on people, not exclusively on other sectors such as economy or technology, though these other sectors need to be considered as well, particularly in their interrelations with people. And particular identifiable client systems normally are given priority.
Activities (interventions) intended to bring about positive change . . .	Here we point to the range of available interventions and raise the perplexing issue of just what *positive* change is.
. . . for specifiable clients and stakeholders.	These constitute conceptual and practical "people" focal points for what goes on in OD, and with whom.
. . . directed toward improvement of the human condition, guided by humane values.	A wide scope of personal, professional, and social responsibility is intended here, and the matter of humane and humanistic values becomes of paramount importance with respect to both clients and to more remote stakeholders who may be affected directly or indirectly by OD.

| ... by means of significant application of knowledge rooted in the social and behavioral sciences. | Use and usefulness become central, with ideas for application drawn from a broad range of knowledge bases relating to people, from the intra-individual to society as a whole, drawing on traditional and emergent disciplines. |

In formulating the above, establishing historical context, we also considered a number of oft-cited and substantially useful definitions. Particularly, we considered definitions originally noted by French and Bell (1999) and others cited by Huse (1980), Cummings and Worley (1975), Beer (1980), Beckhard and Harris (1987), and Rothwell, Sullivan, and McLean (1995.)

OD Terminology

We now consider some substantive issues emerging in OD terminology.

Systems

Frequently the term "system"[4] or "whole system" is used to denote what (or who) is to be subject to change. Less frequently it is made clear just how the subject system is to be *bounded* or, for that matter. what is meant by "whole system." Is it a specific subunit, for example, information systems (IS), in a very large organization that retains OD consultation? Is it indeed a huge company, for example, one of the Fortune 500 in its entirety, that is to be changed? Or is it a ten-person team in a regional law firm? Or do we ever point to a "system of one," as perhaps in individual executive coaching?

As we interpret it, the systems concept adduces a *holistic* approach. This orientation is historically rooted in Gestalt theory[5] and subsequently elaborated and adapted emphasizing the unity of any given entity. A system is not to be regarded as a collection of mechanistic activities. Wholeness implies the organic interdependence of various "parts" to the extent that they are differentiated, either structurally or perceptually, working together, toward some identifiable goal(s). So far so good.

However, what is less often noted in the OD literature is the concept of *salience*. Essentially one cannot attend to all parts simultaneously, even while appreciating the holistic pattern. Something needs to stand out to provide a focal point for attention. Indeed, what is salient shifts over time and may vary among different observers at any one time. Accordingly, while various participants in the unfolding of an OD event may superficially agree on certain ostensible "facts," ambiguity, uncertainty, and multicausal change are constant companions.

The Lesson? When we identify any unit (company, team, task force, management level) as the arena within which an OD involvement is to occur, we need to recognize simultaneously:

- The holistic nature of *this* system (often a subsystem within a larger systemic entity); and
- The *differentiated* importance assigned to some event or circumstance existing at a certain time within the system (and/or subsystem) that is the focus of a particular OD involvement.

The issue of *strategic* consideration enters here, but needs to be joined by the recognition that different people, and indeed different sets of stakeholders, will vary in their perceptions and actions. The OD consultant is an active player in this ongoing definition and redefinition. This affects the nature of intervention as well, recalling both the co-joint effects of *interdependence* and of *differential salience*.

Change

What about *planned* change? Surely OD involves planning directed toward certain objectives, presumably within the framework of humanistic values. However, as the old saying has it, "Even the best laid plans of mice and men oft go awry." Sometimes it becomes necessary to plan on an iterative basis, intuitively or formally revising plans as new circumstances arise. Frequently, changes naturally occurring from other causes in the waves of turbulence that are normal rather than exceptional reduce or obliterate the discernable impact of the change initially planned. Or perhaps the change survives in rudimentary form, quite different from the original formulation. We will consider the concept further in Chapters 5 and 6.

The Lesson? Planning change often runs into *unplanned* circumstances, calling for purposeful revision of the initial change plan.

Behavioral Science

The question needs to be addressed: "What is behavioral science or applied behavioral science?" Is it the same "behavioral science" with roots in the work of the Ford Foundation and with academic input and so-named institutes from the 1950s onward, or has it become synonymous with organizational behavior? Or is it a form of industrial/organizational psychology?

To answer our own questions, we do not believe in such synonymity. Rather, we view (and most definitions agree) the (applied) behavioral science concept as encompassing and drawing basic ideas from a wide range of disciplines: psychology, sociology, anthropology, political science, psychiatry, social economics, history, philosophy, and other fields and subfields concerned with the study of people.

In Figure 1.1, behavioral science is seen as a major field of study and practice, which in turn influences both organizational behavior and organization development.

However, each of the disciplines noted does not necessarily contribute to applied behavioral science equally. For instance, *social* psychology may be more central for purposes at hand than, say, physiological psychology. But even this distinction is not ironclad. As to philosophy, much can be said about teleology (the study of goals and purpose) and about other subfields—ethics, free will/determinism, the nature of human nature—that make a difference in the theory and practice of OD.

The Lesson? Behavioral science, applied and fundamental, to serve the purposes of OD, needs to be broadly based, eclectic yet disciplined, and focused on strategic issues associated with the kinds of improvement in the human condition to which OD aspires. Behavioral science is not a fixed replica of pages from an OD text. It needs to keep up with *new* knowledge generated by numerous traditional and evolving disciplines.

Words constitute symbolic frameworks affecting what OD is, by definition. And eventually words impact all aspects of OD's work, as in statements of values that lay a foundation for interventions to follow.

Values

Why Value Statements Don't Work . . .

You can blather on endlessly about teamwork and trust, but if your people don't see what's in it for them, don't expect them to listen. Nearly all the employees were aware of the company's value statement, but only 60 percent believed the company actually meant it. The brass talked about the "hard" values all the time (e.g., profitability), while "soft" values were discussed far less often; the company's equivalent of "respect for individual" showed up scarcely at all. Yet that is the value employees care most about. Over time, self-interest distorts corporate values. (Corporate values) have to be compatible with the culture that is already there; pretty words won't bloom in the wrong soil.

Figure 1.1. Positioning Behavioral Science

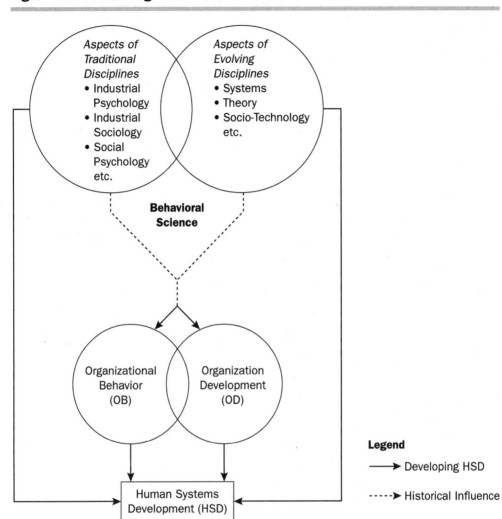

Aspects of Traditional Disciplines
- Industrial Psychology
- Industrial Sociology
- Social Psychology etc.

Aspects of Evolving Disciplines
- Systems
- Theory
- Socio-Technology etc.

Behavioral Science

Organizational Behavior (OB)

Organization Development (OD)

Human Systems Development (HSD)

Legend

⟶ Developing HSD

----▶ Historical Influence

Adapted from *Human Systems Development* by R. Tannenbaum, N. Margulies, and F. Massarik (eds.). Copyright © 1985 by Jossey-Bass, Inc. Reprinted by permission of Jossey-Bass, Inc., a subsidiary of John Wiley & Sons, Inc.

This does not sound terribly encouraging. What is OD to do if knowledgeable observers of the corporate scene assert, "Value statements don't work"?

The issue relates to whether value *statements* don't work or whether values are not relevant. Few would argue the latter. Yet it is apparent that which is stated— often loudly with considerable bombast and public relations emphasis—is not implemented nor "bought into." We have been engaged in consultations where this was blatantly the case, as is shown in the following:

▶ CASE IN POINT

Joseph Jones, president and CEO of a large regional bank, is meeting with the executive vice presidents (EVPs) to review the mission statement for the next decade. He opens the meeting with a request for candid expression of opinion by all concerned.

An administrative associate at this point distributes some hard copy material, while at the same time the first transparency is projected on the screen at the end of the executive conference room; here is an (abbreviated) summary of key value statements:

This (bank) is committed to the following:

- To assure profitability;

- To provide outstanding service to all its customers;

- To respect our employees individually and in their work together;

- To serve the needs of the communities that we serve;

- To enhance the natural environment;

- To serve the best interest of our stockholders; and

- To respect ethnic and gender diversity.

Considerable discussion ensues. Minor changes in wording are suggested. Instructions are given to the public relations representatives to prepare a video on the topic with appropriate animation and narration. The meeting ends on a self-laudatory note.

Shortly after the meeting is over, two events occur:

1. A financial report is received by the CEO stating that significant losses were sustained in business lending due to several large real

estate loans in default, calling for major realignment and perhaps closing down of an operation with a workforce exceeding 180 employees. This unit is headed by a woman, Andrea Rossi.

2. In the hallway, on the way to the men's room, the CFO and the CIO are overheard in conversation as follows:

CIO: "You know . . . I never trusted that b—h. I knew she would s—w up. It's those HR guys; they put her on the job."

CFO: "I don't believe all that touchy-feely bunk out of HR! Let's just go make money . . . skip all that other stuff".

The CFO adds an ethnic slur. (Andrea Rossi is black.)

The CEO is busy reviewing the public relations proposal for interpreting the values noted in the mission statement: "We'll sure have to make this look good. If we keep having problems like these with real estate and with the bottom line, none of this mission thing is worth a hoot." ◀

Whatever the circumstances, reflecting both on Thomas Stewart's observations and on the experience in the bank, it is clear that OD needs to focus on underlying genuine values beyond hype and superficial assertion. Indeed, OD's approach needs to take account of the *several* stakeholders, such as those mentioned in the bank's avowed mission statement, with efforts addressed to optimizing value satisfaction among them. Reality suggests, however, that optimization at equal levels among all these stakeholders is rarely possible. Tradeoffs need to be taken into account, and the overall picture needs to be recalled, recognizing that there will be losses as well as gains for particular stakeholders. *Awareness of long-term consequences* on the part of the OD consultant is critical, in contrast to narrow short-term service to any particular stakeholder, even if he or she is identified as "the direct client." Organizations must face, and act on, moral dilemmas.

Following is an example of such a dilemma:

▶ CASE IN POINT

If an OD consultant is asked by a client to plan a team-building meeting for sales personnel on Martin Luther King's birthday, how should the consultant react? Does the decision depend on . . .

- The consultant's own ethnicity?
- Community values and expectations?
- Real urgency in meeting scheduling?
- The client's views?
- Client pressure?
- All or none of the above? ◀

With pervasive concern regarding what values are, we must examine the concept in some depth. We note that substantial systematic treatments of the value concept abound (see Bouglé, 1926; Pepper, 1958; Rokeach, 1973; Rosenthal, 1984). These should serve as background in OD, counterbalancing the often-casual usage of the term.

- Roy Wood Sellars, in his introduction to Bouglé, observes that, "The history of society is a history of the differentiation of values . . . but values can mingle and interact upon one another in the unity of society" (Bouglé, 1926, p. xxxxi).

- Rosenthal (1984) considers the word "self" as a significant concept in the study of values. She refers to ideas such as "self-fulfillment," "self-identification," "self-sufficiency," and "self-determination" as representing important contemporary value positions. With autonomy of the person as a core value, we observe that many humanistic value statements are based on this position and incorporate OD-linked approaches such as empowerment and voluntary collaboration.

- Pepper (1958), in a lengthy and complex treatment of values notes, "[in] the last few decades a great division has sprung up between those who conceive value theory as the study of value *terms* and those who conceive it as the study of value facts between the linguists and empiricists."

- Rokeach (1973) observes that, "To say that a person has a value is to say that he (sic) has an enduring proscriptive or prescriptive belief that a specific mode of behavior or end-state of existence is preferred to an appositive mode of behavior or end-state." Institutional as well as individual values can be discerned.

We surmise that the idea of value cannot be used lightly; yet it does not in itself constitute a sufficiently clear beacon to enlighten OD consultants who wish to be "value driven" in their professional efforts. In each source cited, substantial complexity is encountered. Gellermann, Frankel, and Ladeson (1990) have made major contributions in addressing this issue in an OD context, as has Kaplan (1998).

Surely values are rooted in the cultural milieu in which individuals—and groups, organizations, and institutions—live and indeed are immersed, often taking specific value configurations for granted, without conscious explication. Organization development consultants—and managers—must make their choices based on explicit consideration of personal and social responsibility. This is not a simple task, requiring knowledge of both heart and mind.

Science itself encompasses values from the earliest days when it was intertwined in philosophy, religion, and statecraft: Visalius' values, Hippocrates' values, Machiavelli's values! And value assumptions abound in the works of ancient Arab philosophers, to Aristotle and Plato. Throughout, choice is an *essential* element in the delineation of values in practice, and the OD consultant makes choices in this context. A frequent inquiry to this point, addressed in both casual and serious discourse, is "Would you do OD for the Mafia?" Even sadder and more destructive examples in genocide come to mind. It is both banal and laden with horror to conjure up value assumptions engendered in the Holocaust and the destruction of Jewish life in Europe. And "scientific inquiry," for example, lethal experiments on twins or the disabled, or "purity" in the sense of a strong blue-eyed "genetically superior" race—these positions were adduced and formulated as compelling *values* in Germany in the 1930s and 1940s. More recently, "ethnic cleansing" in Kosovo and African tribal warfare constitute massive value aberrations.

The Lesson? The OD consultant cannot take for granted what is a "value" nor the specific values to guide the OD effort. A conscious definition of value positions *chosen,* and an understanding of the complexity that underlies the choices involved, is essential if OD is to live up to its ethical as well as to its practical realization. With this in mind, we suggest, by way of reminder, some specific criteria for identifying values in OD.

Some Criteria for Identification of Values for OD Consideration

- Values are basic orientations toward self and society, including individuals, groups, organizations, cultures, and the environment.

- Values are not temporary day-by-day preferences or transitory tactical determinations. However, over the long term, these preferences need to be consistent with fundamental value orientations (for example, preferring vanilla ice cream over chocolate ice cream is not a "value," but rather a preference; on the other hand retaining one "high profile" spokesperson, such as an athletic star or entertainer, for an advertising campaign will need to be consistent with the sponsor's basic value structure).

- Values need to be intrinsic to the individual and to the organization. They cannot be "window dressing," for strictly external or for "cosmetic" purposes. They need to be fully integrated with and central to OD's fundamental commitments.

- Values need to be acted on (or restrained) by action. Relevant here is the old saying "not just talking the talk, but walking the walk." As a corollary, you must also *not* walk the walk that is contrary to the articulation of an intrinsic value position.

Management

We shall consider three topics in "management" as aspects of "the way in" for OD practice:

- The nature of management support;
- The bounding of the management-intensive systems within which OD takes place; and
- The relationship to the human resources (HR) function.

The Nature of Management Support

Definitions of OD frequently call top management support a sine qua non of effective OD intervention. Indeed, much is to be said in favor of this position and for this stance toward top management by the OD consultant. There are questions, however, regarding what is meant by "top management support" and whether OD can or cannot be implemented at all without such support. And indeed there is a question as to who and what is "top management" in the rapidly shifting organizational forms that abound. Let us take these issues one at a time—first the meaning of "support" and second the nature of "top management."

▶ THE STORY OF MOREAU

Monsieur Moreau is CEO of a worldwide luxury goods conglomerate. The company has about $4.5 billion U.S. sales and controls or owns product lines in the following: fragrances/perfumes, precision watches, champagne, high fashion, and quality leather goods and accessories. Monsieur Moreau has just received an e-mail from Señor Abardo, an executive at a beverage subsidiary in Barcelona, Spain, to the effect that the subsidiary has retained an international OD consulting firm to address certain issues of conflict and tension in management teams in Barcelona and to re-establish harmony and, it is hoped, lagging profitability at this moderately important profit center.

At this time, Moreau is involved in a major acquisition of a distinguished international auction house specializing in antique furniture and old masters, among other profitable lines. There is likely resistance to this acquisition and possibly other competing buyers in the wings. Moreau is not terribly concerned about Spain, which as an entire market area currently contributes 3.5 percent to the company's revenues and 2.8 percent of its profits. He glances at the e-mail and mentions it to the executive vice president for finance, Monsieur Lavoche. Lavoche nods and resumes discussion of the financial implications of the possible auction house acquisition. No more is said about the Barcelona OD contract.

Is this top management support? ◀

It is helpful—beyond simply answering yes or no to the above query—to consider a typology of management support for OD programs. While not exactly linear, the numbered points roughly suggest a sequence from "great support" to "complete opposition":

1. Direct personal and professional commitment by key top decision-making manager(s) to the OD process and their active involvement;

2. Tacit approval of the OD process and occasional monitoring by specified top decision-making manager(s);

3. Nominal approval of the OD process at the top; details delegated to subordinate operating managers to "carry the ball";

4. Involvement by specified managers in the early stages of the OD process followed by relative passivity, that is, only HR is involved;

5. Resistance by key managers to the OD process, but willingness to let some others in the organization deal with it, sometimes with the assumption that nothing will happen anyway;

6. On hearing that an OD process is proposed, a prompt veto by upper level managers and termination of the incipient arrangement.

As noted, the numbered points above do not fall along a simple continuum; many intermediate stages and mixes of support and lack of support can be found. However, it is evident that proactive OD requires a satisfying support level in order to proceed. This level may not be optimal, but it needs to be good enough to permit reasonable function of the OD process and reasonable prospects of success. The OD consultant needs to make an informed judgment with reference to these matters, taking account of preliminary data available *prior* to full commitment to going forward with the OD engagement.

As to the question "Who is top management?" Consider the example of Monsieur Moreau and his associates. For the company worldwide, he and his immediate group—however structured in terms of networking and influence systems—*are* top management. But when we consider the situation in Barcelona only, within that subsystem Señor Abardo qualifies as top management, together with a particular subset of relevant associates; and the international OD consulting firm might well explore the feasibility of an OD intervention directed toward conflict resolution and team reconstruction in the framework of the worldwide firm within which the Barcelona operation is embedded.

The Bounding of the Management System

Here the issue arises once again: "What is the boundary of the system?" Even considering the permeability of such a boundary and its interaction and interdependence with a broader encompassing system, specific analysis in each instance is required. In the Moreau example, embedded systems relevant to an OD intervention might include the following:

- The organization unit within which conflict and tension resolution may be attempted;

- The Barcelona operation, headed by Señor Abardo and his group; and

- The worldwide operation, headed by Monsieur Moreau and his group.

The Lesson? It is of critical importance, in determination of whether or not to proceed with an OD intervention engagement, to consider both the organizational boundaries/systems perimeters within which the interrelations may occur and the nature and quality of management support—both at the subsystem level and at the whole system level, short term and long term.

For this purpose, a dedicated analytic and predictive process is in order, far beyond the feasibility of "getting a contract" or obtaining an *apparent* buy-in by a particular client, whether manager or management group.

The Human Resources Function

The human resources function and its subfunctions such as training and development constitute both an additional resource and a contact point in the development of OD programs beyond line management. The human resources department in many instances harbors and nurtures the OD function, internally and as a contact point for external OD consultation. At a later point, we shall speak in detail about the *internal* OD consultant and his or her position in the matrix of delivering high quality OD services. For the moment, considering the issue of support, it is important to realize that, depending on the company's total function and the particular niche that HR occupies, HR may either facilitate or impede OD. Much depends on how HR is viewed by various management levels and on its predominant image and impact. Is HR regarded mainly as being involved in routine hiring or downsizing? Is it positioned strategically and involved in the top management decision-making process? This differential positioning varies widely among companies. Some examples follow.

▶ BIGFRAME COMPANY

A major computer mainframe company—a pioneer in this field that had a tradition of "never firing anybody"—has fallen on hard times. New top management is intent on changing the corporate culture and eliminating—if necessary by drastic means—the well-entrenched policy that "we will take care of you . . . we will not fire you . . . yes, we want your loyalty long-term." "Lifetime employment," whether formally defined or implicit in work commitments, is now out!

The newly hired CEO, selected from outside the company, is charged with turnaround and with cultural change. He has appointed (from within) a new corporate HR executive VP, charged with implementing massive lay-offs, whether called downsizing, reduction in force, or whatever. However, even this HR manager has been historically committed to gradualism and to the longstanding Bigframe corporate ethos. He is slow in showing results on the layoff/downsizing front. While his efforts to follow top management instructions are on the way, a number of OD engagements also are going on. Some relate to team building, others to feedback and performance evaluation, still others to career counseling. At the outset these efforts seem to enjoy HR support. Support by top management, however, is soon in question.

Before too long, the HR EVP himself is relieved of his assignment. Now all HR support has disappeared and, indeed, having been associated with the now-separated HR EVP becomes a distinct negative for anyone who has worked within the corporation. And OD in its earlier form largely disappears from "corporate" and is reassigned in bits and pieces to functional divisions, especially under the "training" rubric. Its overall influence is diminished. ◀

Following is a more successful example.

▶ FUNGADGET COMPANY

A major marketer and distributor of toys, starting operations long before the Internet and holding a significant share of the retail toy market, Fungadget creates a mission statement with heavy emphasis on good customer relations and caring response to the needs of its employees. In this context, the HR function is an integral part of the top management team. While most of the operating executives focus on marketing and on the functional management of overseas manufacturing operations, HR is charged directly with the people side of the business. This overlaps in part with marketing concerns (How should the salespeople relate to customers on a human basis, especially those with children in tow?), as well as affecting employees throughout the company, who are regarded as a vital resource in the conduct of business.

The top HR executive, hired in at the EVP level and also a member of the corporate management committee, comes from an academic background (mainly in organizational behavior) and is fully committed to OD, both in relation to applications in the company and to furthering OD as a profession. He has created an advisory council on "corporate human relations," consisting of subexecutives in HR, key operating managers, practice-oriented academics from three universities, and a philosopher who also writes a newspaper column.

Numerous OD projects are carried out on a continuing basis, some with more success than others but with management always conscious of responsibility both to the corporate mission and to the welfare of individuals involved. When separations and layoffs are needed, energies are devoted to career counseling and outplacement. ◀

It is clear that HR needs to be considered in the context of the organization as a whole, consistent with consideration of systems theory and associated modes of thought. Yet under rapidly changing conditions, HR itself is subject to instability. This changeability, of course, has always been a factor. Now the pace has become more rapid and changes have become more dramatic as substantial trends toward disequilibrium (for example, Internet marketing, global realignments, turbulence in organizational forms and functions) become dominant worldwide.

At lower levels as well, this turbulence is manifest. Less attention is paid to formal degrees (even MBAs!) and people from disciplines such as communication studies, English literature, and history are hired as "internals." This makes a difference in the nature of OD within the management framework.

The Lesson? For the OD consultant, it becomes important to consider in depth the nature of the management structure to which OD relates. This goes beyond the presenting "client," of which we shall speak more later. Rather, OD needs to take the broad view of the strands of support that exist and those that are lacking within the organization's line hierarchy, as well as in the HR function itself and the latter's connection both to corporate hierarchy at one hand and to OD activities, internal or external, on the other. This requires purposeful effort by the OD consultant on the way in, explicitly clarifying support systems and boundaries in relevant management structures. As a basis for such effort, we believe that it is essential to proceed in context of a comprehensive framework presented in the next chapter.

A Framework
for OD Consultation

CONCEPTS AND THEORY are omnipresent, whether or not called that. Here we focus principally on a checklist of concepts from which guidelines and theory positions in OD may emanate. Concepts both guide and limit the formation of theory. They help us focus, yet they may limit vistas of that which has been, for whatever reason, excluded. Our list therefore is relatively comprehensive to draw attention to the manifold issues that the OD consultant may need to consider.

The Nine Cs

While we will suggest some approaches to applied theory in OD, here we identify ubiquitous concepts that need to be considered as a basis for "doing OD."

The Nine Cs

1. Consultants

2. Clients

3. Capabilities

4. Contacts

5. Contracts

6. Contexts

7. Cultures

8. Chaos

9. Change

And two integrative concepts, S (Self) and R (Relationships)

Any theory in OD must take appropriate account of the nine Cs and S-R and their significant interrelations, which are illustrated in Figure 2.1.

The boxes are not intended as clear-cut separations. They serve only as descriptive conventions. More importantly, one may visualize a continuing ebb and flow of forces agitating the entire configuration, with shifting salience, differential strategic emphases, and inevitable modifications over time: Chaos and Change particularly denote these process flux.

Figure 2.1. The Nine-C Field

Core Concepts	Consultants (1) and Clients (2) and their Capabilities (3) the Self (S) in Relationships (R)
Secondary Concepts	Contacts (4) and Contracts (5)
Encompassing Concepts	Contexts (6) Culture (7) Chaos (8) Change (9)

The diagram in very complex, despite its apparent simplicity. Obviously, Clients and Consultants are specific individual people and sets of people; Self and Relationships are the core of OD process. And these Clients and Consultants have Capabilities (what they bring to the party), based on personality and propensities subject to influence and change in OD's implementation.

Contacts and Contracts involve specific relationships, particularly between consultants and clients, based on significant interpersonal processes, including trust and implicit and explicit structures (for example, memoranda of agreement, engagement plan, hierarchic relationships, and the like).

Beyond core and secondary concepts, broader vistas beckon, especially Context and Cultures. Much has been written about culture's pervasive influence on "how things are" and "how they are done around here." Obviously, people are key as well, but so are abstractions such as values and physical entities such as buildings, technology, and artifacts.

We need to recall that in some form the various elements that are important in OD interrelate at all times. A kind of "web of meanings" is established, discernable but always shifting, consisting of assumptions and perceptions among people who try to make sense out of what William James, in various formulations, described as that buzzing blooming confusion that is life. Stuff happens in context. People define context. OD is not a box of random pebbles, each separate and apart. We need to look at *patterns* of meaning.

Finally, we come to Chaos and Change. In some sense, these concepts are closely linked. Change, no matter its nature and basis, whether abstract or concrete, involves the epigram, "things ain't what they used to be." As in biblical chaos preceding order, evolutionary sequence, or OD interventions, something typically is shaken in the process. Chaotic circumstances may well occur (perhaps must occur) before something new and different appears, eventually to take hold, and later likely to deteriorate or otherwise change again.

"Change" is of course a *big word* in OD, as indicated by various definitions and indeed as bears in the question whether OD is synonymous with "change management." The Consultant has necessarily *a theory, however called, with reference to his or her self and in the operative relationship with the client as regard to change.*

As regard to the use of theory, it will be particularly helpful here to reconsider the conceptual work of Kurt Lewin[6]. While the *procedure* of Force-Field Analysis introduced by Lewin is well-known as a tool in the study of organization change, recently it has been questioned by some (see Goldstein, 1993) and has been regarded for the most part as a "stand alone" method. But this use has been too limited. Force-Field Analysis calls for updating revision and can be successfully enriched by combining it with other Lewinian concepts such as Life Space Analysis and Vector Psychology (see Leeper, 1943; Lewin, 1936, 1938) and by extending its scope. Primarily, the complexities suggested in the Nine-C Field include the impact of Chaos, and its irregularities need to be applied as we "enter" the life spaces of OD consultant and client, building a unique mini-theory for each engagement.

The Lesson? In evolving OD, it is necessary to consider the wide scope of factors (forces, variables, parameters) that are actually or potentially involved. We propose the nine Cs and S-R, with consultants, clients (self and capabilities), and relationships at the core. The focus may vary, but consciousness of the *big picture* is strongly recommended.

As pointed out earlier, the nine Cs constitute an "array" rather than a linear sequence, and their numbering is not sacrosanct. On the whole, they provide a "heads up" for us to pay attention to a substantial set of variables, whether building OD theory or doing the work of consulting.

Each of the Cs subsumes subconcepts and can be elaborated on. Indeed, any one C, even if taken separately, generates volumes of ideas and a richness of descriptive material. While to unfurl this plethora of information is not our present task, we believe that the consultant needs to be aware of *each* of the nine Cs and of *all of them in concert.* Every OD effort should take account of the relative significance of the emerging pattern and evaluate its relevance for the task. Examples and vignettes appear throughout this book that help to illustrate the relevance of the nine Cs to various consulting scenarios.

Further, some kind of mini-theory, as suggested by expanded Lewinian Force-Field Analysis, may prove useful in guiding each particular OD engagement.

The Nine Cs Checklist form on the next pages will serve as a reminder of the most relevant factors in your OD consultation. The concepts of self and relationship, however, require additional elaboration and are the subject of Chapters 3 and 4.

The Nine Cs Checklist

Instructions: This checklist can be used as a prompt during your OD consultations and for taking notes. Considering the unique elements of a particular consultation, for each of the nine Cs listed below, take a few minutes to think about the information that you have, the information that you want to obtain, and any other relevant questions or comments.

1. Consultants

2. Clients

3. Capabilities

4. Contacts

5. Contracts

6. Contexts

7. Cultures

8. Chaos

9. Change

The Self

MOST OF US normally have little difficulty remembering who we are. We face life with *some core concept* of ourselves that is fairly stable. Indeed, we may agree that, while aspects of ourselves change gradually over time, the core self-concept's continuity appears to be its most salient feature: "I know this is me" and "Yes, this was me ten years ago."

In our search for an understanding of the individual, we may well begin by looking at this stabilizing aspect in our lives. After all, who we think we are and what we feel we are provide a kind of "home base" from which our dealings with others inevitably originate. With OD's people focus, this "home base" indeed is basic for OD consultants, clients, and others involved.

Erich Fromm[7], a psychoanalyst with a concern for broad social issues, has suggested that enlightened self-love and meaningful self-acceptance provide a fundamental condition for the ability to love and for the acceptance of others. The research evidence on this point is not definitive, but there are strong indications that a positive relationship exists between positive feelings about self and capacity to function, closely and effectively, with others.

25

Whatever the asserted significance of self-acceptance, an examination of the self-concept is an appropriate starting point. We can do no better than to raise the question, formulated by J.F.T. Bugental, a humanistically oriented clinical psychologist, in a research context: "Who are you?" (See Bugental & Zelen, 1950; Cheung-Judge, 2001.)

You may want to proceed on this premise, asking yourself, "Who am I?"

- "What is my core self in OD and in my life as a whole?"

- "Is 'being an OD consultant' a primary aspect of my being?"

- "What am I trying to 'prove,' personally and professionally, by the work that I do?"

Analogous questions are faced by clients and stakeholders.

Such questions may seem both self-evident and, superficially, easy to answer. Yet, it is that age-old inquiry for self-knowledge that defies simple reply when we begin to "dig deeper." As a matter of fact, it might be a useful exercise to stop reading right here and for five minutes consider the following:

Ask yourself for *your* self, both personal and professional: WHO AM I?	Conjecture about this: For a given client, how would she/he answer the question: WHO AM I?

As you seek answers, you may have noted that, beyond a certain point, your thoughts and feelings begin to run out. Noting your experience, let us proceed to develop a framework that may help us to understand the nature of the self-concept.

The Levels of Self

We may distinguish several levels of the self-concept[8]:

The First Level: Simple Labels

It is very common to respond to the "Who am I"? question by simply giving one's *name*. The name has become the denotative label par excellence for most of us. As Sandor Feldman (1959), a psychiatrist, wrote in his *Mannerisms of Speech and Gestures*, for most "the name is identical with the person as a being. It belongs to his self."

To the extent to which we feel comfortable with our names as the appropriate symbols of the "me," hearing others call our names, particularly in a laudatory context, is in itself a sort of reward. In Western culture, relationships among people often are epitomized by use of first names or last names. And beyond, intonation and expressive subtleties often "make the difference" (or at least symbolize the difference) in these connections. Is the client (let's call him Joseph Markell) *Mister* Markell? *Joseph*? *Joe*? Or, as his golf buddies call him, *Putter*? Does this affect consultant/client rapport?

A second simple label is our *job role*. It is relatively easy, of course, to identify ourselves as "students" or "executives." But as "OD consultants"? The culture in which we live (and there are important variations) readily uses occupational role as a means for establishing a person's position within a set of social coordinates. "OD" is *not* often used as an occupational label, nor am I likely to introduce myself at a cocktail party with "Hi! I do OD" or "Hi, I am a change agent." Others may differ.

A third such simple label is that of *family role*. Many of us carry at the surface of our awareness something about our position in a lifestyle or family structure: "father," "husband," "mother," "wife." But with changing demographics, these labels become less than ubiquitous. Probably the use of family role as a spontaneous identifying label is greater for persons who are adult members of organized families. Different patterns prevail for single individuals living by themselves or for young people residing in the homes of their parents. Gender identities, too, make a difference here. Again, the influence of the general culture is significant.

Among the relatively superficial, simple labels we have found name, job role, and family role. Although on the surface, they are not insignificant. They provide a basis for *public* presentation, but for most people they rarely address deeper levels of self-definition.

The Second Level: The Acceptable Present

The kinds of things that occupy me these days tend to loom large in the view I develop of my "self." Particularly, I am likely to consider those behaviors that I regard as "acceptable" or at least "revealable," especially those behaviors that are responded to favorably. I may also consider some (but only *selectively* some) of my current concerns and problems.

I may come to think of my self as someone who is busy on the job yet perhaps engaged in a controversy with a business associate. This is "acceptable" from my standpoint because I feel that my actions serve the organization's best interests. Or I may think of my self as someone who has been promoted recently to the position of executive vice president of a large consulting firm—and I feel good about this.

Perhaps most cogently, I may describe myself in terms of a number of relatively laudable adjectives: "I'm conscientious, sincere, loyal, honest, and trustworthy."

Now, greater richness and complexity emerge in my self-concept. No longer do I insist on neat, highly general labels. Now I deal with a series of events in which I am the central character or with a series of adjectives that describe "me." At this level, the situations I mention tend to be those that cause me little anguish or conscious shame, although on occasion they may "open up" my current problems and concerns. Yet they place me in a light that I experience to be largely acceptable to others. But indeed there *is* an affective, emotional component present—an initial sense of emotional meaning. Do I as a consultant share these parts of my self with the client? Is this reciprocal?

The Third Level: The Acceptable Past

In our exploration of who we are, it often seems natural to follow the thread from current and recent aspects of our self-experience to events in the more distant past. Typically, at this level we may initially deal with events once more that we believe to be deemed acceptable. Now we consider some aspects of our life history, perhaps noting when we were married, how our occupational or school career proceeded, past travels, and, in an OD context, recollection and highlights of previous professional activities.

The assumption underlying reflection on these past occurrences in our lives implicitly holds that we might draw some understanding of what we are now by an examination of what we have been (or what we have done) before. This assumption has been subject to much scientific inquiry; certain theories of personality, notably psychoanalysis and other psychodynamic theories, and inquiries making use of life history methods rest on this foundation[9]. These theories insist on a look at the self that extends beyond neutral positive self-report.

Eventually, further attempts to explicate the self-concept may drift—or may be pushed—toward experiences with negative affect, those parts of our "self" that we experience as painful and disturbing. We also need to confront what we *dislike* about ourselves as human beings and in our function as OD consultants.

The Fourth Level: The Unacceptable Present

We now come to the more serious problem areas of our self-concepts. Our attention focuses on deficiencies that we may sense, tensions among opposing aspects of our personalities, and the troubling conflicts between ourselves and other people. Our feelings may range from mild annoyance to frantic anguish.

In this phase, we are moved to deal with present and recent troubling, anxiety producing situations, and we tend to describe ourselves in explicit, negative terms. We may perseverate on our "sins of omission and commission," and we may reflect on our current personal and interpersonal deficiencies. Feelings of guilt, among other disturbing forces, may rise up to gnaw on the integration of our self-concept. When I feel this way can I be/should I be actively involved in an engagement?

On the other hand, we may not always find the words to be specific; we simply may lean on broadly diffuse descriptions such as "I sure don't feel good about what is happening these days," or "I don't know what it is . . . I'm just always getting mad at people." Karen Horney (1937), a neo-psychoanalyst particularly interested in the impact of culture on the individual, has been among the writers who has stressed the significance of a "free-floating anxiety"—incisive but non-specific—as a culture current.

The unacceptable present represents what may be termed the "acute phase" of self-concept difficulty. Such present disturbance, however, does not simply spring up de novum. The past, of course, is never *truly* past. Its consequences continue to make themselves felt across broad sweeps of the human lifetime, and the troubling aspects of our self-concept today are rooted in a set of chronic personal determinants, originating in times gone by. To be effective, professionally and as persons, we need to come to grips with the issues involved.

The Fifth Level: The Unacceptable Past

In describing "what we are like" now in terms of negative events and characteristics derived from a more distant past, we tend to follow one of two roads: (1) we tend to deal with those elements of the past that we have learned to "live with," although we recognize their subjectively unacceptable nature at the time of their occurrence, or (2) we may emphasize those elements that persist in establishing an underlying tone of difficulty and discomfort even to this day, no matter how long ago they took place or how *objectively* irrelevant they may be for events of the present.

In the former case, we say to ourselves something like, "It was really bad, but that was long ago." This view involves no denial of a negative past, nor does it lead to psychological self-flagellation. The latter, however, is unforgiving: It reproaches the self and maintains a persistent state of emotional trepidation, agitating the person as a whole. Under these conditions, all professional practice involving people is seriously at risk.

The Lesson? As OD consultants we need to be clear, especially to ourselves, about who and what we are. We go beyond our stable core self-concept and well may want to reflect on "Who am I?" and on the client's corollary views.

Several levels of self-concept call for our attention: simple labels, the acceptable present, the acceptable past, the unacceptable present, the unacceptable past. In their combination, as total pattern, these levels give content and substance to what we are all about as human beings, with consequences to our life and work in OD. In an analogous context, we need to be sensitive as well to the client's "way of being."

You can use the Thinking About Your "Self" worksheet later in this chapter (see page 34) to begin examining the various facets of your self.

With these challenges, we now come to two helpful approaches, one by Joseph Luft, with a current statement on the "Johari Window" as a model for self-awareness, and, drawing on it, Barbara Brewer's Disclosure Exercise, looking more deeply at the "unacceptable" aspects our selves.

► REVISITING THE JOHARI WINDOW
JOSEPH LUFT

> "Oh wad some power the giftie gie us to see ourselves as others
> see us! It wad fare monie a blunder free us, an foolish notice."
>
> *Robert Burns*

In a new millennium dominated by the information revolution and global commerce, it seems appropriate to re-emphasize the basic significance of the human element. Organizations are complex systems involving technologies, resources, structural design, and personnel. The employee networks, from CEOs to clerks and janitors, operate and run the organization. Hence, human interaction is the pivotal process.

In an effort to illuminate this complex process, The Johari Model of Awareness is offered in a manner that may, hopefully, prove useful (see Luft, 1984). The Johari Model was created by Joseph Luft and Harry Ingham at a Western Training Laboratories lab sponsored by UCLA in the early 1950s.

It was originally called An Awareness Model. It was not until the early 1960s at an NTL program in Bethel, Maine, that I (Joe Luft) made up the name "Johari." As a staff member in a Human Interaction lab, I presented the Awareness Model and called it the Johari Model (for Joe and Harry). A few years later, I learned from a Sikh Indian colleague that the word "Johari" was Sanskrit for "the God who sees within." I am still in awe.

The Johari Model, illustrated in Figure 3.1, helps us to think about those areas of ourselves that are known and unknown to ourselves and to others.

- Quadrant 1, the Open area, refers to behavior, feelings, and motivations known to self *and* to others.

- Quadrant 2, the Blind area, refers to behavior, feelings, and motivations known to others but *not to self.*

- Quadrant 3, the Hidden area, refers to all things *known to self* but *not* to others.

- Quadrant 4, the Unknown area, refers to behavior, feelings, needs, and desires known *neither* to self nor to others.

Figure 3.1. The Johari Model of Awareness

	Known to self	Not known to self
Known to others	1 OPEN	2 BLIND
Not known to others	HIDDEN 3	UNKNOWN 4

When meeting someone for the first time, we tend to form instantaneous impressions of each other. Both individuals can observe certain things that are out in the open, such as physical appearance, facial expressions, and shared communication. In the model, these events are assigned to the Open window, Quadrant 1, that is, behavior and things known to each of the interactors.

In the graphic model shown, information is assigned to a quadrant depending on which of the participants is aware of the behavior. In Q2, called the Blind quadrant, there are behavior, feelings, and intentions known to others but not known to self. Most of us have little habits or mannerisms, such as the way we gesture when we speak spontaneously or scratching ourselves repeatedly, of which we aren't aware, but that others can see.

Sometimes, more serious behavior may be involved. In the January 2000 issue of the American Psychological Association's *Monitor* journal, a study entitled, "Professors' Most Grating Habits" revealed that students were most annoyed by such things as monotone voice, lecture style, talking down to students, poor course organization, and long-windedness. And most of the professors, members of psychology departments, were totally unaware of these perceptions.

In every conversation, attention is usually focused on the Open area, Quadrant 1, what is known to self and known to others. Soon, however, conventional personal disclosures take place: "What's new?" "How are you?" "Haven't seen you lately" "I've had the flu bug all week long," and so forth. Disclosing information from one's Hidden area is usually normal and somewhat predictable. But it can be surprising or even shocking at times. As more and more is shared from the Hidden area, the relationship grows and the Open area, Quadrant 1, expands in size. But the reverse can also happen. If a person's feelings are hurt or if she or he feels unsafe, the Open area can shrink in size as participants clam up or pull back psychologically.

Self-disclosure usually occurs reciprocally and in small increments. When the sense of trust and satisfaction rises, the flow of disclosure from the Hidden area increases. And in times of physical or psychological crises, unexpected feelings and information may suddenly be revealed.

Quadrant 4, the Unknown area, contains the unrealized potentials of the individual that have never had the opportunity to develop. These could include a wide variety of latent talents and skills, such as musical ability, social skills, language, acrobatics, inventiveness, and other great arts. But Quadrant 4 also contains residues of the past such as trauma or abuse or other high anxiety experiences that the individual, for various reasons, has not been able to face. They are buried in the Unknown area until the person grows strong enough or feels well-supported enough to face the problems and to deal with them adequately.

The four quadrants may be applied to behavior in groups and teams:

- The Open area, Q1, in a new group (or new team) is usually small. There is not much free interaction and spontaneity.

- The Blind area, Q2, in a group tends to change very slowly. Members tend to sustain and reinforce their blind boundaries. However, as interaction goes on and the group matures, its members are less afraid to re-examine the basic beliefs of the group.

- As mutual trust increases, there is more disclosure within the group, and the Hidden area, Q3, decreases in size while the Open area grows in size.

- The Unknown area, Q4, changes very little unless the group culture develops soundly and a real need arises for hidden resources. ◀

The Lesson? Based on the ideas presented, we suggest a set of principles of change.

1. A change in any of the four quadrants can affect interpersonal as well as intrapersonal relations.

2. A sense of *trust* tends to facilitate more openness.

3. It is not effective to try to *force* someone to see into his or her blind area.

4. As the open area increases in size, the prospects for interpersonal learning improve.

5. It may be stressful to hide, deny, or be blind to behavior and feelings involved in interaction.

6. As the open area grows larger, communication improves.

7. We are all curious about the hidden areas of others, but social training and simple courtesy restrict our probing.

8. Respecting another person's blind area, Q2, is important in all relationships.

9. The values of a group and its members may be noted in the way unknowns in the life of the group are dealt with.

10. Small groups and teams make up the core life of all organizations, and change within them often depends in good measure on the process of interpersonal openness and sharing reflected in the Johari Window.

Thinking About Your "Self"

Instructions: Fill out the following worksheet, giving as much thought as you can to each question. The following questions are not intended to be exhaustive but should serve to prompt exploration of self.

1. What are the labels that you (or others) give yourself?

   Job Role:

   Family Role:

   Other labels:

2. What are your present behaviors, skills, or traits that you find acceptable?

3. What are your past behaviors, skills, or traits that you find acceptable?

4. Can you see how or if your past experiences have shaped your present self?

5. What elements of your present self do you find deficient or unacceptable?

6. What elements of your past self do you find deficient or unacceptable?

7. Are there steps you can take to remedy your dissatisfaction?

▶ DISCLOSURE EXERCISE FOR THE JOHARI WINDOW

BARBARA BREWER

A useful theory presentation in the early development of the T-group[10] is the Johari window. The purpose of the presentation is to help the participants have a clear understanding of the importance of self-disclosure.

To begin this exercise, present a brief lecture using the Johari Window model to explain the Open, Blind, Hidden, and Unknown quadrants. In the presentation, it is important to use self as a learning instrument; use examples from your own life to demonstrate the concepts of Open, Blind, and Hidden.

I talk about my own experiences when describing the Open area. Everyone can see that I am a woman. They can hear that I have a Texas accent, and I disclose early on that I love groups. In the Blind area (what others know but I do not know), I use a silly example of the time I walked around our small rural town, where I am well-known, with a bra attached to the back of my shawl. No one bothered to tell me of my inappropriate dress until I saw my sister. She, of course, not wanting me to bring shame on the family, exposed my blind side to me. The point being that we all have behaviors that are hidden from self. It can be a caring event to give and receive feedback.

Since I use this exercise in a lab setting that is by nature designed to encourage people to self-disclose at a deep level, the example that I use for the hidden area concerns my own experience of spousal abuse. I talk about being a battered woman and the impact that those scars still have on me in terms of facilitating the group during the conflict stage.

Last, the fourth quadrant is presented. This represents the unknown to self/unknown to others.

After the presentation is given, pass out 2'' x 4'' blank note cards. Ask each person to think about a time, an event, a happening that he or she has not previously disclosed (or which has only been disclosed to a few people). Emphasize that these writings will *never* be identified with the writer (unless the writer decides to make public what he or she has written). Collect the cards. Shuffle. Sit in front of the audience with a trash can handy. Read each card as though you had personally written the card, then tear the card into small pieces and discard into the trash can. It seems to add to the value if two people, a male and a female, take turns reading the cards.

Because I use music to heighten awareness, I choose a meaningful song and ask people to close their eyes and listen to the music. Some of my favorites are "You Must Love Me" by Madonna and "All by Myself" by Celine Dion. If you elect to use music in your sessions, be sure to abide by copyright law. When the song(s) have been played and there have been a couple of minutes of silence, the session is completed. Generally, people will process this exercise in their T-groups, but I stay in the room for a few minutes or until all of the participants have left in case anyone has any immediate questions or issues to discuss.

Note: As with many of the activities that are used in experiential learning, we can cite no specific source of the origin of this activity. ◀

The Lesson? Concern with the unacceptable past in a sense represents our own view of the "skeletons" in our personal—or professional—closets to the extent that we can face them at all. Whether or not we permit others to catch glimpses of what is inside the closet depends, of course, on who these others are, on the *relationships* that we have with them, and on our own *readiness* to reveal—even to ourselves— that which we deem to be unacceptable. Consultants and clients are not immune to these quandaries, and these issues may particularly affect activities such as coaching and negotiation, as well as group process.

The Levels of the Self-Concept: A Summary

The self-concept may be likened to an "onion" composed of several conceptually discernible layers, which in real life, however, do not constitute totally separable categories. There is movement across the layered boundaries with this metaphoric entity, and there are shifts over time. Still, in our attempt to answer the question "Who am I?" these levels serve as a useful guide, delineating those components that are relatively near the surface of our responses, those that are further removed, and ultimately those that require deep and searching inquiry. It is our view that such inquiry is/should be an explicit agenda for the OD consultant, enhancing her or his long-term personal and professional growth.

Toward a Professional Self

The idea of "self as an instrument" has emerged as an avowed concept for many OD people. The recognition that the effectiveness of the consultant could vary with his or her own mental health now is talked about explicitly. While clear intellectually, much remains to be done to fully implement this basic idea. Indeed, OD practitioners are beginning to explore how they can become more in tune with themselves and with others by the use of peer-group supervision, ongoing therapy, meditation, and systematic focusing.

Skills and Abilities

Beyond this central self-knowledge, other learnings matter. Whether one specializes or whether one wishes to be a generalist, knowing much (but not "everything") about basic topics, such as theories of organization, individual and group behavior, communication, power, politics, and conflict, surely is among the most important. Especially for those who favor the generalist emphasis for the OD consultant "for all seasons," a working knowledge of the above *plus* substantial capability in a variety of interventions would seem in order. Importantly, this knowledge needs to be integrated within the total Self, not attached as a simply cognitive appendage.

Ideally, the consultant, as practitioner, has a list of "angelic" traits that include open-mindedness, a keen problem-solving mind, an enhanced ability to communicate and moderate conflict, and the ability to modestly "sell" his or her competence, however defined. There have been several studies that seek to isolate both traits and competencies that an OD practitioner *should* have. For example, Tannenbaum and Sullivan (personal communication, 2001) define a competency as "any personal quality that contributes to successful consulting/management performance." They go on to say that basic areas of competency include relevant knowledge of professional theories, techniques, and methods; human values; self-awareness; and performance skills.

In reality, many a practitioner seems to be a recovering workaholic and high achiever who needs to remember that it is "progress not perfection" that matters. Once more, Self and Self-Concept need to be understood by the *person* who functions as practitioner.

A Re-Emphasis on Values

The authors admit that defining the level of skill and ability for the OD practitioner is somewhat subjective and varies by individual and by institution. Values are less negotiable. As stressed in Chapter 1, values are a basic consideration in a constantly changing business environment. The tools of practice change with time, as evidenced by the "death" of Quality Circles and Management by Objectives (MBO) and the birth of Open Space Technology. But values, for instance, the integrity of the person, balanced concern with the welfare of all people impacted by an intervention, and emphasis on genuine growth reflect exemplary consistencies.

"Physician, Heal Thyself". . . and Your Attitudes

Problem solving becomes an almost automatic response that spontaneously animates the consultant, based on beliefs about how organizations should function, especially with respect to communication, power, conflict, rewards, and risk taking. And yet, because humans are illogical and irrational at times, so practitioners are also swayed by their own biases, emotions, and insecurities. Again, the concept of Self plays a significant role in how the consultant approaches the consulting process. As consultants, we need to be self-aware and to "heal" certain attitudes often ingrained in conventional academic education and in popular thought, as described below.

"Away from Linearity": Conceptualizations Are Linear; Much OD Is Non-Linear

Especially in relations with a client, influenced by natural change at all points as well as by unanticipated consequences during the unfolding of an OD effort, complex engagements do not necessarily follow a neat step-by-step sequence. This non-linearity is exacerbated by the uncertainties brought about by rapid change that is all about us, and that is not likely to go away.

It is possible to *construct* some kind of reality by looking back on a complex real world process and put it into some kind of order. Regarding this, Abraham Kaplan (1998) has spoken of "reconstructed logic." Such efforts are all well and good, providing we recognize that it constitutes an ex post facto endeavor that imposes order through the human eye on that which has involved a mass of non-linear events.

Views of chaos and its resolution partake of similar elements. Vast data sets are recorded, initially appearing indeed, shall we say, *chaotic*. Subsequent analyses, rethinking, and reviewing of the phenomenon generate discernable patterns elicited from initial chaos (see Gleick, 1987, and Prigogine & Stengers, 1984; see also Allaire & Firsirotu, 1989, and Huey, 1993).

"Capturing Simultaneity": Sequences
Can Be Discerned, but Simultaneity Rules

We have noted that some patterns can be elicited from that which initially appears chaotic and idiosyncratic. Surely, search for such patterns is essential, in OD as well as in other professions, to provide a framework for practice. At the same time, we need to be aware that many events of importance occur *simultaneously,* and yet at any given time we attend only to a subset of these simultaneously occurring events. In terms of Gestalt theory, certain events stand out and others fade out. Evidently what we pay attention to (and that which we ignore, per force or by choice) makes a difference regarding what we do as OD consultants. For instance, if I am convinced that I need to involve myself in a one-on-one conversation with a principal client to understand her or his view of a downsizing program that does not (from a client's standpoint) seem to be progressing fast enough, we might not attend as well to significant pressures in the technical and socio-economic environment affecting the organization as a whole. This selectivity has consequences, especially if the forces not attended to eventually prove to be decisive.

Typically, sequence is honored in some sense, for example, diagnosis in a more complete form *is* most important before all details of an engagement are specified (in other words, avoid the "fire, aim, ready" syndrome). Yet there needs to be constant adjustment and readjustment as the OD engagement proceeds as other simultaneous events are apprehended. Perhaps the only exception to this relates to a single intervention in a very short time frame, with the intervention being almost entirely technique, fully standardized, and irreversible once begun.

"Valuing Ambiguity": Balancing Ambiguity and Clarity

To be "transparent" in our professional role, to be suitably self-disclosing, these are values of importance in OD engagements. Yet, and if this be heresy let us not recant it, there are also instances when ambiguity is functional. This is the case in organizations when there is work in progress or a merger negotiation going on and in corporate "face saving" at the announcement of separation of a top executive. ("Joseph Dough, CEO of Biowing Inc., has informed the Board that he wishes to leave his post to pursue other challenging opportunities. His resignation is effective immediately.") And many job descriptions include phrases such as, "and perform other duties not inconsistent with the above (job description)"; indeed if all normal job descriptions were followed to the letter and by these rules only, the job probably would not get done, surely not in a timely manner. In almost all but the most mechanical jobs, there is a *variable level of optimum ambiguity.* This holds as well for different OD interventions (Massarik, 1968).

And as many a competent T-group trainer knows, ambiguity is an important aspect of the development of productive group process, particularly in the group's early stages, when many a trainer (facilitator) may choose to be inactive, opaque in his or her responses for clarification for what it is all about, and purposefully evasive to devolve the burden of responsibility onto the group.

The Lesson? Basically, the skilled OD consultant needs to be liberated from traditional constraints of simplistic thinking and (as the Los Angeles OD Network logo says) reach "beyond our boundaries," especially when existing boundaries have become ossified by conventional prescription. This calls for encounter with non-linearity, with simultaneity, and with sometimes functional ambiguity to implement the actual OD process effectively.

Thus, thought must be given both to requirements of clarity and to the skillful recognition that optimal ambiguity as well must hold an honored place when considering the initial encounter with the client, as the next chapter will illustrate.

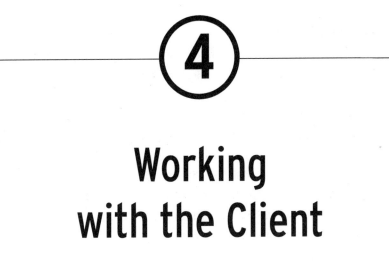

Working
with the Client

WE HAVE NOTED that the OD consultant does not come to the tasks at hand as a "blank page," nor, one may hope, as an automaton simply purveying a set of techniques. As in all professions—and more so than most—the OD consultant brings forth his or her humanness in the very process of doing the work. Often there is implicit readiness for the OD task. As OD consultants—with genuine understanding of self—we often know more than we think we do. We may make many decisions based on our intuition, and such intuition rests on a bedrock of self, experience, and knowledge that is not always in the forefront of our awareness. Further, the best learning seems to come by trial and error, and mostly the latter. And indeed, learning from mistakes is exactly what we may encourage our clients to do. The dilemma forces us to shed the traditional consulting paradigm of "saving face in front of clients" and instead use our total experiences as models from which our clients may learn.

A previous experience by co-author Marissa Pei-Carpenter highlights this point.

► CASE IN POINT

We teach our clients to resolve differences openly in the present process of communication, as opposed to talking later behind others' backs. And yet in years of my engagements with other consultants and clients, we all adamantly agreed not to disagree with each other in front of the client. On one project, my colleague disagreed with my suggestion and argued that the clients would learn much more if they witnessed a disagreement. I reluctantly agreed to take a risk (I realize that for a change agent I am not very thrilled with change), and the results were phenomenal! The client not only learned that conflict was normal and necessary, but that working through the discomfort openly resulted in a very rewarding end product. ◄

Some Thoughts About Technique

Technique—given the OD profession's value position—*should not* (and this is a value term) dominate. What the OD consultant brings to each meeting with the client is really the total self, within which is integrated an eclectic collection of theories, models, experiences, orientations, personal values, principles, beliefs, and long-term characterological patterns. However, if the consultant uses only one particular model, theory, or tool for most every engagement, the self becomes but a shadow, and the intervention relies primarily on the theories and techniques that underlie the model, for example, MBTI (Myers-Briggs Type Indicator), coaching, Schutz' Element B, TQM (total quality management), MBO (management by objectives), diversity, 360-degree feedback. This may be effective when the circumstances of the nine Cs truly are a fit with the proposed model. But even then the Self is a factor, affecting the way in which the intervention is implemented.

The range of techniques available has come to be legion, and herein lies the danger. Specialization becomes vogue. It has become attractive to highlight application of a particular technique by a particular OD consultant and/or the corporate/partnership provider of an intervention. Yet, while value may be provided, questions such as these need to be posed:

- Is this the *right* technique under the circumstances?
- Will the application of the technique likely have lasting impact? Or is it a "quick fix" with short-term euphoria or less, and not much else?

- Is the technique integral to the Self, to the *person* who is the OD consultant, or is it purely a mechanistic appendage, run "by the numbers"?

These questions need to be addressed in *every* instance. One technique does not fit all, even if it is sellable and superficially attractive, or even if the client "buys in"! A dedicated process is required to consider all these elements and to proceed with the engagement, but also to provide the option of saying "no" when professional judgment counsels caution and suspects significant dissonance in line with the nine Cs. Of course, this is difficult when economic considerations become paramount. "Should I go ahead with accepting this contract? I have some professional doubts, but everyone, including the potential client, thinks it's a great idea." And, of course, the money would help.

Ethics and conscience need to be principal guides, which as in similar cases beyond OD, necessarily constitutes a troublesome internal conflict. Organization development consultants, through informal support groups, "kitchen cabinets," and simply purposeful colleagueship, are helped and helpful in addressing these matters.

▶ THE CONSULTANT'S INNER CAULDRON

The client CEO, Dr. Arthur Prolief, at Procom.com has no doubts: "We need a survey to check out morale and to help our human resources people do a better job. We need to confirm the benefits program and working condition upgrades that we're planning. Will you guys do that for us?

Josie Parker, the OD principal consultant, hears this loud and clear. She discusses the possibility of doing this survey with her three associates in a small OD service firm, JRC Development Associates. Among them is Wayne Pelter. Wayne knows the client firm well, having done some work for Procom.com six months ago when he was employed by another organization, Insight/Inside Partners. He recalls that there was a great deal of conflict in the firm's top management team focused around some "tricky behavior" by Dr. Prolief. It seems, Wayne notes, that Prolief is something of an "activity freak." "Some people think he is well-intentioned; others seriously doubt this. Indeed," says Wayne, "Arthur is always looking for something to do that 'plays,' but I think he doesn't have a clue on what really matters." Josie Parker listens well, but she also knows that her firm does surveys very well . . . and they *need* the revenue!

Wayne argues heartily: "Those guys don't need a survey; the top management team needs to get together and begin to work out some of their problems. People all over the organization know there is something wrong at the top." An animated discussion ensues among the several consultants in JRC.

"Of course, the survey probably wouldn't do any harm," Wayne concedes. By this time, Josie is wondering, "Maybe we should go for coaching, heading toward conflict resolution of some kind; maybe we shouldn't do a survey now." What is Arthur going to say? Wayne remains ambivalent about the survey and eventually both Wayne and Josie agree . . .

On what do they agree? And why is this so? ◀

▶ CASE IN POINT

Let's say your expertise is in team building, and you have developed a particular method to create and operate effective teams, which has worked particularly well in the past. You are asked to help an organization that is suffering in morale, and at which in the last year production has dropped considerably. There are no existing teams, and there is little communication both within and between departments. The CEO has heard of your expertise in teams and has called you specifically to "do your magic" with your team tool. The short answer is to please the client and implement a team solution. Those areas that are suffering from "no teamwork" do progress spectacularly. You look good and the client is happy, but the employees are still uneasy, sort of.

Why? In the long run, even more important problems—unclear roles and responsibilities, micro-managers, and a racist culture—are left untouched and eventually deter any long-term benefits that might have resulted from the teaming effort. Your short-term goals, and your unwillingness as self to engage with and consider the broader issues, have limited your effectiveness as an OD consultant. ◀

The Client/Consultant Relationship

It is evident that conflicting considerations co-act. What about the money? And will (all who matter) accept a possible shift from survey to coaching? Or from team building to something else? Everyone's unique personalities, positions, and motivations are at work in the process of reaching a decision. There are no quick answers; each case involves a variety of unique considerations. As a basis for next steps it becomes useful to provide a general framework, focusing on each person as self. From the standpoint of the consultant, Figure 4.1 serves as a starting point[11].

Figure 4.1. The First Circle: The OD Consultant as Total Self

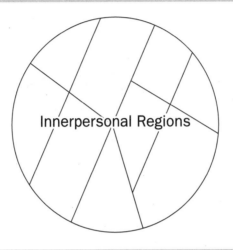

The "first circle" is a metaphor for "the total personality," the self. In Lewin's terms, this includes the "innerpersonal regions" of the person, the "psychologic material," the various characteristics, motivations, and social relationships generally as subsumed in the literature under the rubric of Personality Theory (Lewin, 1935; Argyris, 1957; see also Hall et al., 1985). This is, however, far too broad and complex a topic to allow present substantive review. Yet, the metaphor points to the following: Whoever you are, whatever you see within yourself, and whatever you do not see (including the unconscious and the archetypal) makes a difference . . . when you are yourself and by yourself and when you are with others. And what *you* think about what the others think, now or later, is clearly of great significance.

The Self is an organized whole, with inner relationships among the various elements, both in their convergence and congruence and in their inconsistencies and doubts, as well as that which is not known to the conscious. All this is relevant when the OD consultant moves through the cauldron of determining what should happen in a given client situation, as well as in life in general.

The identical metaphor holds for each person in the client system and for each person in the set of stakeholders actually or potentially affected by a particular OD engagement.

Let us examine the "second circle," partaking of the identical conceptual characteristics—but involving different constellations of elements relative to the principal client. Let us superimpose, with only arbitrary overlap at this point, the "first circle" (the OD consultant) and the "second circle" (the principal client). (See Figure 4.2.)

Figure 4.2. Overlap of First and Second Circles: Congruence

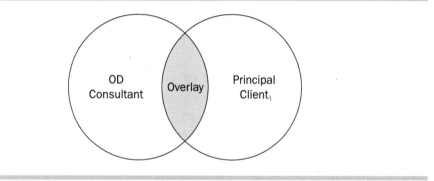

The nature and extent of the overlay is defined by the congruence of styles, needs, objectives, and values between the OD consultant and the principal client. Overlay points to the necessary congruence between the OD consultant on one hand and the client on other. Indeed, the second circle might be expanded to synthesize a kind of shared vector of forces generated by the broader client system. This overlay could serve as a heuristic criterion for whether the engagement should proceed. If there is no significant overlap, there probably isn't anything to talk about. Complete overlay is highly unlikely. However, substantial congruence for key dimensions of self/selves, however measured, undoubtedly is an important prerequisite for a successful OD process, linking consultant and client.

And, finally in this sequence, one stipulates that a given level of congruence is not necessarily fixed. As Figure 4.3 shows, there are alternatives.

Figure 4.3. Altering OD Consultant/Client Congruence

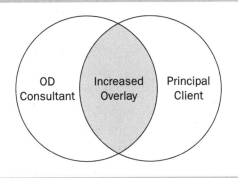

Figure 4.3 points to increased congruence between OD consultant and principal client, as contrasted with Figure 4.2, and serves as a metaphor for rapprochement, conflict resolution, or reduction of dissonance between consultant and client. Alternatively, it constitutes a symbolic representation of shared approaches of "working things out," as the consulting arrangement is considered.

To widen the field of overlap, either or both of the "circles" may put out energy to "get it together." But in the negative sense, either or both may be responsible for "pulling it apart" or concluding that "this just isn't going to work out!" Particularly to get it together, to make it work out, *mutual* effort is called for. As a practical matter, often the OD consultant is particularly equipped by training and background to initiate forces—by way of shifts in relationship style and other interpersonal means—to strive for increased congruence. Sometimes neurotic tendencies in either or both OD consultant and client can split things apart further, suggesting that the engagement will not prove satisfactory and should be terminated at a preliminary or early stage.

The Lesson? The above analysis points to the essential importance of the *total* personalities of all involved in the OD consultation process—and particularly to the "fit" between consultant and client. It is appropriate to address these relationships explicitly, taking nothing for granted and making no unwarranted assumptions, either about the OD consultant's self nor the client's self individually or collectively. A purposeful process is required, focusing on these selves, while considering as well the other external variables among the nine Cs in planning strategy and estimating the chances for success of a given OD effort.

We have just spent considerable time reviewing the concept of self as it applies to both consultants and consultant/client relationships. In the next section, we'll focus our energies on the client.

The Client, Never Singular

So far we often have had occasion to refer to consultant and client, singular. Yet while the OD consultant, in work in progress, is involved necessarily in a relationship with a client, this is never the whole story. The words "a client" in the singular necessarily constitute a misnomer. There never is a single client, even in instances in which one observes what appears to be an exclusive one-to-one relationship[12]. The concept of "client system" perhaps is more descriptive, yet even this formulation does not provide much of a guideline for untangling what is often a complex network of relationships. We need to recall the Gestalt viewpoint: The consultant faces a *pattern* within which a particular client person or client group is most prominent in salience, while the remainder at any one time are background. Patterns and prominence may shift, but a principal client normally (but not always) perseveres in salience throughout an engagement.

While in fact a principal client relationship may constitute a continuing thread, the simultaneous existence of multiple clients creates challenges for the OD consultant. It can prove seductive for the consultant, as well as for the client(s), to assume that this is indeed an exclusive one-to-one association. Inevitably, however, numbers of others co-act within the inevitable network of a consultant/client relationship. Who are these others?

First, there are the specific *organizational others*—superiors, peers, and subordinates—who surround the presenting client. While these may be visible in specific meetings focused on the OD engagement, they are indeed simultaneously present as well even though the principal client and the consultant *seem* to be involved in a one-to-one conversation, for example, in discussing what has happened during a given intervention, what should happen next, and so forth. These others make their presence known within the "psychological field" of the principal client and thus constitute *shadow clients,* sometimes as, or more, influential than the principal client.

Then there are *peripheral clients* within the framework of the organization who variously may support, oppose, or ignore the particular OD effort in process. Previously, we have spoken of various types of support, from top management downward, and in various constellations from enthusiastic involvement to passive acceptance to active opposition that whirl about the implementation of an OD program. These remote client sets may include individuals and subgroups at levels of management other than the one in which the principal client operates. Here the political process within the organization becomes manifest—a sometimes invisible dragon that can spout flames unexpectedly—and surely people with multiple "axes" to grind emerge. It becomes necessary here for the OD consultant to consider or to map these less obvious client sets and to identify their points of relevance to the OD process.

Beyond, there are *stakeholder constellations* not directly linked to client groups. These are constellations of individuals and groups of groups that are affected— immediately, short term, or long term—by the consequences of the OD program. For instance, there are employees at distant locations of a large organization who *may* eventually be impacted. There are unions who *may* have negative or mixed feelings about what is going on in OD. There are the people in communities within which particular companies are located. All these, and often others, need to be considered in the client matrix.

The Client Matrix

- Principal Client(s)
- Shadow Client(s)
- Peripheral Clients
- Stakeholder Constellations

Presently, clients may fall within one or another of the first three categories. We have also included a fourth category of people on the "client side" influencing OD. In addition to these categories there is the personal "people world" of the principal client and, in turn, the personal worlds of all others actually or potentially affected—their families and their friends outside the organization whose opinions matter. This is the world of informal support, of close-in reality testing, of exploration of anxieties and fears perhaps associated with undesired OD outcomes, and of the proverbial "kitchen cabinets" outside the organization's formal structure. Indeed, in the Internet world such constellations go beyond the face-to-face, although this most intensive exposure to feelings of self and relationships with others remains primary.

Again it becomes useful for the OD consultant to consider, map, or otherwise identify these interpersonal patterns by means of ethnographic inquiry, or in informal conversation and purposeful interviews. We turn to an example involving multiple clients.

▶ PLYMOUTH-ROCKHILL REAL ESTATE DEVELOPMENT

This is a family-owned business. It is a fairly small company with fifty-five permanent employees, located mainly at a headquarters office in a prosperous suburb of Boston, Kelpholm. The company develops real estate, primarily single-family dwelling units; these are sold to junior executives and other upwardly mobile population groups on the northeastern seaboard. Some redevelopment is part of the company's mission. The normal operations appear to be in good order, and the company is profitable—and, as noted, privately held.

The company's head is a former lawyer with some additional background in investments—mainly conservative debt instruments. As a young man he briefly worked in a regional brokerage firm. He is the company's founder and chairman of the board. His name is Herman Perando, but he is known to one and all as Hermy.

Hermy, realizing that he "can't do it all alone," has hired a real estate executive as president. (It turns out that the president, Alex Axter, long before there had been a business association between him and Hermy, had dated a girl in high school who eventually became Hermy's wife.)

Alex had attended a management seminar at Boston University. There he learned something about "accountability" and, wanting to be up-to-date, went looking for a consultant who might help in setting up accountability charts for the company.

At the time that Alex was looking for a consultant to help in this matter, Plymouth-Rockhill was involved in a contentious proceeding involving property owners and the Kelpholm City Council regarding rezoning required by Plymouth-Rockhill for a future development.

Eventually Alex locates an independent consulting firm, Organization Facilitation Partners, and meets with its managing partner, Phil Marks.

Organization Facilitation at one time had done a project on accountability for the Kelpholm City Council.

As Phil meets with Alex, it becomes clear to Phil that accountability is not the major problem. He proceeds with careful diagnosis of company issues and of its community and environment settings, as well as internal factors, and concludes that two sets of problems prevail: (1) internal organization, particularly delegation, with Hermy having major difficulties in letting go; and (2) different visions of Plymouth-Rockhill's future as seen by Hermy, who aspires to quantum leaps in company growth, and Alex, who would like to see rapid short-term development and possibly (unbeknown to Hermy!) the sale of the entire company to a nationwide real estate conglomerate, Turtle Place Imperial, whose top executive, on the golf course, has expressed interest in acquiring Plymouth-Rockhill.

To complicate matters, Hermy has a son, Marc, who has graduated from a liberal arts college with a major in English literature and communication and who is looking forward to a career at Plymouth-Rockhill. Marc knows little about real estate, but he is interested in computers and in their application to the analysis of Shakespeare's plays.

Marc also contacts Phil to talk about the situation at Plymouth-Rockhill. (At the time, Marc had been given a nominal job title by Hermy: "Assistant to the Chairman.") Soon Marc develops evident ambition to succeed Alex as president and eventually his father as chairman as well. Marc does not like Alex, and vice versa. Alex keeps pushing "accountability" and offers Organization Facilitation a substantial contract to do the job.

The Kelpholm City Council tightens zoning regulations as agitated home owners protest Plymouth-Rockhill proposals.

Phil is meeting with his associates at Organization Facilitation. The discussion focuses on identifying the principal client and the structure of the client system as a whole, plus key stakeholders potentially affected by outcomes of an eventual OD intervention. ◄

If you were to map or describe this client system, how would you see it, particularly in terms of a Client Matrix? In this instance, who is the principal client? Hermy? Alex? What about the "presenting client," Alex, the person who has directly approached the OD consultant offering a contract? Was he ever the principal client?

Is Marc a shadow client? Is the Kelpholm City Council a stakeholder? And what about the homeowners who are protesting? Are the Plymouth-Rockhill employees peripheral clients, for example, part of the client system? The questions proliferate.

At any rate, at the outset an *initial problem* is defined: "accountability." This problem definition needs to come from the *presenting client* and not be constructed by the OD consultant. Indeed, even at this early stage, the consultant may feel ready to "jump ahead" for a variety of reasons; perhaps because he or she really thinks he or she knows what the problem is or how the client *ought* to see the problem or who the "real" principal client *ought* to be.

In the process of sorting out the shape and scope of the Client Matrix, the OD consultant may want to show professional expertise, to demonstrate insight and competence, and/or to establish rapport or to strengthen an early relationship. This stage may involve a mutual verbal sparring between the client(s) and the OD consultant; each may want to demonstrate awareness of the issues—part of a symbolic "feeling out" and sensing process. Of course, either or both may decide that it's not a good mix and terminate the interaction.

In more desirable circumstances, the OD consultant acts as a caring and intense listener, in a facilitative role to assist the presenting client and eventually the principal client in formulating the problem (or problems) and its detailed ramifications. Whether identified simply as a conversation or "depth interview," or the more sophisticated "phenomenological interview" (see Massarik, 1981), the consultant creates an open forum for exploration of ideas phrased in words, which carry both overt and covert meanings for all concerned.

For the moment we note that this initial contact provides a verbal "open space" into which the presenting client may pour her or his technical and programmatic definition of what this is all about and, more importantly, which may provide a suitable entry or exit point for the OD consultant.

The "opener" is a setting for gauging first impressions. Here, as in other human encounters, much importance rests on a sense of the hot/cold character of interaction, possible fit, or incompatibility. At the content level, organizational issues are clarified and technical strengths and limitations are sensed that may speak for or against the acceptance of the engagement by the OD consultant.

Also there are *shadow clients* that the presenting client carries along, explicitly or by implication, to be determined (or at least hypothesized) by the OD consultant in this initial exploration. By this time the initial presenting problem may have begun to metamorphose into something quite different.

Eventually, a client core emerges and the identity/identities of principal client(s) is/are clarified. Here we find the key people who are in fact likely to be centrally involved in the OD engagement. Ironically, it may turn out that the presenting client is not one of them; this exclusion may be related to lack of influence, characteristics that are seen as abrasive or irrelevant by others who *do* wield influence in the organization, or, in some instances, a voluntary withdrawal for tactical or strategic reasons. The constellation of potentially relevant people, beyond those met in the initial encounter, needs to be conscientiously considered by the OD consultant through interview data or for that matter by secondary information such as working memoranda, e-mail shared by the presenting client, or other documentation.

When the client core has been specified, always *tentatively* and *subject to revision*, the OD consultant must recall that indeed the *internal structure* of this client core is of great importance. Political forces, common thrust and alliances, jealousies, personal and organizational hidden agendas, as well as technical and structural issues need to be considered. Positioned within this configuration is the *principal client*, who may or may not be (have been) the same as the presenting client.

Of course, the client core does not exist in isolation; rather, it is linked to other entities within the organization's framework. The client core constitutes both a structure, embodying formal and informal relationships, and a force field of its own devising. In turn, it is associated with wider force fields of various kinds and shapes, all subject to their own internal forces and reciprocally affecting the client core.

Of further import (related to peripheral clients and stakeholders) are *internal influence groups*. In most every instance, numerous groups, named or unnamed, coexist. *Within* the organization's framework there are structured divisions or departments, identified by function (information technology, operations, finance, engineering, strategic planning, human resources, marketing, Internet, and so on) or perhaps by geographic designation (American operations, the European Union marketing, South Eastasia, and so forth). The structures, and relative import among these, are ever subject to de facto change, often extraneous to the OD engagement.

In labor-intensive concerns, unions and other industrial and trade categories may be of importance. And still at another level, there are corporate boards, especially in large organizations, and committees of such boards. In Europe and in other countries, various board types may exist, including non-executive advisory boards and policy-setting boards. *Professional constellations* within any one organization are another set of groups to be taken into account, such as software developers, trainers, systems engineers, e-commerce marketers—the variety is infinite.

External influence groups too must be taken into account. There are numerous groupings that are for the most part external to a particular organization within which the OD engagement takes place, including government and regulatory bodies, people within a given geographic community, members of a particular ethnic group, interest groups, and a plethora of others.

The Lesson? While it is often convenient to focus on consultant and client, singular, on further consideration it turns out that "client" is never singular. In OD practice, multiple clients form a rather complex picture like that of a rapidly moving and unpredictable dragon and are subject to review. These include the presenting client, who may or may not emerge as principal client. The Client Matrix also includes shadow client(s), peripheral client(s), and stakeholder constellations. Then there are organizational others, a client core, and various internal and external influence groups. All constitute an ever-changing panorama that needs to be scanned and understood throughout the engagement.

The Who Is the Client? worksheet on the next page can help you to organize your thoughts about client systems.

Normally the client is a prime focus for change, with change of some kind indeed pervasive at all levels. It is of importance not to take change for granted, as though it were a simple, self-evident, homogeneous concept. Rather, we need to rethink the nature of change in wide perspective.

Who Is the Client?

Instructions: Consider an OD consultation that you think is or has been particularly complex and list, in the appropriate spaces below, the various client system members.

- Presenting Client

- Organizational Others

- Principal Client(s)

- Shadow Client(s)

- Peripheral Client(s)

- Stakeholder Constellations

- Internal Influence Groups

- External Influence Groups

During this consultation, what major shifts in the above occurred?

Rethinking
the Issue of Change

BECAUSE CHANGE IS omnipresent, it is difficult to define, either philosophically or practically. The question of "What is change?" is particularly cogent in OD, given the extended history of the term "planned change" and the persistent focus, both popularly and rigorously, on effecting change and of dealing with change in one form or another in the OD process.

Beyond the continuing use of the term having to do with changing organizations, we have encountered both "change masters" (Kanter, 1983) and "change monsters" (Duck, 2001), not to mention more lighthearted and extremely popular publications such as *Who Moved My Cheese,* a many-weeks bestseller (Johnson & Blanchard, 1998).

In this chapter, we will examine different interpretations of the concept of change and some applications derived from other fields of study. We will review some conceptual models of change, particularly Lewin, and close with a look at one of the "new science" elements, complexity, and the resulting need for strategy in the practice of OD.

Not to Be Taken for Granted

It is our view that change as a concept cannot be taken for granted, nor is it self-explanatory. In its fundamental form, it is rooted deeply in the traditions of the ages going back to the ancients. Indeed, in a review of an earlier version of this book manuscript, lack of attention to this matter was raised as a point of criticism. While we need not go back to the very beginnings of the controversy (in classic Greek), succinct summaries, such as Mortimer J. Adler's (1978) *Aristotle for Everybody,* are helpful in the present context.

To consider point and counterpoint: Adler notes (as have other contemporary philosophers in their retrospect) that Heraclitus held that everything is always changing and that nothing remains constant or static. On the other hand, Parmenides thought just the opposite—that it is only constancy that matters and that in its fundamental form nothing ever changes. He held that our senses only provide us with false data, suggesting that illusion makes things look different, obscuring their ultimate permanence.

The argument, whatever common sense retorts to its substance, contains elements of truth, both on behalf of the position stated by Heraclitus and for the position held by Parmenides. In one way, the evident "flow" of human existence is all about us (Csikszentmihalyi, 1990), while by contrast some fundamental elements reveal considerable stability. So we may regard the *concept* of organization as a rather constant phenomenon throughout human history, from the caveperson's efforts to organize a hunt to the structure and operations of a company such as General Electric or Apple, or of a particular HMO. In these terms, both *continuous change* and the *permanence of conceptual essences* exist side-by-side.

What do these somewhat abstract reflections mean for OD?

The Lesson? Let's be clear at the outset what we *really* mean by change, past and intended. Let's be explicit regarding what seems to be constant and what seems to be in process. In OD we are part of both continuing flow and stability, including past patterns that have held on for long periods of time. We need perspective on this interplay of change and permanence.

Recognizing conflicting tendencies, we need to abandon the simplistic before/after model of change, even change ostensibly attributed to OD. At best, this model serves as rough, heuristic shorthand; much as it seems appealing at first sight. We never enter a placid entity in the first place; we always come in "mid-stream" and make our way through a muddled, sometimes chaotic situation, when we plan to "intervene" or to conduct some kind of OD program.

And, when we come out "at the other end," we cannot assume that whatever "change" has occurred is uniquely due to our intervention. Past history, too, has left its imprint. Thus, we are best advised to "trace the threads" of our influence—noting the specific forces and non-linear currents that involve OD process in a complex field of pre-conditions, causes, and effects.

The Tao of Change

This theme is taken up by Robert J. Marshak (1994) in his paper, "The Tao of Change":

> After more than forty years of searching for the Promised Land "desired end states," perhaps it's time OD as a profession started thinking about "going around in circles."

Adopting a Confucian and Taoist view, oneness, interdependence, and holistic thought emerge as driving principles. Simple uni-causal models, with direct cause-and-effect relationships attributing a given change to the specific OD effort, are replaced with an understanding of the multi-causal environment in which OD necessarily operates. In this sense, OD change, including its cyclical aspects discussed by Marshak, is characterized by the interaction of many factors, among them the nine Cs.

While moving away from a simple cause-and-effect model, the context of past, present, and future needs to be understood. This holds particularly as we relate to such trends as globalization, crumbling of historic barriers among countries and companies, and the impact of innovative technologies. These matters have been discussed in much detail elsewhere, from varied standpoints, in scholarly literature and in public print, and are beyond this chapter's purview.

The Lesson? As noted in the much-quoted parable, "This is not a billiard ball universe." And even this kind of universe involves complex interactions. Our change interventions always are embedded and intertwined with much else. Therefore, change and outcomes involve both intended and unintended consequences. We need to pay attention to these potentially chaotic conditions and sort out issues in dedicated effort.

Other Disciplines

Given this ode to complexity (or is it a lament?), we are well-advised to consider approaches in other areas of inquiry that may help us illuminate our concerns. For example, consider quantum mechanics, which is discussed in lay terms in Marshall and Zohar's (1997) *Who's Afraid of Schrödinger's Cat?*

In a section entitled, "Identity in Quantum Mechanics," the authors state, "Quantum entities are not really 'things' but rather patterns of active energy. Each has a wave aspect and a particle aspect. Which aspect shows itself at any one time depends on the surrounding circumstances."

OD comment: Organizational entities are not really "things." They are systems/structures for transforming energy. People give energy to the organization. What we need to look at—whether the holistic structure/system as such or the individual human components—depends on the task at hand, for example, large-systems change, change by executive coaching, and so forth. Often we need to look at these manifestations of energy in interconnected context.

Marshall and Zohar go on to discuss change over time: "What persists through change? Is the bare winter tree we see from our window in December the same as the leafy green tree we saw last summer? Is the man standing before us now the same boy whom we once knew?"

OD comment: Of course the "bare winter tree" is not *exactly* the same as the "leafy green tree that we saw last summer," nor is our "old" friend the same person of our youth. Yet we recognize this tree as *this* tree—with its own particular identity—as we recognize the person's core identity. In this sense, we recognize that the organization that we encounter (at an initial contact with a client or in early diagnosis) is not the *identical* organization that existed before we came on the scene. Yet we know as well it is a particular organization, with its own stream of history (and culture), with a reality, and an essence unique to its own existence.

Is the IBM of the millennium "the same" as the IBM of the mid-1950s? A simple answer escapes. Louis Gerstner, Jr., as IBM CEO, likely would have argued that the "new" IBM is quite different, and indeed, in significant ways it is. Yet perhaps there has been an ongoing stream of IBM's position in the economy and society that has transcended changes in technology, product, and environment. It depends on what we *want* to see and on what becomes the focus of our attention.

And the *process* of change looks different to the OD consultant who focuses on teams as the key intervention, in contrast to the one who sees 360-degree feedback as the way to go. There is a different "reality" of sorts in each instance, involving both constancy and identity on one hand and mutability and change on the other.

For another perspective, we turn to the area of change in psychology as considered in the *Handbook of Psychological Change* (Snyder & Ingram, 2000). Michael J. Mahoney, a contributor to this volume, recites six principles associated with change in psychological thought:

- Abandoning simplicity
- The (re)turn of the body in psychology
- Cultures, contexts, feminism, and human rights
- Spirituality, values, and wisdom
- The return of the person: therapist and client
- Measures, methods, and models: promises from complexity studies, constructivism, and dynamic systems theory

OD comment: Surely there is an echo here to much of what is encountered in OD. As we have noted, the illusion of simplicity is just that—an illusion. While it may provide temporary satisfactions of neatness and closure, in more fundamental ways it misleads and provides but the minimal relief of pseudo-success.

The move away from the mind/body dichotomy that has long plagued psychology, perhaps much as the individual/organization dichotomy has plagued OD (and for that matter organization theory, organizational behavior, and various approaches to personal change), suggests that OD, too, must move beyond assumed dichotomies. In psychology, the body has again become a *psychologic* variable, as a legitimate focus of inquiry, in the study of stress, in health psychology/behavioral medicine, even in brain physiology as a cross-disciplinary field, recalling with melancholy the apparent simplicity of phrenology.

We do not claim that one is able to study "everything" in one intellectual or practical gulp, for example, *all* about persons and their organizations at one time. Yet the interplay and the wholeness of people in the organization (anticipated by many early contributors to the field, Hawthorne Studies included [see Roethlisberger & Dickson, 1946; see also Gillespie, 1991]) presage this viewpoint and are best kept in mind in day-by-day OD.

As in psychology, topics such as cultures, contexts, feminism, and human rights as objects and causes of change appear in OD as well.

Psychology, much as OD, has rediscovered the importance of spirituality, values, and wisdom. This increasing "respectability" of ideas that at one time were regarded either as irrelevant or contrary to scientific practice defines an emerging trend.

And there is the "return of the person," in OD the return of consultant and client as flesh, blood, and bone human beings, not as professional automatons.

The Lesson? In many disciplines, complexity, wholeness, avoidance of rigid dichotomies, and sound recognition of values and spirit animate numerous viewpoints and underline the necessity of dealing purposefully with the flow of change in theory and in practice.

For OD practitioners these considerations point to the need for reaching beyond technique or intervention mechanics in the change process, paying heightened attention to the human being as a whole, as we combine uinderstanding of apparent "facts" about people with appreciation of their deeper, complex and spiritual selves.

Conceptual Models in Change

We now return to some frequently used conceptual models in OD relating to change. Sometimes (unfortunately) what change is assumed to mean is pretty much taken for granted. We hope that this is rarely the case for the sophisticated practitioner and thinker alike. Indeed, there are available numerous articulate "theories of change" in OD, some in the group process area and some relating to organizations as wholes[13].

Surely one of the most popular systematic models for change is Kurt Lewin's (1938, 1951) Force-Field Analysis. A key statement of Lewin's position regarding change appeared in the article, "Frontiers in Group Dynamics" (Lewin, 1947). Here, Lewin addresses "quasi-stationary equilibria in group life and the problem of social change," noting that periods of social change may differ quite markedly from periods of "relative social stability." His thoughts on this topic are worth revisiting well more than five decades following their publication.

According to Lewin,[*] "The conditions of change and social stability should be analyzed together for two reasons. Change and constancy are relative concepts . . .

---

[*]Reprinted by permission of Sage Publications Ltd from Kurt Lewin, "Frontiers in Group Dynamics," in *Human Relations,* 1(1). Copyright © 1947 by The Tavistock Institute.

and any formula, which states the conditions of change, implies the conditions of no-change as limit. The conditions of constancy can be analyzed only against a background of 'potential change.'

"In discussing the means of bringing about a desired state of affairs, one should not think in terms of 'the goal to be reached' but rather in terms of a change 'from the present level to the desired one (p. 64).'"

Lewin provides a further example of some mythic significance—one recurring later in this book: "To change the level of velocity of a river, its bed has to be narrowed down or widened, rectified, cleared from rocks. To decide how best to bring about such an actual change, it does not suffice to consider one property. The total circumstances have to be examined (p. 32)."

In this paper, Lewin formulates the well-known three steps: unfreezing, moving, and refreezing. Here he notes that "permanency implies that the new force field is made relatively secure against change." Regarding unfreezing, he says, "To break open the shell of complacency and self-righteousness it is sometimes necessary to bring about deliberately an emotional stir-up (p. 32)."

Let us recall that these formulations, replayed in so many different settings in subsequent—and current—OD practice, were formulated in the 1940s. Yet much of their relevance has been maintained, although criticism has been offered as well. (Lewin would have liked this!)

For example, Jeffrey Goldstein (1993) in "Beyond Lewin's Force Field: A New Model for Organizational Change Interventions" contrasts Lewin's assumptions, which Goldstein holds as being too linear, to a proposed new model seen as non-linear. This latter model is regarded as supporting norms of disorder and non-equilibrium, appreciation of resistance to change, processes of encouraging differences, and allowing self-organization.

Applying Lewin's Change Model

One of the many examples of application of the Lewinian change model is presented in Leonard D. Goodstein and W. Warner Burke's (1991) article, "Creating Successful Organization Change."[*] This article shows how Lewin's change model is applied to a change effort at British Airways:

---

[*]Reprinted from *Organizational Dynamics*, Spring 1991, Leonard D. Goodstein and W. Warner Burke, Creating Successful Organization Change, pages 9-13. Copyright 1991, with permission from Elsevier Science.

At the individual level:

Unfreezing: new top management team

Movement: managing people first, peer support groups

Refreezing: in context of continued commitments by top management: promotion of staff with new (BA) values, "open learning" programs

Structures and systems:

Unfreezing: use of diagonal task forces to plan change, reduction in hierarchy levels, modifications in budgeting

Movement: profit sharing, opening a new terminal and training center, new user-friendly management information system

Refreezing: new performance-appraisal system, performance-based compensation, continued use of task forces

Climate and interpersonal style:

Unfreezing: top management commitment and involvement, redefinition of business from "transportation" to "service"

Movement: greater emphasis on open communications, data feedback, work-unit climate, off-site team building meetings

Refreezing: new organization symbols such as uniforms and coat of arms, development and use of cabin crew teams, continued use of data-based feedback on organizational climate and management practices

The British Airways story and the application of the Lewin three-phase model represents an excellent example of the utility of this framework conceptually and practically. Yet beyond it a still broader paradigm comes to be relevant. We note that in this kind of analysis, two additional elements play a role:

- The time horizon considered, and

- Other variables, both within and outside the organization that may make a difference.

After all, the Goodstein/Burke program had a beginning and an end necessarily within a discrete time period, representing a "slice of time" in the late 1980s and early 1990s. This involved a certain set of conditions in air transport and world economies and within the internal political structure of Great Britain (the era of

Margaret Thatcher), with growing privatization and deregulation. Beyond these conditions, the worldwide economics of air transportation changed thereafter: Trends included the increasing development of "alliances" among carriers, the intensification of global competition, the increasing role of the European Union. Still later trends included heightened globalization, new patterns of competition (for example, Virgin vs. British Airways), and macro-economic cycles as recessionary forces manifest in 2001. In perspective, these elements in turn affect numerous individuals as well as the organization.

In the study reported by Goodstein and Burke (1991), massive layoffs and downsizing impacted more than 20,000 workers, each a "self," and their families and friends. High-level abstractions do not do justice to a deeper understanding of the human meaning of the resulting "redundancies" and dislocations associated with this particular change effort, melding positive organizational outcomes with distressing individual consequences, at least near-term in real time. On the other hand, what about long-term consequences? Easy answers are elusive.

The Lesson? Lewin's model of unfreezing, movement, and refreezing continues to make sense *within a given time frame* and considering particular known or sensed variables. But beyond it, longer time horizons beckon and variables that may once have been considered background come to be front and center. Change is lodged in the evanescent flow of human and organizational change.

And the value issue must not be forgotten. Who gains and who loses in a particular intervention that now has succeeded in a "turnaround"? Top management? Middle managers whose ranks have been thinned, with fewer and fewer surviving in the organization? The many thousands who now are unemployed? Stockholders? The children of the newly unemployed?

As person and as professional, the OD consultant needs to be concerned with these issues of timeline and of the anticipated and unanticipated consequences of intervention, particularly as a time-bounded sequence of unfreezing/movement/refreezing is implemented.

What Is Complexity?

Lewin (1963), as well as Emery and Trist (1975) and Olson and Eoyang (2001), provides source ideas illuminating the nature of complexity especially relevant for present purposes. Koolhas (1982) provides a lively (paraphrased) example:

Four missionaries in a tropical forest are taken by surprise by savages. By an intelligent ploy, they succeed in escaping from the boiling pot and fleeing to the river. There they find a canoe with paddles in it. They push the canoe into the river and step into it while the crocodiles lazily float by. The canoe is very narrow and tips over easily, so the missionaries realize that they have to be very careful if they do not want either to be eaten alive, or (avoiding river and crocodiles) once again risk a fate in the savages' boiling pot.

The question becomes, "How complex is the problem of propelling the canoe in their attempt to escape?" Are there only five variables—the four paddlers and the canoe? What about the distribution of the weight of the paddlers? What about the rhythm of their movements? What about the speed of the stream? What about the rocks they may encounter downstream? What other risks are as yet unfathomed? Are there other savages on the shore? Or the beneficent appearance of a rescue troop of colonial forest scouts?

Koolhas notes, "Complexity is in the eye of the beholder." Yes, we would agree, *and* beyond that there are factors foreseeable and unforeseen, anticipated and unanticipated, that affect what we may recognize as diagnosis, to lay the foundation for an OD intervention, to bring about a desired temporary state (never an ultimate end state) toward which the change effort is directed.

The Lesson? How are we to manage this complexity in dealing with change in OD? It would seem that much that has been presented lays the foundation. Importantly, we need to be open to this complexity at all levels, including that of the self—what we as OD consultants are prepared to see, to apprehend, and to comprehend. If we rethink the Lewinian model, we might consider two approaches:

- Instead of thinking of the particular facilitating and restraining forces around the points of equilibrium, we may want to think in terms of patterns of fractals—the elaborate and ramifying "trees" of *currents of energy* flowing one to the other, growing, collapsing, eventually spending themselves at the end of their hypothetical lifetimes. Here we deal not with neat directional arrows, but with patterns of a convoluted multi-directional nature. In each instance this calls for paying attention to many subtleties, to what goes on at micro and macro levels in the consultant-client relationship and in others of the nine Cs.

- We can imagine the three stages noted as a "movie clip" covering a certain period of "real time," run fast or slow, with a pre-history and a potential post-history, predicted but with unanticipated consequences. As a practical matter, we *bracket the change sequence* as the primary focus at a given time. And in this era of interactive media, we can well visualize inputs by supplemental actions affecting "the movie of change" that we have on our screen. We write new change scenarios as the OD engagement develops.

No automatic formula or stand-alone intervention serves the purpose. Both *deep understanding*, long-term and fundamental, and *strategic understanding*, near-term and practical, need to come together in implementation of the OD change process.

Strategy and Change

We come once more to a point where we might either feel overwhelmed—as by the number of variables previously mentioned (for example, the nine Cs associated with an extended potentially highly complex and convoluted Lewinian analysis)—or where we maintain our sanity by becoming selective in our focus. What is it, here and now, that *really* matters? What holds promise for making a positive difference in the future, in light of values held, for the relevant organization(s) and/or individual(s)? Choosing another term, we need to be *strategic*. Much of the management literature uses (or overuses) words such as "strategic thinking" or "corporate strategy." The roots of the term are linked with military operations, often distinguished from "tactics," while present usage between these two concepts often blurs. Typically, strategy is regarded as long-term whereas tactics are viewed as responsive to more immediate requirements and opportunities, in context of an encompassing strategic plan.

A classic statement of the meaning of strategy, in military context, states that strategy is "the use of the engagement to attain the object of war . . . it must therefore give an aim to the whole military action . . . strategy develops the plan of the war and links the series of acts which are to lead to it . . . much more strength of will is required to make an important decision in strategy than in tactics . . . in the latter we are carried away by the moment" (Von Clausewitz, 1965, pp. 115–118).

Strategic thinking in OD calls for *selectivity* from among the many variables that may be considered. Within the framework of this selectivity, tactics in OD (a concept rarely noted) are more closely associated with problem solving and ongoing interventions. As in war, OD strategy and tactics are inevitably interrelated: If we do not succeed at the tactical level, solving current problems as they arise (including, for example, dealing with client anxieties or glitches in the human resources information system), we may not "live to see another day" in planning strategic large-systems change looking three years ahead.

In this vein, Robert H. Schaffer (1988) notes, "Managers should stop berating themselves for their tactical preoccupations. There is no way that they can ignore the demands of current performance: stockholders want returns, banks want to be paid up. Top management's success is measured by quarterly results as well as strategic thrusts." And in an article appearing in *The Industry Standard* (the newsmagazine of the Internet economy), Larry Dones (2001) addresses issues of strategy and its limitations under the heading, "Strategy Can Be Deadly: Long-term planning is making a comeback. And that's not good." He points out that spending months on a "hefty five-year plan . . . stuffing it in a three-ring binder and pray(ing) the market will hold still as they execute it" may well be a waste of time and concludes that "worrying less about strategy and more about execution is the key to winning a revolution" (Dones, 2001, pp. 74–75).

The Lesson? In seeking change, in context of particular values and aspired results, the OD consultant (a) needs to be aware of the many interacting variables *and* (b) needs to be selective, taking account of long-range strategic implications while executing effectively in terms of short-term tactics. This viewpoint argues against mechanical application of any particular intervention type or change approach *unless* conditions (a) and (b) are conscientiously met. Strategy is selective, guided by strongly held positions of what OD is trying to accomplish. It is also selective in making immediate, short-term, and long-term determinations of what needs to be done tactically to achieve the basic goals of an OD effort. It all has to fit together.

OD Versus Change Management

Late in the 1990s and in the early 2000s, the word "change" became a point of contention between those referring to OD in some historic sense and those proposing a new profession, change management, as an alternative (Worren, Ruddle, & Moore, 1999). It is the thrust of these authors' article that OD as currently practiced should be replaced by "change management" in the sense that this term is used in the large consulting firms. Miles K. Davis (undated) has provided an excellent historical review and analysis of thought on this topic in a paper, "Change Management: Not Your Father's OD." As Davis concludes, he compares OD and change management in terms of polarities: OD with humanism and democracy as underlying values, while change management emphasizes organization survival and viability and shareholder maximization. In turn, he contrasts the theories and analytical frameworks of change management and OD, with the latter based primarily on human processes and individual/group functioning, while the former is presumed to link primarily to strategy and alignment of people, process, structures, and culture in the cause of strategic corporate change.

A helpful response to this asserted polarization appears in Farias and Johnson's (2000) "Organizational Development and Change Management: Setting the Record Straight." We believe that Farias and Johnson are quite correct in their rebuttal to Worren, Ruddle, and Moore, noting that "OD has grown from its roots in human relations variables to focus on strategic issues as well and on the adoption of more holistic and integrated models of organization." Further, they point out correctly that "OD has nurtured an interdisciplinary approach from its inception."

There is no doubt that the large consulting firms, once nurtured by their accounting forefathers and committed to corporate business models, would focus on bottom-line considerations "at the end of the day" and on the renewal and extension of contracts with major client systems. Yet as Davis (undated) notes in quoting one consulting firm's approach to change management, "We help our clients derive new kinds of business value by focusing on the human dimension of business. Successful change requires an expertise in *both* our human performance and in its connectivity with the strategy, technology, and process related elements of an organization." Evidently, we note a crossing of lines or, better, an assertion of integration among human and non-human, for example, structural, economic, and other factors external to the person, in the cause of change. Farias and Johnson again have, as we see it, the correct perspective when they point out, "OD professionals understood and adopted a holistic and integrative perspective on organization change long before the large consulting firms did so. It would appear that integrated methodologies were only recently developed in the major consulting firms." They conclude that, "In their efforts to convince the reader of the necessity of a new discipline, Worren et al. misrepresented (and rejected) current OD theory and practice and its contribution to large-scale change" (Farias & Johnson, 2000, pp. 376–379).

The authors cited do not report on one other important element, perhaps little known in view of the large consulting firm's lack of readiness to disclose: numerous behavioral scientists (including the co-authors) have served as consultants to certain large consulting firms, among them McKinsey, Andersen, and others, on behavioral science and OD-related concepts and practices. Thus, streams of thought, particularly survey research, human systems analysis, small-group process, counseling, and feedback, were infused into general consulting practice.

The actual or assumed tug of war between OD and change management may rather be an issue of "invented here" for the latter, without full tracing of antecedents to original OD formulations. Branding and labeling—let us recall the importance of *words* as an OD issue—are matters of concern and influence the profile and marked boundaries of approaches to theory and practice.

The Lesson? A discussion of OD versus change management may be a storm in a glass of water—no more than waves among small droplets of substance. Organization development has been, continues to be, and needs to be in the future integrative and responsive to many interacting variables, as observed throughout this text. Beyond that, no one owns a field of knowledge as such. Beyond rather unproductive arguments of "Who said it first?" or "Who did it first?" the concept of change, and thus the need to manage change, is fundamental in OD's history, evolution, and current status.

In concluding our consideration of change, it is well to recall that any change effort needs to be placed in the context of values (What is truly desired?), publics (Who is affected by it?), and time (What is the time horizon within which a particular change is to be implemented? How long should it last before another change overtakes it naturally or is induced by one or another means?)[14].

In the next chapter, we consider change as it specifically applies to cultures and the culture concept.

Changing Cultures: Concepts and Constraints

FROM THE EARLY 1980s on, the concept of culture has come to be a widely noted construct in OD practice, including the work of Deal and Kennedy (1982), Schein (1997), and others. These authors, drawing widely on experience in consulting and organization theory, established a contemporary starting point for the analysis of organization culture as a basis for change.

Defining Culture

Schein (1985) defines culture as follows:

> A pattern of basic assumptions invented, discovered, or developed by a given group as it learns to cope with problems of external adaptation and internal integration that has worked well enough to be considered valid, and therefore to be taught to new members as a correct way to think, perceive, and feel in relation to those problems. (p. 9)

While the contributions of Deal and Kennedy and of Schein are significant in their own right, it is necessary as well to re-examine the classic roots of the culture concept, which antedate by centuries the more recent interest in corporate culture. A number of publications of older vintage come to mind.

For instance, Kroeber and Kluckhohn (1963) provide a critical review of concepts and definitions relating to culture and an overview on different uses of the term, in varied perspective.

Frequently noting that culture is a "complex whole," the following sub-concepts are revealed in the comprehensive listing of definitions:

- Knowledge
- Belief
- Law
- Custom
- Acquired habits and capabilities
- Property
- Etiquette
- Industries
- Religious order
- Material objects and technique
- Tradition
- Instruments
- Buildings
- The things that people have
- The things that people do
- What people think

This mélange of subconcepts, drawn from the work of a set of distinguished anthropologists and others, suggests both the strengths and weaknesses of the culture concept: It is very broad and complex and by its very comprehensiveness includes a vast agglomeration of detail.

This inclusive character of culture is emphasized further in Kroeber and Kluckhohn (1963), who cite T.S. Elliot to the effect "that culture has organization as well as content . . . it is not merely the sum of several activities but *a way of life*" [emphasis added] (p. 81).

Culture and OD

What is the OD consultant to do? On one hand culture presents itself as an encompassing way of life. On the other it brings forth an overwhelming amount of detail. Much can be said about both sides of this apparent polarity, from detail to broad sweep. For OD, detail may provide diagnostic data to guide a specific engagement, while the broad sweep highlights social forces impacting client system and external public, for example, economic conditions, environment, and so forth. The danger exists, however, of becoming trapped in the detail or alternatively of being led toward unwarranted conclusions by apparently far-reaching but shallow generalization.

From an OD standpoint, it is most important to note that genuine understanding of the nature of a particular culture is of great significance, but that such understanding does not come easily. It requires both intuition and training, particularly ethnographic skill development—including observation and interviewing. A variety of roles, specific in anthropology and ethnographic fieldwork, come to the forefront (see Leiter, 1980; Merton, 1981; Sanjek, 1990; Spradley, 1979). Just because somebody is "doing OD" in other contexts, for instance coaching, survey feedback, or team building, does not *ipso facto* qualify that person as an acute analyst of culture.

A further complicating issue has to do with the relationship between a given culture and the geographic and/or sociologic unit to which a particular description applies. Popular, although rampant with oversimplification, are responses to queries such as, "Is there an 'American culture'?" "A 'British culture'?" "A 'Scottish Highlands culture'?" Similarly "London/Mayfair"? "Wales"? "Barbados"?

A similar recitation of culture types applies to "corporate culture." Is there a "U.S. corporate culture"? Are there specific cultures for given industries? Steel? Air transport? Retailing? High technology? E-commerce? And what about differential companies within any of these sectors? A common sense response no doubt would point to a mixture of internal consistencies, general similarities, and unique characteristics for any of those mentioned.

The issue becomes no simpler when we look at a given company and its subcultures. For instance, what about internal differences within large multinational organizations doing business in major culture areas such as Southeast Asia, Eastern Europe, and France? Or differences between professional specialties? Similar analysis may be applied to most any country and subregion within a country and to most any organization within one of these geopolitical entities, plus variations in industry and culture of a particular company.

And, as noted, different professions have their own cultures. Is the culture of physicians in private practice similar to that of aeronautical engineers? And how about similarities and differences between the Internet entrepreneurs and middle-aged school teachers?

"Family cultures" also may be observed: Amish, newlyweds, a matriarchal extended family, a foster home, a gay couple, a widow living with her helpers and friends.

Overlap and distinctiveness, convergence and difference. Such dynamics characterize most any culture sets that we encounter. The conceptual Culture Relationship Map shown in Figure 6.1 may be helpful to provide guidelines to OD thinking for purpose of culture analysis.

Figure 6.1. A Culture Relationship Map

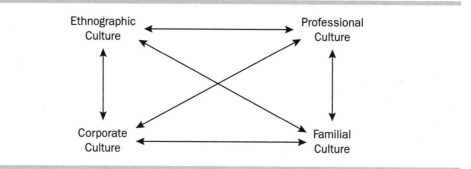

Note: Arrows suggest interrelations and interinfluences.

The vertical arrow on the left of the figure might suggest exploring the relationship between a particular ethnographic culture (perhaps Singapore) and a given corporation at that location (perhaps "Singatek"). At the same time, an additional relationship might lead from corporate to professional, examining the particular technical subcultures within Singatek (engineers, research scientists). Then there is a further set of relationships between family values as they affect the balance between work and home life in Singatek, as we look at the corporate/familial connection.

All relationships to the four major rubrics here indicated a need to be explored in an effort to understand the culture constellation of a particular corporate entity relevant to a particular OD engagement. The key here is not to treat any one of the rubrics as though it were self-contained and separate from the others; rather, the interrelations and overlaps as well as distinctiveness need to be noted. Once again, we address non-linearity and apparent chaos to be sorted out in skilled and perceptive analysis by the OD consultant.

When we speak of *culture* change in OD, we may frequently overstate the case. It is difficult to change an *entire* mass culture or a complex culture, even by major intervention. Culture change is not simply a matter of modifying one aspect of a culture or overlaying an approach such as "empowerment" over a cultural bedrock that has been severely hierarchic for decades. Nor is a program of instituting teams across a set of corporate divisions a sufficient means for changing culture fundamentally. Perhaps contrary historic values and assumptions about the world may operate as substantial and pervasive forces and constitute viscous structures that would need to be altered if fundamental change were to take hold. This may be a matter of many years of iterative effort, one following the other, sequentially and simultaneously dealing with varied organizational and human styles of "doing things."

The Lesson? Cultures *can* be changed, but if the culture is well-established such change requires major interventions over lengthy periods of time. It is not sufficient to change one aspect of a culture and to assume that this is equivalent to genuine, lasting, whole-culture change.

Culture Change Dimensions

We would prefer to set more modest objectives. Perhaps we could address change in terms of clearly identified cultural dimensions, such as a significant move from a heavily Theory X culture toward a Theory Y culture, acknowledging that some Theory X assumptions will not be completely eradicated, especially if the intervention is short-term and technique-oriented[15]. Key managers, broad client systems, and stakeholder support provide strategic leverage points to move the change.

Every culture change of course develops its own dynamics, and its success needs to be assessed against the degree or rigidity or malleability that predisposes potential success or failure of a given OD intervention. Surely a clear understanding in the context of the multiple culture categories noted in the Culture Relationship Map in Figure 6.1 needs to precede any serious effort at culture change.

In many instances, it is hoped that the particular dimensions chosen in a quest for culture change may prove to be strategic, eventually diffusing a desirable change throughout the organization. We recall the internal interdependence in complex systems, realizing that this "cuts both ways": a given intervention may be designed to impact positively on some dimensions, such as the spread of collaborative working modes, but in turn it may collide with countervailing pre-existing forces in the culture that are rooted in well-established bureaucracy and rigid internal boundaries. Then the question becomes: Will new collaborative methods prevail long-term or, over the long haul, will there be a regression to bureaucracy, perhaps with a different face?

We believe that certain dimensions constitute particularly viable starting points for long-term culture change. These dimensions are listed in no particular order and among themselves are interrelated.

Mission Statements. Such statements are designed to place in writing (and into other media) the important directions that an organization is intended to pursue. These statements are heavily interwoven with the fabric of avowed values that may, however, not necessarily come to be acted on in management practice or in the organization's ongoing operation.

Leadership Styles. These involve role models and exemplary behavior among managers and others, for example, collaborative and team ways of doing things.

Rituals, Including Celebrations and Public Events. Here we deal with the "face" of the company, the way it wishes to be perceived, both internally and externally, depending on the nature of the event and circumstances. A stockholder's meeting, a retirement dinner (a classic example from gold watch to humorous roast), the unveiling of a new product, institutional ads, the introduction of an incoming CEO, all these constitute visible culture symbols.

Buildings and Workplace Organization. Among the most obvious expressions of an organization's character are the locations and physical structures within which companies are housed. Even in these days of Internet and virtual organizations, there are important visible embodiments of company character in structures that contain them. These structures in turn speak in the company's voice to the community and public at large.

Resisters to Culture Change

As one considers the practical interventions in efforts to change cultures, it is of critical importance to revisit the old parable to the effect that we must learn to change that which we can change, but to recognize as well that which heartily resists change, given available time and resources. These impediments to change have in common the quality of being historically grounded and of being supported by oft-recited ideology or frequent usage. The following are illustrative.

Stories About the Founders

Both old and new companies develop well-articulated stories regarding "the founders." The issue is not whether these stories are true in an actual sense. They do, however, provide a set of perceptions that then are integrated into subsequent value systems that guide important aspects of the organization's operations. Although many founding stories feature the company patriarch, there is growing variety these days to include such elements as high-tech startups begun in the garage and the high-school dropout as entrepreneur.

On occasion, revisionist stories are promulgated asserting that "new truths" have been found or that some initial "facts" have been proved incorrect. At the same time, the circumstance that certain founders *did* live and *did* leave an imprint on the organization in one or another form are frequently encountered and need to be considered in the development of an OD change approach.

The Principal Language

The principal language can be viewed in the sense of native spoken and written usage, but also in terms of the special languages, dialects, or symbols specifically in use, for example, when you say "I'm at 590," the in-people know that means that you are at headquarters. Or in former days, being a "hat" meant being a supervisor. And what about the "the suits"?

Significant Milieu Shifts

Broad cultural milieus indeed do change, albeit typically at a very gradual pace. A significant alteration, such as major leadership shifts or active social movements, is usually necessary to bring about dramatically new conditions, for example, the fall of the Berlin Wall or Japan's post WWII demystification of the emperor.

In situations involving a merging of cultures, these forces of impediment take various forms, but some kind of resolution reflects eventual change. An example follows.

▶ TWO COMPANIES MERGING: "AND THE WINNER IS. . . ?"

Under conditions that in a prior era would have been considered unthinkable, two very large corporations, one U.S., one German, each principally engaged in the manufacture and marketing of transportation equipment and related products, develop plans for merger, read "acquisition." It is evident that major differentiated cultures play a role—that of core European cultures, Germany, and the United States, and two corporate cultures, also recognizing additional subcultures for each company, divisions, professions, work units, and so forth. (See the Culture Relationship Map in Figure 6.1.)

By culture-specific confluences and divergences, as merger talks go forward, significantly different management styles are revealed, while much is said initially about a "merger of equals." Soon it develops that the German partner emerges as the more influential. Executives originally associated with the U.S. partner leave. At the same time, efforts to integrate various U.S.-linked operations with German operations prove to be failures.

There is much conversation about complementarity of products and synergy. Practical outcomes are invariably influenced by the degree to which coherent relationships are established among people and products originating in differing cultural milieus. In this instance, key leadership by the German "partner" becomes dominant. The merger spawns a new German company, struggling, however, with a burden of technological and financial problems. ◀

Beyond mergers, which in a sense force culture change, we must recall that cultures *are* always changing on their own, although sometimes with glacial slowness. This holds particularly true for core values and central mythologies. Typically, large corporate cultures with many components and reinforcing stabilities over many years duration do not "turn around on a dime." Witness change efforts in companies such as IBM or AT&T. But eventually change they do, as they alter fundamental operating procedures and missions. Failure to do so effectively likely leads to the culture's and company's decline.

More fluid rapid changes in the high technology area in companies, driven by values such as "innovation" or "revenue growth," with other core values insubstantial, have been reflected in rapid rises and sudden demises. The concept of "reinventing the company" has come to be popular to maintain responsiveness to fundamental changes in technology, markets, and economics (see Hamel, 2000; Naisbitt & Aburdene, 1985; Reinventing America, 1993).

As we consider the culture concept in OD, we suggest some guidelines:

1. Culture needs to be described from the "inside out" in terms of the meanings of activities and events attributed by the members of the specific culture to what is going on, not by dispassionate external assertion.

2. Culture is an *organic whole*, not a collection or even a mosaic of disparate dimensions, although such dimensions can be analyzed as a matter of convenience. Each culture constitutes a Gestalt, a complex pattern of activities and events and artifacts that are interrelated in numerous ways. At any point in time, one or another element or subpattern of elements may be salient as "figure," while the rest are less distinct, as "ground." Thus no single culture dimension is to be interpreted in isolation.

3. Culture, especially if large in terms of territory or population or high complexity, necessarily includes subcultures, each in turn an organic whole and each part of a further encompassing organic whole.

4. Culture is not a thing. It is a *process* over time involving many interrelated participants in many forms of activity.

5. Culture at its historic and committed levels—deep culture—often survives in fundamental respects even beyond major change effort from the outside and beyond many change efforts from the inside, depending on leaders' *leverage* and *internal infrastructure.*

6. Organization development efforts to further "collaboration," "teams," "Theory Y," and other approaches have themselves spawned the outgrowth of specific normative assumptions about what a culture *should be* or become. Such approaches must always recognize the limiting and facilitating forces present in the established pre-existing culture.

The Lesson? The complexities of culture need to be recognized and thoroughly understood if we wish to affect culture change.

Changing large cultures always involves dealing with vast congeries of overlapping and interlocking settings. Within these constellations, it is important to attend not only to visible manifestations, such as in public representations, open rituals, and mission statements. Rather it is essential to examine the *underlying forces*, particularly linked to established values. Such values in turn ramify and are reflected in views and actions of the various client systems and stakeholders. One-gulp efforts to change a culture as a whole quickly face serious obstacles.

While recognizing the wholeness of culture realistically, culture change efforts may be best advised to focus on selected culture dimensions and on strategic leverage points for change. The latter include key managers and their interrelationships with other client systems and stakeholders and pivotal persons and subgroups in organization networks that *significantly* affect "the way things are done" and "'what we stand for." The focus cannot simply be on "cosmetic" change or on realignment of externalities. A fundamental "building in" process needs to occur with the principal participants, influential managers, and network leaders with leverage in the culture system—and with the reinforcement and validation of the changes by the "grass roots" as well. Openness, dissent, and dialogue play important roles in the process of culture change.

The concepts of self, client/consultant relationships, and change permeate every facet of the consulting process. While these elements must always be kept in mind, it is also useful to consider more detail-oriented issues associated with various phases of the consulting process. In the next chapter, we will look at entry, contracting, and engagement.

7

Getting on with It: Entry, Contracting, and Engagement

ON THIS CHAPTER, we will address some of the practical and relational issues of entry, contracting, and engagement.

Entry

As we have noted earlier, entry into an OD engagement is only *sometimes* linear: A client senses a problem and finds an external OD consultant, they meet, and the engagement goes forward. But often the entry process is more circuitous: The OD consultant is referred by an accountant who had worked in the particular client system. The potential principal client ignores this referral. Other things have taken priority. Eventually the potential client and the OD consultant happen to see each other at a social function. They have a good conversation and decide to meet more formally to explore the possibility of working together on a major long-term culture change project. However, the OD consultant is over-committed and reluctantly postpones "serious" client conferences for about two months. By that time there is an "economic crunch" and the presenting problem has shifted in character. Six months later client and OD consultant meet once again and eventually establish an entry point for what proves to be a successful long-term association.

Gaining entry in an OD consultation arrangement often is not a simple matter. Referrals, shifting time schedules, and altered circumstances all affect the possibility of establishing a beginning point. And of course such beginnings provide no assurance that the client/OD consultant relationship will "take," that is, whether it will have viability and durability after it begins. Entry involves a kind of balancing act, calling for not too much nor to little follow-through—all conditioned by coordinated conscious realism regarding prospects ahead.

We have already identified the concept of presenting client. Now we need to consider further the nature of the presenting problem as it affects the entry and engagement.

▶ THINGS ARE NOT ALWAYS WHAT THEY SEEM

"Hey, all I want you to do is to make up a questionnaire. I need that to figure out who ought to be a partner around here."

These words are spoken by a large, burly man who might have played right guard for the Green Bay Packers. Actually he never played football but at an early age he started an accounting firm and is a successful CPA. His name is Roger Lebensman, and he exudes an air of brusqueness and impatience in his contact with people, although when he is working on an accounting problem he displays meticulous care and almost compulsive attention to detail.

Roger goes on to say, speaking to the potential OD consultant, Myra Holbein, "Sorry to be so short with you, but that's all we want."

An outside observer might detect a slightly macho quality in his style, with a veiled attempt to overcome this tendency.

Myra says, "No problem. Let's sit down and talk about it. When would you like to do that?"

Roger, trying to slow down the pace of his demands and the speed of his expression, comes back with, "Why don't you first meet with my managing partner, Hank Brumberg. He understands all our problems and you guys can work it out from there."

Subsequently, Myra meets with Hank. Hank is very candid: "Ole man doesn't want partners—well maybe one or two—but mostly he just wants to do something to show that he's with it."

"So what does Roger 'really' want?" Myra responds.

"Well," Hank continues, "He wants the firm to grow, but he really is something of a control freak. I tell ya, you know his heart is in the right place; we all want the firm to grow, but for this we need more real involvement and quite a few more new partners, but we still want to give Roger his due." (Some present partners think that Roger should retire soon.)

Myra gets the sense of what is going on. It surely is not a matter of making up a questionnaire. Rather, there are deeper issues involving Roger's own status and view of himself, perhaps Hank's role in an expanding organization, and still-unknown issues among existing partners, seniors and juniors, all of whom have their own motivations and relationships to one another and to the profession.

By now it is clear that the presenting problem is not synonymous with a set of more basic issues that need to be addressed if the OD engagement is to have meaning. Simple in-and-out focus on a questionnaire to determine "partner-potential" isn't it.

Following the initial encounters with Roger and Hank, Myra consults with her OD colleagues and as a result proposes an opening "retreat" to sort out the issues. Hearing of this proposal, presented by Myra to Hank, Roger goes "ballistic." The profanities uttered are not reproduced here ("bunch of touchy-feely talk," "a lot dumbheads," are some of the milder comments). At any rate, Roger makes it clear that he will not attend the retreat, but that he will not actually block it by withholding funding: "Let Hank and Myra and those touch-feely guys do whatever they want. They don't really understand what's happening here."

The retreat is planned and scheduled two weeks in the future, at a highly esteemed hotel, on a mountaintop near Los Angeles. After two hours of conversation and open discussion among present partners and selected seniors of the firm, the door to the conference room suddenly flies open and with some bombast Roger appears and, interrupting whatever is going on, says, "All right guys, here I am. I don't know what the hell this is all about." He pauses, then continues, "Okay . . . okay . . . I'm okay with you, Myra, and all you blabbermouth guys. Go ahead and do whatever these OD idiots want you to do." Roger sprawls on the couch, shuts his eyes, and *pretends* to go to sleep.

As to the entry process: Myra meets again with Hank, shares with him her observations about Roger and his style, and provides a preliminary statement, noting her views. Subsequently, Myra meets with Hank and the core client group. (Roger intentionally absents himself, although invited.) Two more retreats are planned, as well as a set of carefully structured interviews and administration of brief life-preference inventories.

Preliminary discussions take place with a search firm ("headhunters") to consider succession at the managing partner level. A time schedule is established, considering both a Plan A assuming all goes as expected and a Plan B allowing for some contingencies. Suitable budgets are worked out, developed by Myra on behalf of the OD group, reviewed with Hank, and finally approved (wordlessly but with inchoate muttering) by Roger.

After this beginning, the OD engagement did get underway, later involving coaching, counseling, assessment, and partner selection, with eventual heightened success by an expanded firm. (Roger did *not* retire soon, but eventually became chairman of the board of a larger organization that by then had acquired the original Roger Lebensman Associates, CPAs.) ◄

As is clearly illustrated by the preceding story, the presenting problem as described by the client is not always the issue actually requiring attention. The OD consultant must make an effort to get to the underlying problem and then to work with the client to resolve that problem.

Once the client and consultant have agreed that they can work together on the problem, some type of contract is typically signed.

Contracting

We need to consider both the psychological and the procedural worlds associated with entry and contracting. These two worlds are closely interrelated. Fundamental to all this is the relationship between OD consultant and client core.

In the instance of Myra, Roger, and Hank—and in most analogous situations—a good deal has already happened by the time the explicit "official" entry is formalized and financial arrangements are agreed on. Indeed, a kind of "underworld" of relationship already has established a complex structure for what is to follow. Who is the core client after all? Is Roger part of this or not? And who bears ultimate fiscal responsibility—Hank or Roger? Evidently both legal and personal issues are involved.

Fundamental to what is to follow is the matter of trust. Yet inevitably such trust is itself variable and may be challenged or may deteriorate, depending on numerous factors occurring within the engagement's evolution.

Under conditions of genuine long-term trust, formal financial specification becomes almost irrelevant, yet may serve as routine albeit necessary accounting validation. Under conventional business conditions, some formalization is typically appropriate, particularly noting the ephemeral nature of trust and potential shifting of alliances and commitments. We note the following typology of contract arrangements.

The "No-Contract" Contract

Here trust and a hypothetical handshake are all that matter. The OD consultant and the client core agree on *some* basis of compensation. This basis may vary widely.

Under conditions of the no-contract contract, both parties continually rely on one another's good faith. In turn, either party, unless otherwise verbally specified, is free to terminate the relationship. The risk then is one of possible lack of continuity for the core client and one of uncertainty as to compensation and/or professional trust for the OD consultant. On the other hand, the mutual freedom experienced and the emphasis on voluntary commitment to the tasks involved adds a qualitative benefit to the work undertaken. Brief documented agreements serve as backup, and some basis for billing needs to be determined, no matter how.

The Open-Retainer Contract

Here the OD consultant and the core client agree on a fixed payment, on a periodic basis, for services rendered. These services may be described in general terms but need not be meticulously documented.

Often the periodic retainer is paid routinely, on a monthly basis. Periodic progress reports, to review accomplishments to date and future projections, are essential.

The Per-Project Contract

Here the OD consultant and core client agree on a generally specified set of tasks to be performed by the OD consultant within a specified time frame. The latter may be fixed or flexible, depending on organizational and practical circumstances.

A total amount of compensation is determined, and a *periodic payment schedule* is stipulated, often in writing, with the assumption that the agreement document provides stability and clarity.

The question remains as to how much detail is required. This issue is particularly cogent under conditions of rapid change: If such conditions call for significant revision in the project plan, does this need to be specified once more by formal document or is it just simply "worked out" in real time?

The issue at hand is one of flexibility when the basic parameters of the project are defined in advance, as well as protection of the contracting parties.

Payment by Billable Time Period

This is perhaps the most conventional billing procedure found in many professional firms, such as attorneys, accountants, and various general consultants.

Here a daily or hourly rate is specifically agreed on, perhaps variable for consultants at differentiated levels of presumed competence or experience, for example, partners or senior consultants and principals may be billed at one rate, seniors at another, new associates at still another, and so on. *Billable hours* are "the name of the game." (Just what counts as billable often is a matter of some dispute and interpretation by client and by consultant.) Billing on an hourly basis fits this pattern, in this sense reflecting an effort to respond specifically to precise time spent in particular activities. Quality of service rendered or success attained do not enter the calculation directly. Only by contract extension or repeat business are success and quality measured.

As an alternative, *rates-per-day* may be agreed to for particular consultants or consulting skill levels. These fees are typically billed on a monthly basis.

It is evident that, when this type of payment mode is chosen, both parties need to be clear as to selected rates, in particular regarding alternatives, for example, shifting certain tasks, perhaps those requiring less skill or experience, to lower billing scales, while reserving those at higher levels for the more costly compensation structures.

Index-Linked Compensation Structure

Here a daily rate might be determined based on a multiple of a publicly held company's stock price, specified for a particular day of the month, or for a monthly average.

One of the co-authors has experimented with this mode of compensation in long-term OD consultation for a large financial institution listed on the NYSE, by loading its closing NYSE stock price on the last business day of a given month, multiplying it by a factor (for example, 20), and using the resulting product as basis for the *billing per day*, with monthly invoices submitted according to this daily rate. Many variants of this procedure are possible.

The applicable concept notes that if the fortunes of the company are on the rise, this would be reflected in compensation to the OD consultant. One might hope—although this is surely not conceptually assured—that the OD consultant's efforts, particularly to the extent that large-systems change is involved, are reflected in the compensation structure. Yet obviously one cannot argue that there is a clear-cut relationship between the OD intervention and stock market behavior; OD consultation at best constitutes only one modest element.

Taking compensation *directly* in stock or stock options represents an additional alternative.

It is evident that these various compensation modes are practically and symbolically reflective of the relationship existing between OD consultant and client. Not any one of the above obviates the necessity for genuine human trust in the relationship, and this may be said for most any consultation, but is particularly crucial in the OD process, wherein positive human values at all levels play a central role.

French and Bell (1999) suggest that some measure of informality may be preferable in the contracting phase. It is our view in this matter that judgments need to be made on an individual basis, considering both the temperament and operating style of the OD consultant and the cultural assumptions of the client system within which the contracting process takes place. In the experience of the authors, widely differing patterns prove effective. In one instance, months of dedicated practice, including complex interventions, proceeded without a piece of paper stating the nature of the contract formally on the table, in pure trust, with subsequent success and long-term association. In other instances, it would have proved useful (learned by bitter experience) had "front-end" specificity of the nature of the contract been agreed on, perhaps saving everyone (particularly the OD consultant) much grief.

▶ TRUSTING TOO MUCH

Following an intermittent series of exploratory meetings involving a U.S.-based external OD consultant, an OD colleague based in Switzerland, and the key representative of the core client system headquartered in Germany, planning sessions were scheduled at the principal consultant's office in California. Only the key client representative and the consultant were present; the colleague from Switzerland was unable to attend. Because of this absence, this informal session was not intended to reach definitive conclusions. Progress seemed to be made in discussion of general guidelines for a long-term engagement. The principal client representative himself, at a prior get-together near Frankfurt, had prepared in handwritten form a six-month compensation schedule for the principal external consultant and had signed this schedule.

Shortly following his departure from California, the principal client, without having raised any questions in person regarding the nature or quality of the collaboration to date, sent a highly negative and manifestly abrasive letter terminating all arrangements, in spite of the existence of the signed, although informal, handwritten agreement. Thus the potential client reneged on all verbal and de facto agreements, and the matter was terminated on mutually hostile terms. ◀

What happened? Who was at fault? And would a "formal" agreement in writing at an early stage have solved the problem? Or, given the varied temperaments and value commitments of those involved, might failure have proved inevitable?

There are no infallible crystal balls in matters of this nature, even if agreement is on paper and explicit. It seems essential to consider legal aspects, temperament and culture, and the multiple pressures operating on each of the key participants in the essential drama of contracting. In spite of the admittedly litigious society in which we live, we confess that we abhor long, wordy "legalese" contracts. As a value and as operating guidelines, trust remains fundamental.

Once some type of contract has been agreed to and both client and consultant concur on the nature of the work to be done, both parties must be aware that this work may be of a changing nature and that flexibility is paramount to the engagement.

Engagement

"Rules are made to be broken . . . and plans are constructed to be destructed."

This parable may overstate the case, yet asserts a measure of reality. We recall that some years ago, "long-range planning" was the rage; any company that was not engaged in such a process was regarded as behind the times and as shortsighted. Increasingly it became apparent that long-range planning efforts often came into conflict with the unexpected and deteriorated or simply were shelved. We wonder how many long-range planning documents circa 1980 still rest in musty corporate archives, if they have survived at all. Eventually "strategic planning" came to the forefront, and the consequent "strategy" at this writing continues to appear widely in academic discussion and in corporate activity. For the most part, quantum differences in the speed of change make it difficult to adhere to a steady planning horizon.

And so it is with many OD engagement plans. Likely they need to focus on selected key *variables* as these present themselves in turbulent environments. Still, engagement *plans* are essential in one form or another. Such plans, however, need to be iterative, that is, they need to continue to a point in time at which significant changes may call for modification, or even for drastic revision, of that which had been planned. In order to develop such iterative planning, the OD consultant needs to be carefully attuned to the emerging patterns of organization life and to the individual experience of the principal client, client core, and of other systems and stakeholders.

Flexibility is essential. It cannot be assumed that stability governs most present-day systems. Rather, the capacity for addressing differences over time, promptly, becomes a sine qua non. This requirement has important implications for OD consultant styles and, for that matter, for the effective selection and training of OD consultants. As noted, being wedded to a single technique or intervention type may be stultifying and not in the best interest of engagement success, unless only short-term application is desirable. For instance, at the outset a massive survey feedback program may have been designed, but soon thereafter a number of divisions within which this program was to be implemented are spun off or dissolved. A job redesign approach, together with counseling and outplacement, may become more appropriate, something that could not have been foreseen.

What about the organization structure to support the iterative planning process? We have found it necessary to extend such structures beyond one individual principal client, even if she or he ostensibly represents the client core. Alternatively, an "engagement guidance committee" in a given situation may be formed, linked with, yet independent of, the organization's formal structure. It should provide a basis for reality testing of what goes on during the OD process, with various viewpoints represented and open dialogue encouraged. While this is the ideal, it is recognized that those who participate in this activity rarely are free of the burden of positive or negative stimulation by their own reference groups, their differences in temperament and political agendas. All this too needs to be taken into account, for better or worse, in the development of an OD engagement.

Predicting Behavior and Visioning in OD[16]

In planning OD engagements, relationships with clients and others necessarily involve making some predictions (or best guesses) regarding *how the clients will perceive a given situation* and how they might act on the basis of their perceptions. The issue is generic, yet concretely relevant in OD. The creation of visions for personal and organizational futures is particularly cogent in this content. The framework proposed here, based on but extending Lewin's (Leeper, 1943) life space analysis, provides a systemic way for thinking about and visualizing perceptions and potential actions based on these perceptions. It harkens back to the root notions of the OD consultant and client as self, previously considered, to be understood in present time and space during an OD engagement.

In order to predict subjectively where to go and how to get there, a simple approach of "mapping" is suggested. This is the case, particularly as the number of variables (including the nine Cs) necessarily point to a whole system that is complex and perhaps chaotic. The need exists, therefore, to sort out this complexity and chaos purposefully, with special focus on the consultant. Of course, this may be attempted verbally, but often a "visual aid" of some kind is helpful. As an additional aid in this direction, we attempt to quantify the *size* of a "psychological region" in the sense that its size serves as an indication of resistance (solidation), a possible unwillingness to "go there."

We have proposed the notion of solidation as "the most generalized form of resistance" to locomotion (that is, restraining "going there"). Any potential activity offers an amount of *resistance,* which is directly proportional to the amount of *time* expected to be spent in this activity and to the amount of *effort* expected to be spent in this activity. This relationship is shown in the following formula:

$$\text{TIME (T)} \times \text{EFFORT (E)} = \text{RESISTANCE (R)} = \text{Solidation (S)}$$

Expenditure of *resources* might well be included in E, especially in organization settings.

Let us take two brief examples:

1. A consultant is to conduct a one-day team-building program in a highly cooperative client system.

   T: would require relatively little time

   E: would require relatively little effort

   S: as $T \times E$ is relatively small, resistance (R) would be low, assuming that other Cs are consistent with this intervention.

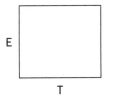

T × E is relatively small, solidation is low, and the activity makes low demands; thus this activity is readily doable.

2. I (FM), not exactly an aspirant for the decathlon team, am assigned to lead an "Outward Bound" trust-building exercise.

   T: it would require a long time for me to get into shape

   E: I would have to expend much effort (even paying a personal trainer) to get ready and to learn more about Outward Bound

   S: as $T \times E$ is large, resistance would be high, that is, for me, a potent barrier, with the Cs serving only as minor background.

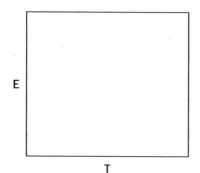

T × E is relatively large, solidation is high, and the activity makes considerable demands; thus, this activity probably won't happen.

It is an important point that, in addition to being defined by T and E, the nature of the resulting resistance (S) must be described in terms of positive or negative valences (V). Clearly, if in addition to major expenditures of time and effort, the consultant and the clients "feel good" or "don't feel good" in varying degrees about what is proposed, this will have massive (but not necessarily decisive) impact on the nature of resistance.

Sometimes it is evidently necessary "to bite the bullet" as in the following example:

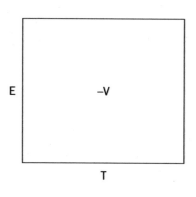

A lengthy, costly corporate program of restructuring is being planned. T × E is relatively large, solidation is high, *and* distinctly negative valence (–V) is in evidence. As OD consultant, I "feel the pain," but realize that in reviewing and thinking about the nine Cs and having weighed the long-term benefits against the near- and medium-term problems for all involved, "this just has got to be done."

The Lesson? At the outset of an OD engagement, the consultant may wish to map her or his life space, including the self that he or she brings to the task, and the anticipated life space of the principal client, considering time, effort, and valence of proposed and potential activities. This effort involves a constellation of *mini-hypotheses* about T/E/V, not statistically testable but explored in the crucible of interaction with the client. This calls for positive and negative feedback at all levels, explicating verbal and nonverbal confirmation, doubt, and disconfirmation on what is more-or-less doable. All these aspects may be sketched at any one point in time, realizing that with passage of moments, minutes, hours, or days, *the constellation shifts.*

Internal Versus External Consulting

Fundamentally, the consulting process is characterized by many generic qualities consistent across a wide range of real-life situations. Understanding of the self and of the client systems and stakeholders and deep knowledge of intervention approaches appropriate to the system(s) involved are illustrative of such consistencies. While many of the issues discussed so far in this chapter apply to both internal and external consultants, there are some differences between the two worth considering (Block, 2000). Some of these differences seem fairly clear-cut; others are subtle. Some key interrelated dimensions highlighting these distinctions are shown in Table 7.1.

Table 7.1. Internal/External Checklist

Issue	Internal	External
1. The Political Framework	The internal consultant is directly enmeshed within the client system's political framework. The consultant is part of this political framework as a person and in his or her professional role.	The consultant is connected with the client system's political framework, but by way of metaphor, has one foot in/one foot out. Yet he/she is affected directly by the political framework of external consulting firm and/or consulting community.
2. Specific Hierarchy	The consultant is positioned specifically within an organizational hierarchy, including accountability and reporting requirements to person(s) at other (normally higher) levels of this hierarchy.	The consultant relates to the organizational hierarchy and is accountable, but not in direct organizational responsibility.

Table 7.1. Internal/External Checklist, Cont'd

Issue	Internal	External
3. Permanence	The association between consultant and client system is relatively permanent in the sense that an employment contract is statutorily defined. It is clear, of course, that in times of rapid systems change, forced reductions, layoffs, and shifts in organization structure, stability may prove to be illusory.	The association between consultant and client system is defined as transitory, even if this association endures over considerable time periods.
4. Organizational Blinders	The risk of entrapment by "organizational blinders" is relatively high. Being enmeshed in the political system and directly impacted by hierarchy, wishful thinking, and unconscious response to conditions in the client system is considerable, particularly as the consultant's relatively permanent livelihood is at stake. Sometimes the internal consultant may find it hard or even impossible to speak his/her mind due to political pressures within the organization.	The consultant is not immune from the risks associated with organizational blinders. Again, wishful thinking and unconscious response may take their toll. Yet the defined transitory role of the consultant and his/her option to move outside the specific client system, with possible opportunities for livelihood, derived from several systems or under the "umbrella" of a consulting firm providing direct employment, modifies the potentially coercive impact of organizational blinders. Yet again a different set of blinders may be derived from the consulting firm and/or the consulting community.

Table 7.1. Internal/External Checklist, Cont'd

Issue	Internal	External
5. Organizational Insight	The relatively permanent association of the consultant with the client system provides her/him with considerable continuing bodies of data relevant to diagnosis and insight. This ongoing data flow must be evaluated, however, in context of the risks engendered by the organization blinders. The internal consultant may have more information to work with, but must be particularly cautious with interpretation in view of blinders issue.	Diagnosis and resulting insight are more artifactual, yet perhaps more focused and purposeful, than is the case for the internal consultant who, as noted, is immersed in an ongoing data stream within the client system. For the external consultant, more sparse yet more focused data may result in a higher level of diagnostic insight.

The Lesson? In each of the five points identified in the checklist, two aspects may be noted: (1) differences in degree, not kind, prevail, and (2) there are tradeoffs. For instance, the external consultant may function with a higher degree of independence than the internal consultant. On the other hand, the internal consultant may have available a significantly greater volume of current data regarding the client system's operations. Yet, once again the external consultant, being more independent, may be less affected by "organizational blinders," although other kinds of "blinders" derived from the consultant's own or employing system generate limitations. And both internal and external consultants are accountable to various stakeholders directly or indirectly. Understanding of self and commitment to values of individual and organizational health are essential for both internal and external consultants.

In reflecting on the factors involved in "getting on with it," it is apparent that no one formula serves. Some summary guides may be of some help, in the form of a brief lesson statement.

The Lesson? "Getting on with it" and entry *can* be simple and linear: A client may sense a problem and find a consultant who "fits the bill," and the OD engagement goes from there. But often the entry road is bumpy and non-linear. Detours and delays, in both client system and consultant world, may arise. The "presenting problem" may turn out to be misleading or substantively irrelevant, and the eventual "actual" problem may require several redefinitions before more work can be undertaken. The "cast of characters," clients and others, may expand to many people and publics and involve varied pressures, motivations, and attitudes.

All this needs to be accurately perceived and thoroughly understood by the consultant, as foundation for what is to follow.

- By the time you get to contracting, there is already a history of contact between client and consultant. The joint issues of *trust* and *fiscal procedure* must both be taken into account when various contractual arrangements are considered: the "no contract" contract, the open-retainer contract, the per-project contract, billable time, and index-linked compensation are all possibilities.

- Engagement planning, with focus on selected key variables, is necessary, but flexibility in this phase of the OD process is essential, as organizational life continues to be turbulent.

Although at this point the OD consultant may have a good idea of the issues to be addressed, further diagnosis will almost certainly be necessary, as is explored in the next chapter.

Diagnosis
and Turbulence

TRADITIONAL APPROACHES to organization theory stipulate a predetermined order, seen as desirable for attainment of organizational goals, for example, an organization chart, a set of documents describing a particular system's functions, a given span of control, job descriptions, and eventually hard copy and/or computerized instructions on "how things ought to be," sets of normative statements. Practice teaches, however, that quite often these hypothetically desired structures are not stable, not objectively clear, nor practically functional. They move with some volatility from one state to another. Whatever is deemed to be objective and normative at any one time is subject to wide individual variation in perception and to realignment. Much energy is devoted to seeking common denominators, to assure organizational activity within bounds deemed to be acceptable, targeting a given goal in context of broader goals or purposes, these also subject to interpretation. Especially in high-tech and dot-com systems, but also in brick-and-mortar organizations, the need to cope with changing conditions and turbulence is pervasive.

Creating Coherence and Focus in Diagnosis

In this sense we see diagnosis as involved with a continuing effort to impose coherence on incoherence, some pattern on apparent chaos. These turbulent conditions put in question the notion of taking a fairly static hypothetical "snapshot" of what's happening at time "A" and simply using this snapshot directly as a basis for action at later time "B" and at still-later time "C." In traditional diagnostic style, a dominant assumption of relative stability reigns. There may well be a "fine print" admission, often implicitly, that things do change. Yet, it is the relatively stable organization pattern that often has been used as a basis for diagnosis, often establishing the foundation for subsequent intervention.

In rethinking diagnosis in conditions of turbulence, it is important to pay heed to ongoing change, recognizing the essentially fluid character of events and the requirement of reviewing and revising the diagnostic process within the ongoing OD program. Changing conditions suggest that to be effective, consultants must:

- Note significant changes that may make a difference in relevant parameters—in client attitudes, personnel changes, aspects of the nine Cs—and adjust the diagnostic process accordingly;

- Cope with apparently chaotic conditions, and within them find some *temporary order* as basis for intervention; and

- Continuously be aware of the implications of this *spiral of diagnosis and rediagnosis* to guide interventions that are truly appropriate in response to rapidly changing circumstances.

It is clear that diagnosis itself is, of course, an "intervention," and that basic diagnosis has taken place already at entry, contracting, and engagement planning. Whatever modes of inquiry are used in iterative diagnosis, the process, to the extent that it involves people in the organization, proves to be an intervention as well. Thus, while diagnosis necessarily *is* an intervention, "making waves" in already roiled waters, its explicit and intuitive insights, at any one time, ideally do provide a guide to future action and for *subsequent* intervention.

Some diagnostic focal points (related to aspects of culture) follow, along with some questions that may be used when considering these points. Data associated with these focal points must be viewed in *patterns*, rather than each separately.

Searching for significance and holistic understanding beyond rote observation is essential. Further, the diagnosis may need to select from among these focal points given limitations of time and resources.

Diagnostic Focal Points

1. The organization's *key people*

    Who is the client?

    Are there other principals?

    Who are the stakeholders?

    Is anyone else involved?

2. The *social economic context* in which the organization is positioned

    What community does this organization reside in or serve?

    What are its primary markets?

    What current economic conditions affect the organization?

    Is this organization bounded by governmental regulations?

    What are the major external pressures?

3. The *physical structure* of the organization

    What are the buildings like?

    What qualities does the architecture reflect?

    What is the surrounding area like?

    How is the office laid out?

    Do structural factors facilitate or impede communication?

4. The *internal structure* of the organization

    What information can you glean from reporting charts, annual reports, or job descriptions?

5. The client's *organizational setting*

    What is the environment *within* the client's offices or plant?

    What is the furniture, technology, and equipment like?

6. *Publications and other visible materials*

   What information can you deduce from the appearance, form, and content of advertising, customer mail-outs, e-mail, websites, sign boards, and logos?

7. Identification of *individual informants*

   Who are the people with knowledge about the organization's interpersonal networks?

   At what levels of the organization can these people be found?

8. *Sociometric networks*[17]

   How can these be directly measured or indirectly identified (for example, multirelational sociometric surveys, network analysis by questionnaire, sketching/mapping of important relationship patterns, per key informants, and so on)?

9. *Flash points*

   What are the significant actual and potential conflicts and disagreements? Are there any additional potential areas of conflict, that is, "smoldering fires," possibly leading to future eruptions?

10. *Forces of cohesion*

    What is holding all or any subgroup together?

    What are the shared ideologies, mythologies, traditions, and "stories" retold over time?

11. *Heroes*[18]

    Who are the persons seen as most admired, present and past?

12. *Enemies*

    Who are the persons or organizations, including other companies or institutions, who are seen as seriously aggressive or hostile toward a specific organization or who need to be fought, contained, or destroyed?

The Lesson? It is not possible to diagnose "everything," especially under conditions of turbulence and unpredictable change in organization life. Some diagnostic focal points need to be considered—we have suggested an even dozen—as we try to identify some coherent patterns as a basis for what is to follow in the OD process.

Modes and Strategies in Diagnosis

Much literature is available on the various *modes* of diagnosis—far beyond this book's intent[19]. Two principal diagnostic modes are observation and dialogue.

We can connect these modes and the diagnostic focal points by way of the following example. We can point to "looking" as in observing the organization's physical structure (3) and reading the organization's publications (6). And we can readily connect "talking" with the process of dialogue with key people (1) and in conversations leading to identification of individual "informants" (7).

As another example, we may "take in" visually the office setting (5) as we look around during a meeting with the principal client (1). Or, as we examine a plaque commemorating the company founder (3 or 11), we ask for an explanation of some of the symbols in the plaque (5) from an old-timer at the plant (7).

What is of importance are not bland-looking/talking "raw data" as such, but rather the analysis and interpretation of data and the attribution of meanings by the OD consultant. This is not a "book-learning" process. It may involve some pre-existing capabilities on the part of the consultant developed further in *experiential learning*[20] as by case study, internships, and group-process experiences.

We believe that deeply probing (phenomenological) interviewing provides an excellent approach to diagnostic data collection (see Gubrium & Holstein, 2001; Massarik, 1983; Nichols, 1995). Starting with a simple broad inquiry, such as "What's going on around here?" The consultant then pursues issues as authentically raised by the respondent. This process offers insights elusive in more direct question-answer interviews or questionnaires/surveys.

Further, "being a fly on the wall"—as an unobtrusive or indigenous observer—may serve well in sensing important subtleties helpful in diagnosis.

As noted, in many instances diagnosis needs to be rapid, particularly if an OD involvement is intended to be responsive to crisis or to quickly changing circumstances. It's one of those situations where it is necessary to be quick *and* to be as right as possible under the circumstances. This kind of philosophy often is at odds with traditional academic thought and with approaches that call for diagnosis requiring a lengthy period of time, permitting detailed examination of numerous data points.

Instead of seeking to maximize accuracy in every detail, as may be aspired to in a more stable world, one often must "satisfice" (see March & Simon, 1958). It is necessary to be "good enough," not perfect. This approach is particularly cogent because natural change, in concert with rapid tactical operational changes, for example, responding to shifting consumer tastes or market volatility, may suggest that a long-term diagnostic process may be overtaken by events and thus prove irrelevant. Therefore, we present an approach for more timely short-term diagnosis.

Suggestion 1: Start with What's Available, Whatever That Happens to Be

Here we adduce the principle of equifinality[21]: There are many ways for getting there, and most any starting point is good enough providing it is not also a stopping point. Such a starting point simply may involve conversations with the potential client (almost inevitable anyway) and others who happen to be present, reading material in reports relating to the company, or discussion with most anyone who has a viewpoint regarding the organization.

Each or all of these items provide the OD consultant with some initial impression. In this sense, we can begin the diagnosis process at any one of many possible points. Some minimum amount of credibility and relevance undoubtedly needs to be considered; following this initial exploration, other data points need to be determined. Both intuition and systematic theoretic perspectives provide guidelines.

What is *not* to be done? Due to time constraints, no recommendation is made for a large-scale, carefully designed diagnostic survey. No suggestion is put forth for a massive interviewing program, with attention, for example, to stratification by management level, geographic location, or professional specialty, as might be implemented in relatively stable systems and with considerable time availability.

Suggestion 2: "The Hunting of the Snark"—Follow the Trail

Beyond the first impression, we seek a subsequent systematic basis for understanding the situation. As with the mysterious "snark" of literature, just where this quest may lead is not entirely clear. Again, both intuition and analytic thought are mobilized. The task to follow has more in common with the hunter in poorly charted territory or with the detective's ambiguous clues than with the hypnotic research scientist in narrow but precise experimentation. Like a detective, the OD consultant observes, one clue leading to the next. And perhaps the OD consultant encounters "blind alleys," bits of contradictory information, or some reassuring indications of convergence. The question of what is "truth" remains tentative and subject to revision. The stereotype of the detective who asks for "just the facts" is inaccurate. Concepts and practice theory determine even what facts are noted at all and, of course, how these "facts" are interpreted in context.

We postulate *a universe of data points.* These are manifold and varied, and the boundary of this universe is loosely defined, including information both within and outside the organization. The data points have in common some relevance for understanding various aspects of the organization, as presumed relevant to the OD process.

Having made a start in exploring this universe, the OD consultant now proceeds with an examination of consistencies and inconsistencies, based on what is observed and what has been heard and understood.

Suggestion 3: State Diagnostic Findings

As patterns emerge in this search for diagnostic understanding, contradiction and ambiguity remain uneasy companions. Yet as patterns are found, held tentatively, they need to guide the OD engagement with a sense of conviction. Even noting that "nothing is forever," some credible basis for intervention needs to be established. Such diagnostic findings are, of course, subject to change as later experience or circumstance may warrant.

Suggestion 4: Recall That the OD Consultant Is Not a "Blank Slate"

The OD consultant's humanness, discussed in Chapter 2 on The Self, always is an active ingredient throughout the engagement in all its phases. What the consultant brings to the diagnostic effort as a person constitutes an important basis for what is seen and understood and determines the nature and quality of the resulting diagnosis.

Accordingly, there is not a single "diagnostic" for a given situation. That which is diagnosed may well vary among OD consultants, given their styles and their readiness or indeed eagerness to see certain things in certain ways.

The Lesson? When it comes right down to it, "looking" and "talking and listening" are the principal modes of diagnosis. Deeply probing and unobtrusive methods often are most helpful. Instead of committing to elaborate "by-the-numbers" diagnostic plans, we suggest short-term diagnostic approaches starting with what's available, then following an evolving trail of clues. Eventually stating findings clearly sets the stage for next steps. The impact of differences of perception among several observers and the need to revise diagnostic findings when changing circumstances warrant must be kept in mind.

Regardless of the time allotted for diagnosis, at some point the OD consultant will need to make decisions and suggest an intervention or intervention program to the client. The next chapter (Chapter 9) focuses on the intervention concept and on the process of choosing appropriate interventions. Chapter 10 presents a variety of intervention scenarios.

Doing Something About It: The Intervention Concept

WHAT DOES IT MEAN to "intervene"? As we look at various dictionary definitions, the word connotes something like . . . coming between two entities . . . or interposing one state of affairs onto another, or for that matter . . . to come between disputing people . . . to intercede . . . to mediate (conflict resolutions?). Or else, "We enjoyed the picnic until a thunderstorm intervened" (*Random House Dictionary*, p. 999).

While containing some kernel of credibility, for many professionals engaged in OD, these definitions don't sound quite right, or at least they do not represent the essence of what we intend to be the meaning of "intervention."

There is something linear in the meta-meaning of "intervention." It suggests some interaction between two entities, one coming into the other as a sort of one-two punch; perhaps what is going on in entity B (the organization) and what is to be improved by entity A (the OD intervention) is seen somehow as a straight line A—B. In this sense, the intervention notion goes along with the "planned change" concept. Someone, the OD consultant, in concert with others, for example, managers, plans to bring about some (hopefully positive) alterations in what goes on in B (the organization).

It is quickly evident that this A-B presumed sequence is enmeshed in a web of values, implicit or explicit. If planned change is to occur, it presumes to be "change for the better," which raises the question, of course, "What is better?" "Better" is a relative term, not only in comparison of "before" and "after," but also as it relates to a congerie of stakeholders, some of whom may be affected positively and others negatively by a particular "intervention." As we reflect on the above, an intervention is not a simple matter, not a given technique that is just turned loose on the organization's system to "improve" it. Interventions do not involve obvious sequences with clearly predictable outcomes "for good."

Then there is, of course, a question of *who* is doing the intervening, the style and character of the OD consultant, and the complex interaction between the OD consultant (one or many) and the "target" of the intervention—the system that is to be affected by it, managers, co-workers, and others, within and outside. All of these interactions cause ripple effects that may reach even remote stakeholders.

Seeking Context

What are the practical implications? It is our position that interventions, as the term is currently used in OD, must be placed in the *context* in which they exist and unfold. This argues against the often-simplistic application of one given "technique," no matter how well-crafted, unless full attention is given to the complexities, sometimes labyrinthine, in political, social, and environmental terms, that confront the "intervenor." We believe that we must rid ourselves of conceptual adherence to straight-line sequential formulations when we speak of interventions, addressing instead the realistic, convoluted, multi-layer, and colorfully interactive settings in which OD in fact operates, with anticipated and unanticipated results.

In essence, as we consider the concept "intervention," two questions arise:

1. How should interventions be regarded? As specific *techniques* to be applied, or as integral to broader (and partly unpredictable) context?

2. What is the underlying grounding of the choice of particular interventions?

In response to question 1, it is evident that in many instances interventions are applied on the basis of ill-defined or incomplete psychological maps, for example, poor, little, or no diagnosis may stem from sets of tacit assumptions made by the

OD consultant and from other sets of assumptions made by the client. One must distinguish here between *superficial levels of agreement*, as might emerge from relatively limited or perfunctory diagnosis, as indeed may have involved both OD consultant and client, in contrast to *fundamental understanding* of prevailing circumstances and projected consequences. Here it becomes appropriate to consider distinct scenarios, including worst-case scenarios as well as idealized hoped-for outcomes. This calls for consideration of numerous variables, some beyond the immediate field of view of either or both OD consultant and client. As a practical matter, the development of *multiple scenarios* of intervention implementation and assessment are necessary to provide a beginning for most any sort of OD effort. Let's remember that, beyond interventions, many other factors operate and interact to bring about change.

In response to question 2, it is appropriate to probe, for individual OD consultants and for others, the *motivation* for choice of a specific intervention. It is clear that individuals differ in their preferences, including what they wish to do in their professional roles and what they think is "best" under given circumstances. Under *any* circumstances? There are those who like to work with teams primarily, others who place main emphasis on the psyche and on personal dynamics, and still others who choose to intervene exclusively in terms of "big picture" issues relating to strategy or to broad corporate redesign.

Among all of these, there are OD consultants who follow the pattern of "Johnnie One Note": They do a particular thing and that's that. They may try to apply an intervention simply because it is their specialty, without clear-cut focus in context of what is required, as long as the client buys it. This may be the case even when diagnostic data suggest otherwise. It then becomes necessary to rationalize that this particular intervention style is appropriate and thus is put forth as the "intervention of choice," although there may be serious countervailing considerations[22].

Here it is important that the OD consultant be directly open to input and capable of assessing whether a particular intervention reflects his or her stylistic preference and whether it is appropriate from other standpoints, short-term and long-term, to attain desired objectives.

As a basic procedural recommendation, it is important that we use one another's insights in choosing intervention patterns. This may involve conversing with colleagues active in the same engagement or personal "shadow consultants" who can help us think through issues and the testing of our preferences against those expressed by others, including clients. The Intervention Choice Worksheet on the following pages may be useful in this effort.

Intervention Choice Worksheet

1. Briefly describe the proposed intervention.

2. List the clients and stakeholders to be affected by the specific intervention.

3. Among these, who is the *principal* client?

    a. Who is in the core client system? Name the people.

    b. Who are possible additional clients? Stakeholders?

4. Is the implementation of the intervention likely to create positive and/or negative consequences (as seen by *each*)?

    a. For the principal client?

    b. For whom in the core client system?

    c. For other clients or stakeholders?

5. Within what time frame?

6. Are there tradeoffs: gain for one or another client or stakeholder, loss for others? In what respect? With what short-term and long-term consequences? (Is this a zero-sum game or win-win?)

7. In what respect does the specific intervention chosen respond explicitly to specific data emerging in diagnosis?

8. Am I (and/or my immediate colleagues and beneficiary professional associates) "specialists" in this intervention?

9. Am I proposing this intervention (a) because it really fits the current or projected diagnostic analysis, (b) because I am most comfortable with this involvement style, or (c) both of the above? Have I done "due diligence" to determine this?

10. Could someone else do all this "better" in terms of likely results and particular client/stakeholder needs? If so, how do I refer the client to someone else and dissociate myself from the presented task?

11. What alternative intervention(s) should be considered (were considered) that might be almost as promising, or more promising, to achieve particular results, beyond the intervention now being considered?

12. How does the specific intervention fit into a broader program of desired change? Is there such a program in hand? Short-term? Long-term? For whom? And with what lasting effect at all levels?

Often, as in the above discourse, we have spoken of "intervention"—singular. Purposely, we have not used the term *interventions* in order to highlight (for purposes of clarity) one particular *component* in a potentially complex OD program. Essentially, it is the OD *program*, whether called an engagement plan and whether explicitly delineated or implicitly assumed, that guides the OD process. The OD *program* is the explicit *plan* (as in "planned change," when this traditional term applies) as specified *at a given time*.

Having noted the changeability of internal and external environments, it is evident that any plan or engagement, as formulated at a given time, is itself subject to change. It is likely that any ironclad plan determined a priori runs into unexpected circumstances as well as those presumably foreseen.

When we speak of conditions as prevailing "at a given time," we adduce Lewin's "life space" as background construct. This refers to a *temporary* ephemeral structure of perceptions, consisting of activities that are perceived or conceived by the acting person as alternative behaviors. It provides a *mental map* for where you are and where you want to be and for possible steps in-between.

OD Technologies and Their Classification

Early historical summaries regarded T-groups and similar methods as just about synonymous with OD intervention—or at least as the basic touchstones of the OD field (see Bradford, Gibb, & Benne, 1964; Siroka, Siroka, & Schloss, 1971). Whatever the circumstances in the 1950s and 1960s, particularly from the 1970s to the present time, this has changed dramatically. Widely varied intervention technologies and related styles, from high simplicity to complex "bells and whistles," have come onto the OD scene. There is now available a vast array of interventions, addressing anything from highly individual change to vast "whole systems" change. The variety found in OD as a field of practice itself has been profoundly affected by external demand and by internal ethos as cultures and professions have changed.

With all this, it is tempting to try some sort of classification. Yet this may not be particularly helpful, as suggested by the general lack of practical use of prior classificatory schemes. A paper by Ginger Lapid-Bogda is helpful in this connection.

► OD INTERVENTIONS OR "HELP! WHAT DO I DO NOW?"

GINGER LAPID-BOGDA

The most complex display of the variety of interventions used by organization development consultants can be found in Blake and Mouton's (1983) "Consulcube"* from their book *Consultation.* This three-dimensional cube looks at who the client is (called "units of change"), the consultation style used ("kinds of interventions"), and problem(s) diagnosed ("focal issues"). See the layout below.

Units of Change	Kinds of Interventions	Focal Issues
individual	acceptant	power/authority
group	catalytic	morale/cohesion
intergroup	confrontation	norms/standards
organization	prescriptive	goals/objectives
larger social system	theory/principles	

Schmuck and Miles (1976), in *OD in Schools,* construct an intervention cube that adds dyad/triad to the "Unit of Change" dimension and role to "Focal Issues." The Schmuck and Miles Intervention Dimension includes consultant style and the process used by the consultant (that is, data feedback, process consultation, task force establishment, and so forth). W. Warner Burke (1982) provides a readable narrative of these and other intervention typologies in *Organization Development: Principles & Practices.* But do OD consultants actually use cubes in making determinations about how to intervene in client systems? We might use one, after the fact, to describe what we've done. We might also use a cube before an intervention to assess our options. However, the remaining sections of this paper depict more of what we actually *do* using analysis and intuition. They are, I think, the mind and guts of our work.

---

*Reprinted with permission of Grid International Inc., Austin, Texas.

Organization Diagnosis

Consultants have models, categories, and working theories (implicit and explicit) about how organizations work, how people behave, and how change occurs. These help us and our clients make sense out of an otherwise chaotic world; without them we wouldn't know what questions to ask, how to organize data, or how to engage in dialogue with a client about organization problems or growth. These models also limit us as we leave elements out of our models. At one time I added strategy and positioning to my conceptual framework and later I added vision and the importance of leadership in setting vision and strategic direction. Now that I look for these issues, I actually see them and work with them in most of my consultations. In sum, we intervene where we see weaknesses and strengths, but what we see is determined by the models we use.

Hurting Systems

The organization diagnosis would tell us which part of the organization is in the most pain and, therefore, the most potentially motivated to work on change. The mottoes, "no pain, no gain" and "when you ain't got nothing, you got nothing to lose" apply here. One client came to me with a "presenting problem" of lack of teamwork. The diagnosis stage indicated an all-out racial war. The issue behind this was a leadership vacuum of ten years. But the obvious pain was in the racial conflicts, which is where the client members were first willing to do the work.

Success Interventions

The client and client system may need to experience something successful together before they are willing to work on deeper, more powerful issues. Or the client may need to have a success with the consultant before the client will use the consultant on a more complex or more expensive problem. I came upon this latter aspect with a client who wanted to use me in an action research project *after* they had seen me do something. They, however, could think of nothing for me to do with them—I was supposed to come to a meeting with them and do something! After I got past my resentment at "being on stage" and my nervousness ("stage fright"), I worked with them to explore how the position they put me in reflected some of their own issues and then discussed what they hoped might result from our working together. I got the contract.

Domino Analysis

I first heard this term from Dick Beckhard in a presentation. As a problem area surfaces, it requires us to ask, "What is the cause of the problem?" and then to ask the question again and again until you get to the root problem. Once at the core, the intervention can begin. A large-scale contract presented our consulting team with a "presenting problem" of morale. This was, however, a symptom of departmental chaos: Every department lacked coherent structure, policies, and communication systems. Behind this was the core issue of managerial competence and leadership. The managers were all very inexperienced and they felt neglected, at best, to victimized, at worst, by the parent organization. So we began our intervention through intensive management coaching and, during the group feedback segment of the action research project, the managers facilitated the meetings with the OD consultant in the role of coach and backup support. This was done to enable the managers to be proactive at each step.

Backup Method

While this sounds like the domino analysis, it is quite different. In the "backup method," the consultant is the artist. If the intervention is the drama, the consultant is the stage director. Here, the consultant asks, "If this intervention is to be successful, what other elements must be in place?" These elements are not core problems; they simply help things along. A recent contract for a three-day retreat with a management team of thirty people focused on direction and purpose for an entire organization. "Backing up," my co-consultant and I met with the leadership pair for a consultation to explore their individual and common values and visions in preparation for their presentation at the retreat. We also requested that the managers do some preparation regarding their visions and values for their departments. These "backup" interventions allowed the retreat experience to become more thorough, reflective, and mutual.

Historical Successes and Failures

In determining an appropriate intervention for an organization with a particular problem, an assessment of the organization's history of OD successes and failures can tell the consultant what might and might not work with the client. It can tell you what may be the effect of a certain process, as well as what type of "halo effect" an intervention may have, simply because it is similar in method to a prior positive or negative intervention process.

As an example, a human resource group with whom I consult requested a team-building retreat in spite of having had a prior negative experience with a team-building retreat. The obvious question was why they wanted it. The answer given was that they felt they needed it. As I explored with them why their prior experience had been negative, two themes emerged: The agenda had been the manager's, not the group's, and the consultant had colluded with the department in not facing highly conflicting issues. As a result of this information (and so as not to encourage a negative "halo effect"), the intervention design was as follows: (1) generate the issues needing attention by having each group member anonymously complete two 3" x 5" cards—the first card answered the question, "What two or three issues do we need to deal with that would be easy for us?" and the second card responded to the question, "What two or three areas do we need to address as a group that are difficult for us to deal with but which would add great value to our organization if we could deal with them effectively?" (2) collect the cards and read them out loud, (3) divide the group into small groups of three or four people and have each group design the next two days, (4) compare and combine designs according to group consensus, (5) negotiate the consultant role regarding confrontational consultant behavior (which they preferred to call "gutsy"), and (6) do it.

Consultant Strength and Stretch

At the negative extreme of consultant strength would be the consultant who is so specialized that every consultation intervention, no matter what the client needs, is, for example, "quality circles" or "team building" or "work redesign." At the extreme of consultant stretch is the consultant who has been wanting to try an intervention so that the next client, regardless of the organizational issues, receives that intervention. The extremes aside, most competent consultants do factor strength and stretch into their practices. My own example feels like true confessions of a consultant. I am quite adept at group process (strength) and have a limited attention span (forty-five-minute intervals, at best) for facilitating task-only problem-solving meetings (weakness). Consequently, if the client needs task-specific group problem solving, I often break participants into small groups where they facilitate themselves, or I coach the head of the group in task-specific meeting leadership and then support the leader through process consultation and make task-related interventions only when the group gets "stuck." My true confession relates to stretch: With any client I always look for some way(s) to do something new. I look for what is unique about the client and the client's issues to assess how I can be creative and stimulated. This approach, I think, keeps me vital and authentic as a consultant and person.

The above items are a beginning exploration of what I think real consultants do. They do *not* use "cubes" or any other mechanistic categorization of interventions as a priori categories. They develop congruent approaches from experience, reading, talking with colleagues, and self-reflection. In doing the self-reflection, I realized that I believe an intervention actually starts when the client make the decision to act by calling the consultant. Consequently, the intervention stage doesn't occur after diagnosis, but starts with the initial call. Peter Block (2000) explores these early interventions in *Flawless Consulting*, particularly those related to contracting and resistance. In all this our own styles as unique human beings are basic. ◀

An OD Intervention Study

As promised, we will not propose any strict categorization of interventions. But it may be useful to consider an overview of OD consultants' reports on some approaches they favor in their professional work. For this purpose we formulated a comprehensive list of, shall we say, mostly "interventions" (but also activities, tools, tests, and so forth) as a basis for a survey addressed to the OD Network members in 1998. The list devised was intentionally broad and "scrambled" in order to avoid reflex and halo effects and to encourage thought, item-by-item, by the 131 respondents. (There was follow-up to reach a subsample of those who did not respond to the initial mailing.)[23] Lists as used for the purpose noted are themselves "time-bound" and reflective of "what's out there." For instance there is no "Appreciative Inquiry" in this list and for other reasons no "MBO." And, as expected, some of the categories overlap. Taken as a whole, this list constitutes a heuristic device and conversation starter, not a conceptual dictionary. Without explicit statistical treatment, we compare three subgroups within the ODN sample: internal consultants, external consultants, and "others." In some instances there is some overlap in these categories, especially in human resource management and academic roles. The results of this survey are shown in Table 9.1.

Table 9.1. Frequency of Intervention Use

	Internal (n = 39)	External (n = 51)	Other (n = 41)	Number of Asterisks
Action Research	*69.2	**80.4	58.5	3
Business Process Analysis	53.8	45.1	53.7	
Case Method	10.2	21.6	14.6	
· Coaching	***97.4	***96.1	*75.6	7
Computer Games	2.6	2.0	0	
Communication Interventions	*79.5	***94.1	56.1	4
· Conflict Management	*71.8	**82.4	*75.6	4
Confrontation Meetings	25.6	33.3	41.5	
· Culture Change	**89.7	*72.5	*68.3	4
Customer Satisfaction	33.3	29.4	17.1	
Diversity Training	35.9	27.5	26.8	
Empowerment	48.7	*62.7	53.7	1
Enneagram	2.6	2.0	0	
Ethnography/Anthropology	15.4	9.8	9.8	
Evaluation	56.4	39.2	46.3	
Experimental Approaches	15.4	19.6	17.1	
Family Business	2.6	21.6	12.2	
· Feedback	**84.6	*76.5	*65.9	4
360-Degree Feedback	53.0	56.9	53.7	
Force-Field Analysis	*66.7	52.9	36.6	1
Future Search	38.5	41.2	46.3	
Gestalt Approaches	12.8	29.4	24.3	
Grid	7.7	5.9	9.8	
Human Resource Mgmt.	43.6	29.4	41.5	
Information Technology	30.8	9.8	22.0	
International OD	28.2	23.5	26.8	
· Interpersonal Exercises	*66.7	*62.7	*65.9	3
Intergroup Activities	53.8	56.9	*61.0	1
Jungian Approaches	17.9	25.5	26.8	
Labor Relations	10.3	11.8	17.1	
Large Systems Change	*64.1	*68.6	53.7	2
· Leadership Training	**82.1	**82.4	*75.6	5
Learning Organization	*76.9	56.9	*63.4	2

Table 9.1. Frequency of Intervention Use, Cont'd

	Internal (n = 39)	External (n = 51)	Other (n = 41)	Number of Asterisks
Life/Career Planning	30.8	31.4	31.7	
· Management Development	*66.7	*70.6	*61.0	3
Market Research	2.6	9.8	7.3	
Myers-Briggs (MBTI)	*61.5	54.9	46.3	1
Observation	48.7	37.3	24.4	
Organization Design	**82.1	*60.8	51.2	3
Organization Diagnosis	*76.9	**84.3	56.1	3
Organization Prescription	38.5	13.7	12.2	
Outward Bound	5.1	5.9	7.3	
Participation	51.3	49.0	36.6	
Performance Measurement	*69.2	39.2	43.9	1
· Process Consultation	**82.l	**88.2	*73.2	5
Psychotherapy	0	7.8	0	
Psychoanalytic Approaches	0	2.0	7.3	
Quality of Life	12.8	11.8	22.0	
Re-Engineering	30.8	33.3	39.0	
Sensitivity Training	7.7	11.8	22.0	
Simulations	33.3	31.4	19.5	
Small-Group Training	56.4	*60.8	51.2	1
Sociotechnical Systems	56.4	35.3	34.1	
· Strategic Planning	*76.9	*72.5	*70.7	3
Survey Feedback	*69.2	51.0	41.5	1
T-Groups	5.1	9.8	12.2	
Tavistock Method	7.7	7.8	12.2	
Teaching	35.8	37.3	34.1	
· Team Building	**87.2	***94.1	*73.1	6
Third-Party Interventions	33.3	29.4	29.2	
Time Management	15.4	17.6	22.0	
Transition/Change Mgmt.	*64.1	*70.6	53.7	2
Total Quality (TQM)	38.5	37.3	22.0	
Visioning	*61.5	*68.6	48.8	2
Work Redesign	43.6	37.3	31.7	
Workforce Diversity	23.1	27.5	19.5	

Some broad-brush findings may be of interest, with the renewed caveat that things may change, and indeed probably have changed, since these data were collected. We consider three top categories of reported frequent use:

ubiquitous	90 percent and up***
very widely used	80 to 89 percent**
widely used	60 to 79 percent*

As shown in Table 9.1, the following interventions (listed alphabetically) received one, two, or three asterisks for *all* of the respondent categories:

- Coaching
- Conflict management
- Culture change
- Feedback
- Interpersonal exercises
- Leadership training
- Management development
- Process consultation
- Strategic planning
- Team building

The interventions most frequently reported as used are coaching and team building.

One may note the changing tides of professional interests and shifting visibilities. "Grid" (as in Blake and Mouton's Managerial Grid®) shows little application, nor does "sensitivity training" (at least by that label), although small-group training appears with a substantial percentage, in the 50 to 60 percent range. Some other items, while not in the top-rated range, appear in respectable proportions:

- Business Process Analysis
- Empowerment
- Evaluation
- 360-degree feedback
- Force-Field Analysis

- Future Search
- Large systems change
- Learning organization
- Organization design
- Organization diagnosis
- Transition/change management
- Visioning

One may surmise that at the time of this review some OD intervention styles are used by almost everybody. For instance, "coaching," which ranks as number 1, no doubt has gone on in one form or another since inception of the field, but more recently the term "coaching" has come to be attached to this essential process. A similar statement may apply to the term "feedback."

Once again we must recall that words define important aspects of the profession and that labeling plays a significant, perhaps essential, role. Yet such labeling raises fractious issues of meaning and debatable definition.

With all this we cannot quite extricate ourselves from the jungle of words and their consequences. Surely designations included here are at different levels of abstraction. Even those that are conceptually comparable are subject to varied interpretation by the respondents, a difficulty that of course affects survey research in general. Yet with all these caveats, this overview may set the stage for dialogue on OD's emphasis and trends in professional practice.

In the chapter that follows, we provide a mélange of intervention scenarios, not as rulebook or systematic inventory, but rather as approaches illustrating OD intervention styles that we have experienced.

It is *not* our intent to be exhaustive or to classify, nor to argue that any of these scenarios represents "the right way," although we have endeavored to include examples of those interventions chosen most frequently as reflected in our survey. For the sake of brevity, many phases of the work are not explicitly recounted (for example, activities variously associated with the nine Cs). We warmly invite dialogue with the reader to explore these issues in further depth within the bounds of realistic collegial collaboration and shared learning.

10

Intervention Scenarios

ON THIS CHAPTER WE PRESENT twelve "disguised" case studies of interventions that are illustrative of particular phases of the process and one contributed case.

► COMPANY BEEN AROUND

"Company Been Around" has been servicing its customers well for five decades, and most organizational members are content but not particularly motivated. In the last five years, there have been more and more conflicts among departments. Decision-making processes are taking two to three times longer than before, and customer complaints are up. Sales and margins have not been affected (as yet?) so the P/E ratio is stable; thus there is not a lot of immediate "bottom line" impetus to change.

Intervention: Creating Vision and Mission
An OD consultant has been called to advise the top management team (three directors). After collecting data, interviewing a cross-section of people

across levels and functions, observing meetings, observing customer interfaces, looking at financial data and production trends over the last ten years, and examining the business environment, the following "opportunities for improvement" are noted:

- There appears to be organization-wide confusion as to the company's direction, including specific goals and objectives, vision, and mission: "what we are about and why we're here."

- There is an abundance of ideas but a lack of clarity on their relative import and various interpretations on the CEO's (the founder's son) present intentions.

It is the goal to provide the organization with a clear understanding of its new visions and missions, translating these into specific objectives for management members to plan and to work by.

Methods

This intervention is conducted in a retreat-style format, where individuals are asked to create vision statements jointly, then evaluate them as a group and prioritize them. (Some small organizations have all of their members participate, while large ones include senior managers, who then communicate down into the organization by department/division).

This process begins with a brainstorming-type session looking for breadth of ideas, then narrowing down to a subset of ideas while maintaining commitment to the resulting decisions. It is important to assure clarity, laying the groundwork for eventual changes and new ways of "organizational being"; with individual differences of perception and crosscurrents of forces this is no mean challenge.

Specific tools include *storyboard methodology* and *group exercises.* The former is used to elicit input in a non-threatening way from all organization members present, rather than simply asking members to churn out answers in the usual brainstorming mode. While brainstorming is useful in generating ideas, it usually is heavily biased toward more verbal members who are also "quick on your feet thinkers." Often those who like to "mull over" the problem first before jumping in are less likely to contribute in such sessions. In storyboarding, specific ideas are written on Post-it® Notes and placed on a cork board or similar surface. Participants can then review these ideas in a more leisurely manner, during breaks and dedicated meeting times, allowing for some reflection on the breadth and scope of the problem. Consistent with our view, this is designed to encourage thinking in terms of complex systems, rather than relying on simplistic linear models. A further advantage of using storyboarding is that it eases the often-frenzied job of the recorder who must try to capture all of the ideas generated in rapid brainstorming quickly and legibly. Computer enhanced voice recognition, as the technology permits, may help as a backup.

The use of group exercises in this intervention has a two-fold purpose. The first is to allow all participants together to generate a "group product" that is truly a synergic result of individual inputs. This systemic, "sum is greater than the whole" product enhances psychological "ownership" of and commitment to the product. This is ultimately critical in communication, action, and follow-up after the retreat is over.

The second purpose is to move the participants to come up with a product that is concrete and specific, rather than just a recording of individual thoughts. As we know, more traditional meeting "minutes" are often relegated to the "circular file" back at work, while the approach here proposed seeks, with some established success, longer-term impact on the organization's style and strategic planning process.

Value of Vision and Mission

In earlier days, a sense of direction for a company was the concern of only a handful of people at the top. In start-ups, it was typically the prerogative of the founder(s) to set that direction. If you didn't like it, you could go and work somewhere else. In addition, it was believed that people in the rest of the organization didn't even care if there *was* a direction, since they were only compensated for "doing their job." Organization development theory challenges these belief systems and suggests that there is much to gain if the entire organization is clear on the purpose, vision, and mission of the company, ideally involving every individual in that organization.

The benefits are three-fold. First, knowing the ultimate direction, the individuals in the organization develop a sense of purpose and an understanding on where and how their particular jobs fit into the "big picture." It *connects* the individual to the organization and allows for a sense of pride—assuming that the mission is something to be proud of. For example, people who worked for Ford in the early days could be proud of being a part of a company that brought commuting power to the masses. Similarly, those who worked for Apple could say they helped bring computing power to the general public. Thus the job becomes more than just "widget processing."

Second, having a resulting clear set of goals gives departments/ groups/divisions a common "sheet of music"—in contrast to separate uncoordinated "notes"—and minimizes conflict among different functional groups whose members might otherwise see themselves as competing for the same limited resources come budget time.

Third, having a vision and mission gives most of those involved a sense that the organization is proactively setting forth on a meaningful path. This sense of control is important, as individuals tend to think the worst in an atmosphere of uncertainty, a premise supported by organizational behavior theory. The creation and recasting of visions and missions often brings new life into tired organizations, and in new companies defines constructive direction. Companies must be aware, however, that technological, financial, market, and other external factors will likely limit and/or facilitate that which is envisioned.

Resources

Creating Mission/Vision

Senge, P.M., Kleiner, A., Roberts, C., Ross, R.B., & Smith, B.J. (1994). *The fifth discipline fieldbook: Strategies and tools for building a learning organization*. New York: Doubleday Dell.

Watkins, J.M., & Mohr, B.J. (2001). *Appreciative inquiry: Change at the speed of imagination*. San Francisco, CA: Jossey-Bass/Pfeiffer.

Facilitating Retreats

Owen, H. (1997). *Open space technology: A user's guide* (2nd ed.). San Francisco, CA: Berrett-Koehler.

Rothwell, W., Sullivan, R., & McLean, G. (Eds.). (1995). *Practicing organization development: A guide for consultants*. San Francisco, CA: Jossey-Bass/Pfeiffer.

Group Exercises: Buy-In

Currin, N.H. (1996). *Team based decision-making*. Lakewood, CO: Team Learning.

Scholtes, P.R. (1988). *The TEAM handbook*. Madison, WI: Joiner. ◀

► COMPANY EC

A well-established company, a conglomerate, operating in twenty-three countries worldwide is in need of a boost of energy. New products in the chemical sector are lagging, and competition from smaller companies is getting stronger. The organization's ability to learn quickly and to transfer that knowledge internally has been severely hampered. Much energy is spent instead on infighting and in competing for resources among divisions.

Interventions: Strategy Meetings/ International Team Building

The CEO and SVP of the Belgium office realize that there needs to be an intervention to reverse the downhill trend. The OD consultant hired begins with *observation* and *interviews* to assess the situation. The first strategic meeting is planned for two months forward and includes activities to try to bring the group together in more social situations, as well as specific meetings for strategic planning.

The resulting social activities prove to be a disaster. Those assembled refuse to mingle as a group; instead, pairs and trios keep together and/or skip programmed events altogether, much to the consultant's chagrin. After the second day, a kindly vice president from Sweden pulls the consultant aside and says, "We really appreciate your good work trying to get us to work together, but forget the social activities! You have to remember, you have thirteen different individuals—some prima donnas—from different countries. They've been at war with each other in more ways than one. A few social get-togethers just aren't going to heal the rift. Nothing you could possibly do could get these men to actually like each other; they don't even want to get close, like some of you Americans. What will work is if we all feel that there is a common business goal that we can concentrate on and that's it."

With these words came a most useful lesson in *international team building.* The remaining two days of the retreat were spent in work sessions, building a common vision, objectives, and goals for the company's top leadership to work on and looking for viable strategic plans in a changing market.

Resources

Facilitating Strategic Planning Sessions/Retreats

Senge, P.M., Kleiner, A., Roberts, C., Ross, R.B., & Smith, B.J. (1994). *The fifth discipline fieldbook: Strategies and tools for building a learning organization.* New York: Doubleday Dell.

International Team Building

Francesco, A.M., & Gold, B.A. (1998). *International organizational behavior.* Englewood Cliffs, NJ: Prentice Hall.

Gardenswartz, L., & Rowe, A. (1992). *Managing diversity: A complete desk reference and planning guide.* Homewood, IL: Business One Irwin. ◄

▶ COMPANY OILSTEP

This is a large international corporation in oil and natural gas exploration, production, and marketing. The culture of the organization, formulated mainly in an environment of the 1960s, is now ill-suited to meet the current challenges. Workload distribution is uneven, with the top levels working on weekends and many newer executives being bored, waiting around, and doing very little. Many people feel powerless to change the things blocking progress in the organization.

Interventions: Changing Organization Cultures and Large Systems Change

The intervention program is designed to provide the organization a means by which to "shift fundamental gears"—to see and do things differently, moving away from well-established operating procedures, mentally and physically, and to recognize the changing environment in which the organization operates, possibly including changes in upper and mid-level management.

Methods

The long-term intervention is begun with a "temperature check" or *survey feedback* mechanism that allows the researcher/practitioner to determine a baseline of organizational attitudes and behaviors, particularly to examine the values underlying the attitudes revealed. Issues of lacking trust, procedural error, and faulty detail abound. Once this current state is identified, one can then articulate the wishes for desired future state.

The most time-intensive aspect of this intervention involves the task of designing the multi-faceted "how to" to move from the current to future state. A *Force-Field Analysis* tool helps the group to identify both areas of focus and next steps in change, determining the configuration of pushes, pulls, and obstacles that must be addressed, concretely and operationally.

A many-pronged approach includes *training,* both for management and staff, *changes in the reward system* to reinforce changes in attitude and behavior, development of *new organizational initiatives,* and various *adaptations of systems-oriented change efforts.* Ongoing diagnosis and re-diagnosis are crucial to keep things on the right track in this connection.

Why Focus on Culture?

Efforts to improve organizational cultures constitute a fundamental strand in systematic large-scale organization development. Organization development theorists have long pointed to the unwritten rules or "atmosphere" that exists in organizations that silently steers the day-to-day operations and the ways in which people interact with one another. For many companies, their unique cultures have largely been shaped reactively, sometimes based on strong leadership characters, environmental forces, and markets. The resulting cultures may not necessarily foster the most effective management styles or create appropriate work patterns under changing conditions.

Frequently, cultures that result from a restrictive, top-down "Theory X" orientation exhibit fairly low levels of creative thinking and learning. Conflict avoidance, poor communication of expectations, and poor performance at all levels may result. Large organization change efforts then seem indicated. But attention must be paid to the strategic factors that emerge in considering the nine Cs and their interactions.

In COMPANY OILSTEP, the intervention program, starting with Force-Field Analysis, seemed to be successful in about two-thirds of the division. But just as results became evident, the company merged with a still larger oil giant, altering almost every aspect of operations and the resulting culture mix. It was now moot to attribute even positive change to the OD interventions.

Resources

Changing Organizational Culture

Rothwell, W., Sullivan, R., & McLean, G. (1995). *Practicing organization development: A guide for consultants.* San Francisco, CA: Jossey-Bass/Pfeiffer.

Force-Field Analysis

Lewin, K. (1951). *Field theory in social science.* New York: Harper & Row.

Large Systems Change

Emery, M., & Purser, R. (1996). *The search conference: A powerful method for planning organizational change and community.* San Francisco, CA: Jossey-Bass.

Owen, H. (1997). *Open space technology: A user's guide* (2nd ed.). San Francisco, CA: Berrett-Koehler.

Survey as an Organizational Change Tool/Survey Research

Krant, A. (1996). *Organizational surveys: Tools for assessment and change.* San Francisco, CA: Jossey-Bass.

Sudman, S., & Bradburn, N.M. (1982). *A practical guide to questionnaire design.* San Francisco, CA: Jossey-Bass. ◄

► HEALTHCO

With the inevitability of managed care, the county hospital system understands that the way of doing business has changed for good and that the mission statement introduced two years ago is no longer idle rumination but a wake-up call for all healthcare workers. The traditional rift between doctors and everyone else has to be healed, as well as the conflict between practitioners and administrators, the way patients are treated, and the conflict among shifts.

Interventions: Survey Research and Future Search

An OD practitioner is invited to aid in the change effort, moving from a very deep-rooted "private hospital for the wealthy" orientation to a managed and preventative care approach. The current state of the organization is investigated using a *survey research* tool, for all key sub-populations, including follow-up with initial nonrespondents. The results show that there are three problem areas that are affecting the organization's profitability and performance. First, the relationships between functional areas is strained, particularly between doctors and nurses, doctors and administrators, and between workers on different shifts. Second, customer satisfaction is questionable; many customers (patients) are going elsewhere, if they have a choice, due to the long wait times and a notably poor referral process to specialists. Third, the management attitude, despite words like "respect, dignity, and professionalism for both employees and patients," seems to be, "do your job as you are told or lose it." Based on these predominant themes, feedback to the management team is provided by the OD consultant, with the purpose of gaining buy-in and commitment to a very different future state.

To create the new concept for the organization, a *future search* technology is used, involving the entire organization. It was decided that in order to bring about such a radical change in organizational culture, and to become a symbol of an increasingly participative approach, more than top-down mandated change was required. By means of the *future search retreat,* a new organization was described, including a modified mission, a new vision of what the organization would look like, and what behaviors would be expected: by job categories, to implement the newly articulated values, and per revised mission and vision.

Shortly following the retreat, key management figures were invited to spearhead the planning and implementation stage for moving the organization to do things differently and to reward those who support and implement the change.

A marked shift in the organization style became evident about sixteen months after the initiative began. In the third year, *profitability and service quality indices* reflect major improvement, with an increase in admissions and patient/customer satisfaction.

Resources
Future Search Conferences/Retreat

Axelrod, R. (1995). *The conference model™: Approach, perspectives.* Wilmette, IL: The Axelrod Group.

Weisbord, M., & Janoff, S. (1995). *Future search—An action guide to finding common ground in organizations and communities.* San Francisco, CA: Berrett-Koehler.

Survey as an Organizational Change Tool/Survey Research

Cummings, T.G., & Worley, C.G. (2001). *Organization development and change* (7th ed.). Cincinnati, OH: Southwestern. ◀

▶ NIFPY COMPANY

A very large and well-known not-for profit organization is going through a change in the nature of its financial support. The old way of thinking about services—almost exclusively relying on wealthy people to come forward and donate very large sums—is seen as a paradigm of the past. Key leadership positions must be filled with individuals who not only have a creative vision for the future but who are also able to "sell themselves" and the organization to a wider public in a way that is rewarding for themselves as well.

Volunteer dropout rates are higher than ever, and the most common reason for leaving is associated with disappointments in working with the public, with little success or recognition. The new director realizes that what is required is a dramatic shift in managing the "volunteer workforce." For example, volunteers need to be educated just as much as employees to understand the optimal way to function to support the organization's mission and objectives. The director called for assistance through an OD contact made at last year's HROD conference.

Interventions: Interviews and Training and Development Planning

Extensive and intensive *interviews* were conducted with employees in key leadership positions and with volunteers to obtain current perspectives and to assure investment by client system and stakeholders. The results were surprising to the organization's staff leadership. Many volunteers were bitter about their experiences working with public and staff. What had originally attracted them to the nonprofit area was being overshadowed by the apparent "do as I say, not as I do" behavior by the staff, particularly by those in top leadership positions. Conflict abounded.

Based on these results, several additional interventions were designed. A number of conflict resolution sessions with top administrators and volunteers were implemented with somewhat mixed results. However, eventually agreement was reached on a *training and development plan* for the volunteers including *sales training, communications,* further *conflict resolution,* and sometime later *leadership training.*

The interventions took place over a two-and-one-half-year period, and by then the resulting operations began to show some improvements in terms of fundraising results, volunteer attitudes, and management's understanding of changing roles responding to significantly different external conditions and markets.

Resources

Communication Skills

Clampitt, P.G. (1991). *Communicating for managerial effectiveness.* Thousand Oaks, CA: Sage.

Conducting Interviews

Block, P. (2000). *Flawless consulting: A guide to getting your expertise used* (2nd ed.). San Francisco, CA: Jossey-Bass/Pfeiffer.

Conflict Resolution

Crawley, J. (1994). *Constructive conflict management: Managing to make a difference.* San Francisco, CA: Jossey-Bass/Pfeiffer.

Fisher, R., & Ury, W. (1991). *Getting to yes: Negotiating agreement without giving in* (2nd ed.). New York: Penguin.

Leadership Development and Training

Covey, S.R. (1990). *The 7 habits of highly effective people.* New York: Fireside.

Davis, B.L., Skube, C.J., Hellervik, L.W., Gebelein, S.H., & Sheard, J.L. (1996). *Successful manager's handbook: Development suggestions for today's managers.* Minneapolis, MN: Personnel Decisions International.

Heider, J. (1985). *The tao of leadership.* New York: Bantam. ◀

► COMPANY STICKUMS

A diversified paper products and reproduction machinery company has had a history of being on the forefront in experimentation. Yet currently both marketing problems and people problems are pointing to some serious emerging issues that must be addressed. The OD consultant finds that a limited number of managers are continually asked to make complex and urgent decisions. As a result, more than 50 percent of decisions are bottlenecked, with no relief in sight. People are content to follow orders and look at you blankly when asked to take any initiative. The latest management approach to "empower the people" has been an object of ridicule and a source of jokes by the water cooler, and even on the golf course. Employees act by routine; they are "good soldiers," but unable to "think outside the box." Creativity seems to be lacking throughout the organization.

Interventions: Participation and Empowerment

The OD consultant seeks approaches to create mechanisms in the organization that will expand decision-making capabilities and responsibility to a wider number of people at various levels in the company and to think and behave more flexibly to gain more accurate information for decision-making purposes from those employees closest to the problem, the *"shop floor."*

As in the early phase of many interventions, it appears useful for the organization to conduct an *audit* of the current status of participation in the company. What are some of the employee attitudes in terms of how they view their situation? Are most employees prepared to make suggestions to improve their own work environment and, if so, are these suggestions attended to by management?

This baseline "temperature check" could be accomplished using a company-wide survey. Yet, in this instance, much time and extensive resources would be required; thus, a survey is considered not to be feasible. Instead, *focus groups,* using a cross-section of the organization, are chosen. This technique requires the consultant to extrapolate from the possibly limited data to *"frequency of themes" analysis* and to sense "what's hot and what's not."

Methods

The need for a greater level of participation and empowerment in the company was clearly established, and a variety of intervention vehicles were considered. For example, there was discussion of *quality circles,* an intervention based on involving more lower levels of management and workers in designated decision-making processes. This practice was popular in Japan and implemented in the United States with mixed results[24]. In this instance, this was not found to be the intervention of choice in view of time and resource constraints. Rather, interventions used included *seminars in creativity and decision making* for all employees and a program instituting *company-wide incentives* for employees to make suggestions, for example, "bright ideas" campaigns, with substantial cash rewards for money-making ideas, the amounts varying to reflect the projected return on investment (ROI) linked to a particular idea. Union cooperation had been secured, especially noting the financial incentives included in this program.

There was no systematic follow-up survey because of an impending reorganization. "Grapevine" comments were generally positive, especially regarding heightened feelings of "they're listening to our ideas now and that's a good thing."

The Value of Emp-ment and Participation

To assure greater commitment by people to the organizations, many organizations, particularly in the 1970s and 1980s, sought to foster extensive and intensive participation and empowerment initiatives. Today, most multinational and Fortune 500 companies have implemented some efforts to bring decision making closer to the shop floor.

One lesson that has been learned is that empowerment and more employee participation do not become possible overnight if the organization has been under a mechanistic Theory-X orientation for a long time. Any employee with lots of enthusiasm and bright ideas who joins a "mechanistic" company is quickly "put in his or her place" if always told to "speak only when spoken to." In fact, there is a psychological term used to describe the state one can reach when told over and over again, "thanks but no thanks"; that term is "learned helplessness." Here people become so frustrated that they become numb and their attitudes turn sour or apathetic. "Just tell me what to do. It doesn't matter what I say; there is no one who listens or cares, so why should I bother to care anyway?"

Unfortunately for organizations, this attitude costs money, both in faulty work processes when carelessness becomes a norm and/or when there are only a few people at the top of the organization who are allowed to be creative. The most dangerous situation that can then arise is "group think," where an erroneous decision is implemented because no one cares or because individuals are afraid to contradict the prevailing group's decision.

Resources
Creativity

Higgins, J. (1994). *Creative problem solving techniques: The handbook of new ideas for business.* New York: New Management.

Empowerment/Participation

Byham, W. (1990). *Zapp! The lightening of empowerment.* New York: Bantam. ◄

► CAR-GO COMPANY

An automobile industry giant is experiencing good times. Market share is up, shareholders are happy, and employees are not on strike. Managers are at an annual HR seminar put on by headquarters, where they are rewarded symbolically and practically for their good work. One of the presenters talks about *valuing diversity* and how attitudes are important in creating an environment in which people are encouraged to perform at their full potential. The rather homogenous audience begins to think about the implications, both personally and professionally as this relates to their own operations. However, one of the site managers realizes that the rumblings he has heard at his plant might be indicative of tensions of some kind beneath the surface. The approach he had been using was "to go in and resolve" the seemingly minute and annoying difficulties that had been coming up. He now recognizes that these typically have involved employees of different races and age groups. Instead of things getting better, new problems seem to keep cropping up, from complaints on what music should come over the intercom to the smells from the microwave. So, armed with the speaker's business card, the manager makes the call to the OD consultant.

Intervention: Diversity Seminars

The consultant and manager go over the complaint/problem logbook and note the increasing amounts of time and effort the supervisors are having to spend to resolve these matters. An approach is suggested by the manager, by which the employees would be educated regarding "people differences" and asked to take responsibility in contributing to a healthy, safe, and relatively stress-free work environment. The union was asked to assist in the design of the intervention and, after the rationale was explained, agreed to do so. The issue of difference was highlighted in several *half-day seminars*. Key concepts in valuing individuals and the benefits of working in a high potential, satisfying organization were communicated. Cultural and gender issues were openly discussed in the seminars, and *lecturettes* illustrated the ways in which employees could work through differences and learn to resolve conflicts, particularly those that stemmed from differences in work style.

Six months after the seminar sessions were delivered, a *follow-up study* was done, and the site manager reported that the complaints/problems as recorded in the logbook had dropped by 47 percent. *Focus group interviews* were also conducted, and the staff reported increased satisfaction with the work environment and self-reported increased output in production. The production output total numbers were up only slightly, but the marked differences were drops in absenteeism and safety-related down time.

Resources

Diversity Training

Gardenswartz, L., & Rowe, A. (1992). *Managing diversity: A complete desk reference and planning guide.* Homewood, IL: Business One Irwin.

Thomas, F.R., Jr. (1991). *Beyond race and gender: Unleashing the power of your total work force by managing diversity.* New York: Amacom.

Focus Group Interviews

Rothwell, W., Sullivan, R., & McLean, G. (Eds.). (1995). *Practicing organization development: A guide for consultants.* San Francisco, CA: Jossey-Bass/Pfeiffer. ◄

► COMPUFIX

The company is a medium-size computer sales and service firm. While the firm as a whole has been successful, now the entire accounting and IT units seem to be falling apart. Several subgroups are in all-out war with each other. The atmosphere is tense and work suffers. People are coming to meetings with magazines and extraneous work, which they surreptitiously complete when they think no one is watching. Some try to play computer games at work. Meetings are a waste of time, with arguments breaking out or someone always needing to "get more information" from someone not at the meeting whenever a decision needs to be made.

Interventions: Team Analysis, Team Building, and Facilitation

Team-building workshops examining formal and informal relationships and shared goals are conducted for work groups in accounting and IT. After some ups and downs, the plan seems to take hold, and progress is shown by both technical and human resource criteria. But it becomes clear that top management support, long term, is essential and so far ambiguous. The accounting people are still worried about the marketing people and "phony orders." And IT mainly wants to be left alone. Eventually a "Team Support Program" is set up for the company as a whole, top management included. While the industry is turbulent and changing, the team effort and facilitation seem to have positive impact, per informal probing.

Small group facilitation involves working both with the individuals in the group, *one-on-one,* to find out how the processes are currently functioning and in a team development mode with the *group as a whole* to examine what's going well and what's not.

Once an analysis is completed, the facilitator feeds back to the group her or his perceptions on the specific issues facing the group. Common issues for the group include clashes between different work units, faulty communication styles, poor decision making, delays, evasions, inability to resolve conflicts between different members of the group, and—importantly—lack of direction and/or purpose of the group.

The Value of Teams

The concept of teams and group work often is traced to the work of Kurt Lewin, although various antecedents can be identified[25]. A significant amount of research on group process has burgeoned in the past four decades.

Many multinational companies adopted the *teamwork* concept, reaping the benefit of group synergy, a systemic concept where the group is more than the sum of the individual parts. Since its inception, all kinds of groups have been created and become team tools for implementation: self-directed teams, sociotechnical work teams, cross-functional work teams, and the list goes on. The years have gone by and some of the "jargon" or "fad" labels have come and gone.

On the other hand, sometimes organizations make the mistake of not involving enough people on critical issues that require input to enhance both the quality of the decision made and the intangible process of "buy-in" to implement the decision. For example, regarding product assessment and upgrade decisions, it is incredible how many companies allow a few executives up in "the corporate ivory tower" to make decisions without even asking for information from those who have daily contact with customers. Cross-functional teams that include members from the customer care department, the R&D department, and operations/manufacturing departments serve to improve decision quality beyond the efforts of one individual executive.

Resources
Small-Group Facilitation/Teamwork
Scholtes, P.R. (1988). *The TEAM handbook.* Madison, WI: Joiner. ◄

▶ RIVOLI RIVALS INC.

This is a large leisure industry company: hotels, casinos, spas, and custom tours. The organization has been divided between the two senior VPs, respectively the son of the president (hotels and spas) and the son of the CEO (casinos, custom tours). The CEO is rumored to be ready to hand down the reins by the next board meeting. There is no designated heir apparent, so people have been forced to choose sides via the subtle and not-so-subtle "game playing" that has been going on in the past year. Both sons have adequate competencies. Which son is favored? Is there a succession plan or simple innuendo? What to do next?

Interventions: Executive Coaching, Conflict Mediation, Multiple Consultant Roles, Organization Design

The goals of these OD interventions relate both to people and to organization structure. To face, accept, and use tensions for productive purposes constitutes an aspect of intervention strategy.

The consultants (a team of three) take turns meeting individually with each of the VPs (sons). They explore in caring dialogue the levels and nature of tensions and conflicts manifest and the nature of intrapersonal and interpersonal dynamics. Is the conflict between individuals only? Are there larger rivalries? Is money an issue? Is being "top dog" important for personal satisfaction or for the good of the organization? Rational factors, rationalizations, emotions, greed, policy, and views of the organization's future all blend together. Are conscious or unconscious forces involved? Issues of power and control?

In addition to one-on-one meetings, one of the consultants meets with both sons *together,* once every two weeks.

The consultant plays the roles of mediator/facilitator/coach with some hope for "objectivity"—clarifying and translating messages so that those at odds can move toward hearing one another more openly and realistically. As mediator, the consultant recommends some "fair" guidelines that enhance the quality of the exchanges. For example, one rule assures that each gets a chance at the start to say what the situation looks like from his own viewpoint without interruption. Yet anger and "irrationality" may intrude.

The consultant as facilitator uses short *vignettes* and *examples* of other cases of rivalry and material on alternate organization forms, surfacing new perspectives. One resulting learning points to open recognition that tensions encountered, while uncomfortable, were natural and basically human and that at this stage transcendent agendas of the *organization's* future were also involved.

The interpersonal encounters were now placed in context of a possible redesign of the organization. The rivalry served to enhance satisfaction and executive performance as the two VPs (sons) and the outgoing CEO, with outreach to other executives and to lower-hierarchy opinion leaders, hammered out a new corporate form and business plan.

Ultimately, Rivoli restructured, combining the tours business, hotels, casinos, and spas into one subsidiary, Riv Resorts, and forming another subsidiary, a leisure real estate investment company, Olinvest. The president's son assumed management of Olinvest, and the CEO's son left the company altogether. A new CEO was brought in to head Riv Resorts.

The Value of Conflict Mediation

It is not uncommon for "enlightened" organizations to want to educate many or most of its members on conflict management and resolution, proactively, including "thinking outside the box" to redefine conflictual issues. Larger companies often choose to offer classes on conflict, usually at the management level. These classes instruct managers/supervisors on how to resolve conflict that may erupt in their departments. Unfortunately, one downside of such training is a developing dependence on others higher up the organizational hierarchy to resolve differences. Thus it is recommended that if such didactic presentations, or "classes," are to be used, they are best inclusive of all levels of the organization with appropriate variations in format.

A common source of conflict in large organizations is often referred to as "functional silos." Entire departments/divisions become so loyal to their own sub-organizations that "the big picture" is lost. Marketing thinks that manufacturing can't make the product correctly; manufacturing thinks finance is hallucinating if they think they can make the product with the budget cuts they're enforcing; research and design thinks sales are setting up false expectations with the customers just to make a "quick buck."

These beliefs and unwritten rumors self-reinforce, and soon communication between departments is avoided and/or loaded with hostility.

This intergroup conflict can be addressed through utilization of a *facilitator/mediator,* who serves to re-establish the "whole organization" concept: We are all part of a larger system that has competition out there, competitors who may benefit from the negative effects of our isolated silos. Finding and holding up the common vision is key in turning around deep-seated negativity between departments. Once a critical mass of employees, especially managers, experiences this paradigm shift, other vehicles can be used to encourage more interpersonal connections. For example, creating *visions* and *mission* interests can be used to catalyze the shift, and *cross-functional ("cross-silo") groups* are in a sound position to build positive links toward "whole-organization," unified efforts. Special interests need to be stated and clarified and harmonized with the interests of the organization in its entirety, as it moves to its next developmental stage.

Resources
Conflict Mediation
Crawley, J. (1994). *Constructive conflict management: Managing to make a difference.* San Francisco, CA: Jossey-Bass/Pfeiffer.

Executive Coaching
Douglas, C.Z., & Morley, W.H. (2000). *Executive coaching: An annotated bibliography.* Greensboro, NC: Center for Creative Leadership.

Zeus, P., & Skiffington, S. (2000). *The complete guide to coaching at work.* New York: McGraw-Hill.

Organizational Design/Structure Change
Beckhard, R., & Harris, R. (1987). *Organizational transitions.* Reading, MA: Addison-Wesley.

Tichy, N. (1983). *Managing strategic change: Organization development redefined.* New York: Wiley. ◀

▶ TOYS

This company is a toy manufacturer with a worldwide sales base positioned No. 3 in revenues in a highly competitive—some might say "cutthroat"—industry. The CEO has recently replaced one fired by the board. Sales are down, and everyone is blaming everyone else. The management team and many operating units are in disarray; meetings are mainly verbal battles. The accounting goal seems to be to cover up the financial problems the company is having (possible disclosure violations?). No one has the guts to tell the CEO that his ambitious turnaround plans for the future are not "doable."

Intervention: Feedback

The external OD consultant, a holdover from times when Toys was doing well, reflects on the engagement objective: To provide the organization members with realistic information about the company, focused on the CEO and the accounting situation. Is it possible that real areas of improvement can be identified and accomplished? Tentatively, yes; there is hope for survival. The OD consultant "maps" her and the CEO's life spaces by reflection and conjecture to provide an explicit basis for understanding current circumstances and implementing future action.

Methods

In the first phase of feedback, process information is gathered through a variety of channels, including individual and group *interviews, focus groups,* and *survey instruments.* Interviews are both face-to-face and over the phone; pragmatics, not scientific purity, rule. The content of the data centers on the company's salient concerns: top management and business practices.

Questions are asked in various modalities (questionnaires or interviews), in both open-ended (for example, "What are some of the things that this organization does well?") and structured (for example, "What portion of people in your work group would you say are [scale: very . . . not at all] satisfied with the way this department operates?") formats. Question wording itself can be a crucial variable and should be carefully considered.

The consulting team collates the results, simply using a *frequency-of-themes analysis.* Similar themes are identified within the set of interviews (or other data points) and tallied to ascertain common energy and/or pain and associated variances. Although this procedure in part uses subjective interpretation, it provides basic images of significant areas of concern to be further clarified and validated in the feedback process.

Participants are informed that they will see results in a collated form, without identification of "who said what." There are times, however, when participants are encouraged in the feedback session to take "ownership" of the themes at their discretion and for clarification purposes. This also engenders a *dialogue* among people in the organization at all levels so that possible solutions can be directly discussed and evaluated.

With data available, feedback is initiated. This is usually most effective by verbal presentation, versus more formal and less interactive "paper" report forms. In some cases, interactive computer-based feedback has been found to be useful.

Feedback sessions range from all members of small departments attending to a wrap-up meeting for the entire organization in a large hall. Due to the sensitive nature of some information, care is taken not to use phrases that may identify individual people. Nor should the practitioner entertain any questions such as, "Who said that?"

Intensive feedback is organized for the Toys CEO, to be given to him alone at first and then again later with the executive committee, providing a picture of how matters are seen internally. In addition, a panel of external financial experts provides feedback on the CEO's turnaround plan.

The "bottom line" phase of feedback is "What next?" It is very dysfunctional to ask people questions, "feed back" the information, and then do nothing with it. Failure to follow up by concrete action potentially breeds a hostile and negative atmosphere, impeding future attempts at organizational change. Instead, it is important to stress to the client organization that this information is theirs and that the next step calls for the implementation of dedicated policy actions by management.

One approach on the road to such implementation is the formation of task groups for each of the major "problem" areas that have been identified. Over a six-month period, the consultant meets with the groups to further clarify key opportunities and pitfalls in instituting change, moving gradually to a revitalization of Toys' operations.

By allowing organization members to feel open and safe enough to share their thoughts, beliefs, and attitudes about their jobs, departments, co-workers, managers, systems, and overall organizational functioning, the OD consultant is able to tap into the internal workings of the company. People, not equipment or systems, carry the knowledge of the organization. Self-determination and intentionality for positive change by people involved in the projected change process are core concepts.

Once the information is available, the consultant needs to be able to analyze and organize that data in such a way that it captures the "state of the organization" and then to initiate a process that will assist organizational members, top management included, to become emphatic and motivated, to hear and respond to the relevant organization images, to recognize key problems, and to connect with their own roles in seeking solutions.

Resources
Survey Feedback
Cummings, T.G., & Worley, C.G. (2001). *Organization development and change* (7th ed.). Cincinnati, OH: Southwestern. ◄

► COMPANY COACHWELL

A U.S.-based company has decided to expand its operations overseas, starting with a subsidiary in Paris. Robert P., the SVP for strategy, has been chosen to head the startup and is concerned about the differences in business and people culture in France. Wanting to make a good first impression, and not wanting to commit too many faux pas, he consults with an OD practitioner known for international business practices.

Intervention: Coaching

Coaching is directed at improving the individual and his or her ability to excel in the organization. Thus, it involves working with individuals, up close, who are experiencing a specific problem or opportunities, identified by either themselves or those interacting with them, to promote individual learning in specific areas. Often emphasis is placed on strengthening interpersonal and communication skills through simulations and exercises or in *tutorials,* imparting new information. A combination of these approaches, by weekly work sessions with the consultant and staff, is used to help Robert P. make an effective move to France.

One-on-one meetings with individuals is typically the most effective coaching mode. Usually, the meetings are most frequent at the start, modifying frequency and focusing content as time goes on. Some coaching interventions, parallel to other OD efforts, may extend over years. In some instances, the individual to be coached turns out to be characterologically not amenable to coaching. (Separate therapy may be an alternative.) If severe personality deficits are manifest, appropriate decision makers need to determine whether the person's technical or professional contribution outweighs the impact of his or her people problems in working with others. The affected managers need to understand the consequences of keeping that person in terms of impact on the work environment. If the decision is made to let that person go, then the manager and the OD practitioner need to be clear regarding the legal consequences and tradeoffs involved.

Coaching efforts also play a role in educating individuals in specific skills such as becoming proficient at understanding other cultures. For example, as Robert P. was going to France, and as he had no knowledge of French, his educational/coaching process includes both social and cultural learning and language familiarization. Excellent learning modules are available from government, corporate, and media sources for such purposes for many countries, and include such topics as business etiquette, cultural mores, time perception, formality, and so on.

For Coachwell, Robert P. came to be an effective manager in the Paris subsidiary, continuing in his assignment for two years before returning to headquarters in the United States.

Organization behavior theory rests on the concept that there is a certain "fit" between individuals and organizations, and that there is a definite, yet sometimes unseen, culture that organizations adopt over time that may or may not "fit" with certain individuals. Often, an organization's internal systems do not allow for, or encourage, open dialogue on how to work positively with problem behaviors, which may appear with people who do not "fit in" with the particular culture. For example, if the unwritten rule is that direct communication is encouraged only to the extent that it is not confrontational, it may rather foster avoidance of overt conflict: "I'll just wait for the annual performance appraisal and write her up." Then when the appraisal is written, the manager looks at the employee's numbers in sales, which are high, and knows the employee is expecting a raise. With all this, the manager doesn't have the heart to give her a bad review. So the problem continues. Yet one wonders as well regarding the tradeoff: sales success versus possible endemic lingering interpersonal malaise. Coaching addresses these kinds of issues in the nine C framework. Other interactive variables, including union relations, may affect what goes on in this kind of coaching effort.

Resources

Executive Coaching

Douglas, C.Z., & Morley, W.H. (2000). *Executive coaching: An annotated bibliography.* Greensboro, NC: Center for Creative Leadership.

Zeus, P., & Skiffington, S. (2000). *The complete guide to coaching at work.* New York: McGraw-Hill.

Organizational Behavior Theory/Concept of "Fit"

Cummings, T.G., & Worley, C.G. (2001). *Organization development and change* (7th ed.). Cincinnati, OH: Southwestern.

Frame, R., Hess, R., & Neilsen, W. (1982). *The OD source book: A practitioner's guide.* San Francisco, CA: Jossey-Bass/Pfeiffer. ◄

▶ COMPANY COMMUNI-COOP

Critical business processes that require cooperation among departments are not happening, and the rumor mill seems to be the most powerful communication system in the organization.

Interventions: Improving Communication Effectiveness; 360-Degree Appraisal

It is the purpose of the chosen intervention program to improve the effectiveness and efficiency of communication and cooperation in the organization, between individuals, within and between groups/departments/divisions, and between levels, that is, staff and line, management and staff, supervisors and shop floor, and so on.

The interventions program was started with a *communication audit* to gain clarity on the nature of the problems. To simplify, descriptions are developed, based on this audit, for subgroups in the organization, focusing on where the communication or miscommunication is occurring. An *organization communication map,* showing clear channels and blockages, provides a helpful tool. Subsequent workshops address specifics.

Communication/Miscommunication Between Managers and Staff

Managers often have very little formal training in how to best communicate or relate to their staffs. Instead, their bosses have been their role models, sometimes modeling narrowly directive, even dictatorial, management styles: "Do as I say, or else." Thus, it is not surprising that when people do feel capable and want the space to be creative in their jobs, disruptive communication styles by their manager de facto inhibit creativity and limit job performance.

One tool that is often used to give managers who are looking to improve their effectiveness in managing their people environment is *360-degree appraisal.* Here staff and other co-workers are asked to fill out a written evaluation of a particular manager(s) on a number of criteria, with both rating scales and open-ended questions. For example, employees may be asked to identify three specific strengths of their supervisor and three areas in which they would like to see improvements. On ratings, they may be asked to strongly agree, agree, disagree,or strongly disagree with statements such as the following: "My supervisor is clear in her/his directions regarding my work."

Once all staff and co-workers have completed the evaluations, the consultant tabulates the scores and prepares an aggregate profile for review by the manager in a way that elicits minimum defensiveness. It is important for the consultant to stress that it is indeed difficult to accept and work through negative feedback, while recognizing the potential for improving one's interpersonal relationships and management effectiveness.

Communication/Miscommunications Among Group Members

It is not uncommon to have less than effective communication between members of groups, teams, and departments. Communication style differences and preferences vary between members, and those differences, if not understood and accepted, can lead to member isolation, frustration, avoidance, and conflict. The team or group does not have to be "in trouble" to benefit from an intervention improving communication.

The entire group meets for a few hours to a full day or even longer or more often when needed, depending on the level of blockage to be resolved. Members are encouraged to identify both areas in which they communicate well and those requiring improvement. A *storyboard* method often proves helpful, allowing thoughts to be put into a *visual forum,* encouraging all participants to input their ideas, even anonymously.

Once those assembled feel free to identify both positives and negatives, the OD practitioner directs efforts toward exploring the dynamics of communication differences, noting that predominant styles may be neither right or wrong, but pointing out that unnegotiated differences are likely to lead to personal job dissatisfaction and lowered group output. The participants are then given time to *practice new communication skills* and to develop approaches to bridge substantive and style differences. Interventions may vary in ways to elicit group ideas and in content of focused "lecturettes," but the common thread emphasizes openness, non-defensiveness, listening, and empathy, as well as honing of skills of expression and presentation of self.

Communication/Miscommunication Between Groups

When entire groups in the organization, whether they be teams, departments, or divisions, are involved in communication/miscommunication issues, some *pre-work* is recommended, such as interviewing a cross-section of people from the different groups, identifying key concerns, distinguishing between symptoms and historical root causes, and identifying the key players or major influencers.

Based on the data gathered at Communi-Coop, the intervention may require initial *meetings between the key players* who were in conflict/not communicating effectively to try to resolve any differences before bringing total groups together. If the state of communication is just beginning to deteriorate, then the practitioner should design the intervention to include total group membership. Again, having the groups input their own assessment on how they're doing—both positives and negatives—can begin building the groundwork in having group members work together toward improvement. Some time can then be used by the OD practitioner to educate the groups about how concepts like the "functional silo" come into being and what the groups have in common, seeing the "bigger picture" that can help them move past their differences.

Communication/Miscommunication Between Individuals at Any Level

When individuals are experiencing communication blockages at the same organization level, or across functions or levels in the organization, the OD practitioner can intervene by functioning as a *mediator* or *third-party facilitator.* By getting the individuals to identify and take ownership of the problem, by educating them on the dynamics of communication or miscommunication, and by encouraging and modeling how to negotiate past the differences, a process is implemented to help in "breaking the walls" and to begin opening the dialogue. At Communi-Coop, where not hostility, but confusion and excess uncertainty had been communication blockers, pre-existing goodwill established a sound basis for such dialogue.

The Value of Effective Communication

Improving communication processes constitutes one of the foundation blocks of many organization development efforts. In early mechanistic organizations, communication was easy, one-way. Thus this managerial communication style can best be described as an *arrow* approach (Clampitt, 2000). Arrow managers believe that if a message is clearly sent, it is effective, regardless of whether the receiver understands it or not. The premise is that logic will also prevail and that any reasonable person will "get it" if one spends the necessary time and effort wording a message carefully. If the receiver doesn't "get it," he or she is either stupid or not paying attention or both.

Early organization development theorists went to the opposite extreme and suggested that effective communication was measured solely by the receiver. In other words, a message was effective only if the receiver heard and understood and agreed with the message. Thus, much effort should be spent by the sender in crafting the message to serve the receiver. This style can be called a *circuit approach* to managerial communication. Although this style does embody a fully participative approach and encourages OD values, specifically that employees are worthy of respect and need to be communicated to in such a way that "buy-in" is encouraged, it does take the principle to an extreme that may not be realistic.

The more balanced approach to communication may be what Clampitt (2000) calls a *dance manager's style,* where flexibility and context are stressed to facilitate effective communication and where care needs to be taken in both formulating the message and in modifying the delivery to meet the needs of the audience.

Also, often what is called a "communication problem" may actually be a "will or commitment" issue. For example, the chief complaint of a staff group may be that their manager does not communicate well. Once investigated, it is not that the manager does not communicate well; in fact, he is very articulate in his messages. The fundamental problem is that what the manager is communicating, the content of his message, is not agreeable to the staff. In this case, "You have to do more for less money." Thus, for OD practitioners, effective communication is not just "the truth," but is information delivered in the best possible way to increase the chances that the receiver is going to accept the message.

Another aspect of effective communication in organization theory rests on the answer to the question, "Is the intent equal to the impact?" This distinction becomes even more important in companies where there is a diverse customer base and/or a diverse workforce. In the past, in more homogenous group settings, one could be more certain that, if a message were framed in a certain way, its intended meaning would be actually received. This assumption holds less water in more heterogeneous groups.

Thus, all individuals in organizations need to better their ability to communicate across differences, culture, age, gender, education, family status, religion, and many other dimensions.

At an organization level, OD theorists also believe that more communication is better than less communication in most settings—vastly different than the traditional organization mantra, "Don't tell people more than they absolutely have to know." The detrimental impact of this approach is plainly evident in impending large organizational changes, such as mergers, acquisitions, downsizing, expansions, and relocations. Using mergers as an example, in the past, SEC guidelines on confidentiality before an impending merger were taken to an extreme with *no* news from management the rule. However, there are few mergers or acquisitions that come as a total surprise. One way or another, the "cat crawls slowly out of the bag" and the rumor mill travels faster than a company announcement. Sometimes leaks spread even faster outside the organization, as in downsizing examples, where employees seem to be the last ones to know that there's going to be a mass of layoffs.

Organization development theorists believe that more communication helps people understand and thereby increases the probability of their committing to and accepting an upcoming "change." It is when there are rumors that there is a change, but there is no confirming or disconfirming data, that people begin to imagine the worst. Not knowing, worst-case scenarios often take over—a human tendency that in large measure is remedied by information. People will fill most any information vacuum with pseudo-information often unrelated to fact.

Some traditional senior managers have suggested that the withholding of information is a good method for "weeding out the deadwood," thinking that the poor performers in the organization will be the first to leave, assuming that they are in line for a layoff. However, it is well-documented that the reverse is true, that more often the top performers will leave first when rumors of an impending layoff or merger or "streamlining" are pending. For one thing, they will be the first to be approached by "headhunters" who know their worth. Thus it is critical for top management teams making decisions in a merger or similar effort to communicate as soon as legally possible with those managers they want to retain.

Resources

Improving Communication

Clampitt, P.G. (2000). *Communicating for managerial effectiveness* (2nd ed.). Thousand Oaks, CA: Sage.

360-Degree Feedback/Appraisal

Lepsinger, R., & Lucia, A.D. (1997). *The art and science of 360-degree feedback*. San Francisco, CA: Jossey-Bass/Pfeiffer. ◀

In somewhat different format, Cheryl Gitlin offers a first-person report of an OD intervention scenario in a military/high-technology environment.

▶ STRATEGIC PLANNING AND PARTICIPATIVE APPROACHES AT THE U.S. AIR FORCE SPACE AND MISSILE CENTER

CHERYL GITLIN

Launch Programs is a service provider for rocket launches for the United States Air Force Space and Missile Center. It is comprised of three rocket divisions: Delta, Atlas, and Titan. In the past, Launch Programs strategic planning was not effective, primarily because it was done with a quick-fix mentality and short-term results. According to Peter Senge (1990), quick-fix mentalities make us system blind. There are additional reasons that made it difficult to achieve and implement successful strategic planning at this site: (1) the frequent changes in the strategic planning committee's membership due to transfers to new assignments, members separating from the Air Force, and retirements; (2) stakeholders not comprehending the importance of a well-functioning strategic plan and not being committed to the strategic planning process; (3) a poor communication network throughout the organization; (4) government downsizing, putting tremendous burden on remaining personnel; and (5) lack of trusting relationships and low morale due to espoused values not being visibly demonstrated by behavior in the organization.

I recommended that Launch Programs establish a *steering committee* with a *diverse representation* of the organization. Each division was asked to have a representative participate on the steering committee. Prior to this, only senior management and a few rising stars from middle management were involved with strategic planning. Strategic planning consisted of a two-day off-site meeting and, as I mentioned earlier, it was with a quick-fix mentality.

I remember that when, at a senior management meeting, I asked if they had come up with the metrics for the objectives, I just about had to put on a flak jacket, and the same occurred every time I raised the subject in the next few months. The champions of the objectives came up with smoke screens, resistance, and an abundance of reasons as to why they didn't have metrics or did not need to provide them. Senior management had other government priorities or were away on temporary duty assignments. The absence of senior management and the lack of a well-functioning communication network impacted these results.

An alternative was needed for strategic planning representation and communication of information back to each division. However, to do this, senior management needed to reassess organizational values that drove organizational behavior and decision making and to review some of the tacit cultural assumptions. Also, although the result of the pre-strategic planning assessment administered to senior management was above average, it now raised the director's level of awareness because it didn't match prior expectations. He requested that an *organizational diagnosis questionnaire* be administered to the whole organization. The results of the questionnaire were extremely low regarding leadership, satisfaction with job, morale, and training.

After I coached the director on raising the level of trust throughout the organization, he came to the conclusion that he needed to disseminate the results of the questionnaire to the entire organization, either along hierarchical lines down through the divisions or with the whole organization gathered together. He decided to call everyone together at once, and he titled the meeting "The State of Launch Programs." After he briefed everyone on what was actually going on within the organization, with a focus on how the organization was not meeting the needs of its people, and told them that they would make the necessary changes together, there was thundering applause. This meeting created an atmosphere in which transformative change could take place. Employees told me that they had never experienced such a meeting in their whole military career. We received e-mails and talking papers with suggestions and plans for improvements.

In the next step, the director listened to every level of employee in group meetings, asking for suggestions on improvements for processes. This was an incredible win/win because all the employees had an opportunity to be listened to and to become empowered, and the organization had the opportunity to benefit from all of its intellectual capital. After this series of meetings was completed, the new steering committee for strategic planning was formed.

The steering committee members ranged in rank from colonel to a civilian GS-6. Meetings were held every two weeks. The steering committee and senior management performed a *values assessment,* and each of the representatives distributed the results to their division for feedback and consensus. Then the steering committee analyzed and revised the mission and vision statements based on the assessment results and presented the statements to senior management for consensus. They then distributed the statements throughout their divisions for feedback and consensus.

Next the steering committee assessed current capabilities. They evaluated the key processes and determined whether or not they were meeting "customers'" needs. To determine whether customers' needs were being met, a customer survey on Launch Program's services and processes had been sent out. By means of this survey, Launch Programs was able to ascertain its strengths and weaknesses and to determine whether it was meeting customers' requirements and needed areas of improvement.

After the gap analysis was completed, which considered the results of both the internal and external customer surveys and derived rankings of importance, the steering committee was able to formulate meaningful goals and objectives. Also, due to the fact that the committee was diverse in its representation of the organization, discussions and brainstorming covered all levels and the majority of organizational perspectives. As a result, goals and objectives were formed on the basis of insightful and pertinent data. The statements of goals and objectives were then distributed throughout the organization, by division, for further feedback or consensus.

Next, the members of the steering committee established action plans for attainment of objectives. A few working meetings were held so that members could learn how to write up action plans appropriately. Members chose objectives and wrote an action plan, either with another member or by themselves. The consultants reviewed and revised as needed and then presented the resulting action plans to senior management. Once these plans were approved by the Director and senior management, they were distributed throughout the organization.

By using a proactive, participative approach and maximizing the potential of indigenous intellectual capital, the organization was able to build and enhance relationships with its employees. The relationship-building process improved the level of trust and psychological safety so that unlearning of old style strategic planning could occur. Transformative change and new learning was able to take place. The new strategic planning process and communication network was accepted and successfully implemented.

Resources

Gap Analysis

Cummings, T.G., & Worley, C.G. (2001). *Organization development and change* (7th ed.). Cincinnati, OH: Southwestern.

Organizational Diagnosis

Alderfer, C.P. (1980). The methodology of organizational diagnosis. *Professional Psychology, 11*(1), 459-468.

Bartee, E.M., & Cheyunski, F. (1977). A methodology for process-oriented organizational diagnosis. *The Journal of Applied Behavioral Science, 13*(1), 53-68.

French, W.L., & Bell, C.H., Jr. (1999). *Organization development: Behavioral science interventions for organization improvement* (6th ed.). Englewood Cliffs, NJ: Prentice Hall.

Preziosi, R.C. (1980). Organizational diagnosis questionnaire. In J.W. Pfeiffer & J.E. Jones (Eds.), *The 1980 annual handbook for group facilitators* (pp. 112–120). San Francisco, CA: Jossey-Bass/Pfeiffer.

Participation/Empowerment

Byham, W. (1990). *Zapp! The lightening of empowerment.* New York: Bantam.

Strategic Planning

Hammer, M., & Champy, J. (1993). *Reengineering the corporation for business revolution: A manifesto.* New York: Harper.

Senge, P.M., Kleiner, A., Roberts, C., Ross, R.B., & Smith, B.J. (1994). *The fifth discipline fieldbook: Strategies and tools for building a learning organization.* New York: Doubleday Dell.

Values Assessment

Frame, R., Hess, R., & Neilsen, W. (1982). *The OD source book: A practitioner's guide.* San Francisco, CA: Jossey-Bass/Pfeiffer. ◀

Reflections
and Perspectives

ON THIS CHAPTER, a number of contributors to the field address history and ever-current issues in a spirit of retrospection and reflection:

In the following article, Jerry B. Harvey, looking back at a specific event, ponders the relationship between music, religion, spirit, and organization development.

▶ THE GOSPEL CHORUS

JERRY B. HARVEY

Shortly after Douglas McGregor (1960) published *The Human Side of Enterprise* in 1960, Bob Blake invited him to the University of Texas in Austin to conduct a seminar about his new work. "Who's who" in the emerging field of organizational psychology were on the guest list. Blake didn't invite anyone with a background in organization development, primarily because the field didn't exist at that time and the arguments about who invented the term had not commenced.

The session was held in an elegant Victorian mansion located on the campus. Owned by the university, the mansion was used only for events of extraordinary importance.

If my memory serves correctly, Ken Benne, Ron Lippitt, Chris Argyris, Warren Bennis, Rensis Likert, and several other luminaries who were engaged in the study of organizational behavior attended. In addition, a select group of University of Texas faculty members, university administrative officials, top-level managers from important local and regional organizations, plus a rag-tag group of graduate students (of whom I was one) took part.

The content of McGregor's presentation and the subsequent discussions, to put it mildly, were stunning. Once the session concluded, I doubt that the letters X and Y ever were simply elements of the alphabet for anyone who attended. Electricity filled the air; the excitement was palpable. I think that all of us were acutely aware that McGregor had come up with something big in our field (whatever that field was) and that we were a part of it.

After the formal session concluded, the participants headed to the drawing room for drinks and hors d'oeuvres. Our little cadre of graduate students was thoroughly cowed. The previous day we had been engaged in reading the work of "the Gods"; today we were consorting with them over hors d'oeuvres. That was heady stuff. As the afternoon progressed, though, one by one the gods disappeared, and we began to feel abandoned. It was as if we were suddenly alone in a crowd.

A short time later, from the back of the manor, we heard the strains of live gospel fundamentalist tent-revival meetings music:

"When the trumpets of the Lord shall sound,

and time shall be no more,

And the morning breaks, eternal, bright, and fair;

When the saved of earth shall gather over on the other shore,

And the roll is called up yonder, I'll be there."*

It seems that Douglas McGregor had discovered a grand piano in the music room and had organized the great minds of applied behavioral science into a gospel chorus. Furthermore, he had them belting out old-time-religion hymns in lusty four-part harmonies. They were not just singing; they were singing with extraordinary enthusiasm, as if they were fully engaged in pursuing their God-given calling. All that was missing were folding chairs, funeral home fans, and shape note hymnals.

At that moment, I realized, albeit very dimly, that the emerging field of what is now called organization development (whatever it is) was not, at its roots, a scientific enterprise. Rather, it was and always will be an oxymoronic (sic) secular religious movement. Its fundamental attraction stemmed, not from the results of rigorous scientific investigations, but from assertions of a shared faith that was masquerading as science.

More than forty years have passed since the days when OD had no name. Nevertheless, I remain convinced that, beginning with McGregor, OD has struggled with but has not come close to resolving its underlying issues of incipient spirituality.

By the way, several years later, shortly after McGregor had died, I told his widow, Caroline, about my memorable experience with him and his remarkable performance as director of the "gospel chorus." "I'm not surprised," she said. "When Doug was a teenager, his father was a minister. During the summer, his father would conduct tent revival meetings throughout the South. Doug would play the piano and his father would preach. Very few people know that about him. I've always thought that, if you don't know about his gospel piano playing, you can never understand the basis of the passion that bubbled out when he wrote about Theory X and Theory Y."

---

*Words and music by James M. Black, 1856–1938.

As far as I'm concerned, Douglas McGregor isn't the only person in the field of OD who has played gospel (that is, good news) music on the piano, either literally or metaphorically. Nor is he the only one who has attempted or will attempt, either intentionally or unintentionally, to organize spiritually starved people into choruses that sing rousing four-part, spiritually conflicted harmonies in the name of science. I think he was the first in the field to do it, though, and that his doing it is what made his work speak to so many people. At the very least, he was one of the first, if not the first, member of the profession who, either intentionally or unintentionally, confronted our sense of the spiritual as an aspect of action.

In addition, I am sure that whoever is the last to play that metaphorical piano will close the door and probably shut out the lights on OD, whatever OD happens to be. Shutting out the lights on an oxymoronic secular religious movement? Or an inchoate scientific enterprise? Perhaps not a bad professional legacy for someone to leave behind. ◀

In the context of group training, Norma Jean Anderson reports on music and its role in a learning process[*].

▶ THE USE OF MUSIC IN T-GROUP TRAINING: A SPIRITUAL INTERLUDE

NORMA JEAN ANDERSON

Music has been called the "universal language," and words of affirmation and inspiration have been referred to as a "healing balm for the souls of all members of all nations." And it is for very good reasons that these truths have been proclaimed.

Each member of the family of humanity has *"experienced"* the truth of these claims. They are not things we *"believe"* or have *"faith"* in. Rather, they are what we "know." For each of us has been moved, healed, deepened, and increased by the vast power of words of upliftment wed to the melodies, harmonies, and rhythms of intentionally inspiring song.

Through the avenue of such music, we have been moved beyond the mind and its concepts of isolation and separation and have been propelled into the rich depths of the inner space of the heart, where the true self is *known* and where the unity of all life is *felt*.

So far beyond the mind is the power of inspiring music that it is not necessary to know either the language in which a song is being sung, nor to understand the music theory upon which that song has been composed for one to be touched at deep levels and moved.

All peoples, all tribes, all nations, all cultures, all religions, all groups and subgroups have known this since the beginning. The belief of many of the world's indigenous people, in fact, proclaim the manifest worlds to have been created by the inspired song of the Creator of All That Is. It is no wonder, then, that each new member born into each particular group is customarily welcomed and soothed and nurtured and

---

[*]No specific religious orientation is espoused in this report.

empowered by that group's form of lullaby, meant not so much to lull the newborn one to *sleep* as to inspire the *feeling of safety,* in which relaxation, peace, and calm are available, accessible, and, to some degree, unavoidable.

The three pieces of music I've chosen for inclusion in my work were chosen for the above-mentioned reason. They are rather like lullabies, and they hold the same intention—to welcome each new member into her or his new world: the society of the T-group experience. In this new world, as in all new world journeys, safety is hoped for and feelings of welcome are much appreciated.

Flying Lessons (words and music by Carlos W. Anderson) is the first piece of music used in my design. Its lyrics inspire participants to open themselves up to growth and learning and to be guided by the heart and the mind in their speaking and listening. Its lyrics speak of the available space of a higher perspective on life and its mundane cares and concerns. Its words are set to lively, lilting music, which holds perfect "ground-breaking" effectiveness and stirs the group to a conscious alertness and preparation for participation in the learning experience.

Be (words and music by Carlos W. Anderson) is a gentle reminder for participants to remain in the present of the group experience. Its lyrics speak of the power of the NOW moment to provide clarity. Its music, very much like a gentle lullaby, serves to relax, to calm, and to forward the feeling of safety and authenticity of being.

Holding Hands (words by Carlos W. Anderson and music by Johnny Earl) I use at the closing of our experience together. At this point, we have moved through much together, shared much, learned much, and grown much. We have each gained a deeper understanding of who we are as individual selves, as well as who we are as interconnected members of the family of humankind. The lyrics remind us of the holiness (wholeness) of each. They remind us to honor both. The music these lyric reminders are set to is in the form of the traditional contemporary love song, which is amazingly effective in forwarding the opening of hearts, one for another, for self, and for all. We are physically holding hands during this piece of music. And we are increased by our joining, each of us. We, together through our experience, have become a new world.

Flying Lessons

Mother Love and Father Wisdom

Call to me within

It is time my child

For flying lessons to begin

Raise your mind

And let us find

A starting place to rise above

Let us stretch our wings and sail on love

Love and Wisdom call from within

Your flying lessons begin

Fly high above your many cares

And all your little fears

Love will lift you far from sorrow

Dry your many tears

Mother Father, Love and Wisdom

Show me how to soar to freedom

Deep within me, teach me how to fly

In this moment, we are free to fly

Love and Wisdom call from within

Your flying lessons begin

Begin, my child, your flying lessons now!

Be

Within the moment

Life is forever

We live each moment eternally

No need to question

No need to wonder

For there is only need to be

Hallelujah, just to know

There is only need to be

Be . . . be . . . be . . . be!

Holding Hands

I adore you, and bless you
I now see you free
I adore you, and love you
With God's Love, in me

Amen, Amen, Amen, Amen
I and myself are holding hands

When I tell you "I love you"
I'm talking to me
When I give my love to you
I grow love in me

Amen, Amen, Amen, Amen
I and myself are holding hands

I'm the love God is giving
I'm the love that God is
I adore you and free you
To love and to live

Holding hands is a feeling
Of love free to flow
Holding hands is a feeling
The whole world should know

Amen, Amen, Amen, Amen
I and myself are holding hands
Amen ◀

In the following contribution, Dean Anderson explores how spiritual self-development leads to professional mastery.

► PUTTING YOUR BEING FIRST: THE SPIRITUAL FOUNDATION FOR BECOMING A MASTERFUL OD PRACTITIONER

DEAN ANDERSON

As you begin your training or your career as an organization development practitioner, what is your goal for yourself? How high is the standard you aspire to achieve? Do you wish to become merely competent, or masterful? Competence will allow you to perform the OD craft well and build a successful practice. Mastery will give you such insight into the craft that you can contribute to it with new approaches and methods and be able to respond in real time with such art that you catalyze extraordinary results in the people and organizations you serve.

Both competent and masterful OD practitioners possess a solid knowledge base and sound intervention skills. They understand human and organizational dynamics, they can see complex systems clearly, and they carry a well-packed tool box of techniques and methods. Masterful practitioners, however, possess a unique, subtle quality—a presence, an intuitive sense, a way of being and relating that they did not learn in school or from their direct consulting experience. They grew this way of being from within, through their own personal and spiritual development. And so can you. I wholeheartedly believe that your success as an OD practitioner will be in direct proportion to your spiritual development. In this short essay, I will attempt to describe why.

A Bit of History: The Great Chain of Being

Life has both internal and external dimensions. There certainly are solid, physical objects "out there," as well as less tangible thoughts, feelings, and emotions "in here." Until approximately the Industrial Revolution, social cultures across the globe held a common belief about the nature of reality that included both the internal and the external. Huston Smith (1992) describes this common worldview as the "Great Chain of Being," which depicts reality as being comprised of various levels, beginning with matter, then moving to body, emotions, mind, and spirit.

After the Industrial Revolution, much of Western society began to neglect the internal realities of the human experience and focused almost exclusively on the external physical plane. As a result, traditional management practices generally overlook the internal levels of people's emotions, minds, and spirits and attend primarily to the external levels of matter and body; that is, they focus much more on the tangible aspects of marketplace trends and the organization's structures, systems, and processes than on the "hidden" dynamics within people.

Organization development rightfully acknowledges these external levels, yet also attends to the internal levels of emotions and mind, that is, an *individual's* values, beliefs, and feelings, a *team's* esprit de corps and the *organization's* culture, myths, and norms.

To achieve mastery in OD, however, I believe that practitioners must also include attention to the spiritual level, especially their own.

Different Orientations to OD

There is a wide continuum of orientations with which OD practitioners approach their work. On one end of the continuum are "externally oriented practitioners" and on the other end are "internally oriented practitioners" (see Figure 11.1).

Externally oriented practitioners focus primarily on the matter and body levels of OD—their own methods and techniques, the organization's struc-

Figure 11.1. Orientations to OD

Externally Oriented Practitioners	**Internally Oriented Practitioners**
Technique	Presence
What we produce	How we relate
Practices and methods	Vision and value
Logic	Intuition
Behavior	Beliefs
Provide answers	Facilitate learning
External results void of spiritual meaning	Spiritual meaning without connection to external results

ture and processes, and individuals' behaviors and work practices. These practitioners typically place inadequate attention on the impact of internal dynamics, such as their own assumptions, biases, or style, the organization's culture and norms, or employees' attitudes and feelings. Internally oriented practitioners do the reverse. They attend to and seek to develop the internal domains of people and culture, often neglecting to tie that work to the external worlds of organizational systems, processes, and results.

Mastery in OD requires both orientations. You must attend to and build expertise in the whole spectrum of the Great Chain of Being, as well as see and understand the interconnections among all of the levels as they play out over time. Focusing on either end of the continuum alone leaves out half the equation.

Putting Your Being First

Mastering the whole continuum of OD skills requires that you put your own *being* first, that you actively engage in developing your internal self. You can build competence in the external aspects of OD without turning your attention to the internal aspects of your own personal growth. However, doing your own internal work is a necessary foundation for learning how to facilitate the internal work required in the people and organizations you serve. Intellectual models and pragmatic techniques, by themselves, are never enough for these domains. You must travel the path yourself, learning by direct personal experience.

Taking a multi-dimensional approach to this self-development is most effective. By multi-dimensional, I refer to developing your *whole* self—physically, emotionally, mentally, and spiritually. Any domains you neglect will limit your overall self-development, as all are interconnected.

There are numerous approaches for developing the various aspects of yourself. Figure 11.2 offers a partial list. The key is establishing a long-term practice that positively impacts all four domains. Many self-development techniques impact more than one domain. I suggest that you begin by picking a domain that interests you and learning and using techniques to develop that aspect of yourself. In six months, learn and apply techniques from another domain, then another. Over time you will build the habits and skills of continuously improving your whole self.

Figure 11.2. Multidimensional Self-Development

Physical

Fitness (cardiovascular, strength, and flexibility training)

Nutrition

Relaxation techniques

Emotional

Gestalt therapy

Cathartic release techniques

Mental

Cognitive therapy

Belief identification processes

Spiritual

Meditation

Prayer

Expanding Your Conscious Awareness

The most fundamental aspect of yourself is your consciousness. Putting your being first begins with expanding your consciousness. This is a subtle, yet profound process of developing your *conscious* awareness of the dynamics at play within your own four domains. The more you are consciously aware of your mental, emotional, and physical patterns, the more you can transform the ones that limit your effectiveness in your life and work.

Personally, I began developing my conscious awareness through very simple meditation and relaxation techniques that enabled me to discover what occurred in my body and breath during times of stress and high performance. This awareness of my physical reactions soon led to deeper insights about my conditioned mental and emotional reactions. I began to see the fight-and-flight behavior patterns my ego generated as ways of defending myself and bolstering my self-image. As I became aware of these dynamics, I learned how to deal with them effectively and lessen their negative impact. With my ego in less control of my behavior, my spiritual and intuitive capabilities began to come forth. During this time of intense personal development, I noticed a profound positive shift in how I worked with clients and the results that we collectively were able to achieve.

Increasing your conscious awareness will put you in touch with the deeper aspects of your spiritual self, which, ultimately, will be the foundation of your mastery of OD. When you quiet your mind and emotions, your spiritual essence will shine through, and a whole new capability will emerge.

What Is Spiritual Development?

By spiritual, I am not speaking about any particular religion, dogma, or socially accepted set of mythical beliefs. In fact, you can be spiritual and follow any religion or no religion. Being religious and being spiritual are two distinct phenomena.

Spiritual development warrants a book in itself. It is challenging to discuss because the spiritual domain has different dynamics than the mental, emotional, and physical domains.

Basically, being spiritual begins with turning your awareness inward and attuning to the consciousness within you that lies beyond your ego's mental and emotional conditioning. It is the process of quieting your ego's fears and wants (through mental, emotional, and physical practices, as well as through meditation or prayer) so you can directly experience the pure consciousness that is the source of your being. By detaching from your conditioned ways of perceiving, you can more directly experience reality (both internal and external) without mental and emotional filters. This puts you in touch with the essential life force—Spirit—that animates all existence. In other words, spiritual practices increase your ability to consciously experience spirit. As you develop this direct connection to spirit through your own deep connection to your self, a whole new way of being, relating, and working emerges. Then, that subtle quality mentioned earlier, that presence and way of being required for mastering OD, grows within *you*.

Consciously breathing is a very simple, yet profound and direct tool you can use at any moment during client work to disengage your ego and connect more deeply to yourself, your intuition, and your clear insight. Try it now. On your next breath, focus consciously as you inhale and you exhale. Allow your breath to flow in naturally, without any effort on your part, then completely relax into your exhale. Let it flow out freely. Don't push or hold, as that activates your ego's control mechanism. Just surrender into your breath's own motion. As your breath flows out, sink into that space at the end of your exhale just before the next inhale. Feel the quiet, still place that exists there. Sense everything occurring inside your body and outside in the world. Simply allow everything, including yourself, to *be* in this present moment.

This exercise might take all of ten seconds, yet done consciously and consistently over time, it will open a doorway to access your spiritual self in your work. Do it often. No one will ever know, but you will see the benefits of bringing your deeper self to your clients.

The Benefits of Your Personal and Spiritual Development

There are numerous benefits that you will derive from putting your being first and developing yourself spiritually, mentally, emotionally, and physically. I will discuss the five most pertinent to becoming a masterful OD practitioner.

1. Increased Choice and Options

As you turn inward and expand your awareness of your fundamental assumptions and beliefs about people, organizations, and change, you will increase your ability to see and acknowledge other worldviews. This will provide you increased choice about your consulting style and behavior as well as about the techniques and methods you use and how and when you apply them.

2. Improved Performance

High performers in every field ultimately discover that they perform best when in an internal mental and emotional state, often referred to as the "flow" or "zone." As you develop yourself mentally and emotionally and learn how to overcome fears, doubts, and other self-limiting dynamics, you will find that "flow" of high concentration and confidence occurring more often within you, thus improving your consulting performance and results. For more information on this internal aspect of high performance, see Csikszentmihalyi (1990).

3. Increased Centeredness

As you do your own inner work, you will reduce your ego's conditioned, automatic reactions to difficult situations and events. This will enable you to operate with greater calm and centeredness. You will be able to see challenging situations with greater clarity and be able to sense what is required of you to positively influence them.

4. Increased Ability to "Trust the Process"

People bring more of themselves to challenges or change when they feel safe, supported, and able to contribute. Spiritual practitioners consistently report the existence of a deeply rooted, fundamental spiritual truth that creates for them a profound sense of personal safety, support, and confidence. The "Great Wisdom" traditions of many religions have described this truth for centuries. I can confirm its impact on me throughout the years of my own meditation practice. This truth is easily described using language from the new sciences.

The new science literature describes living or human systems as "open"; they continually import information and energy from their larger environments that enable them to self-organize out of chaos into higher orders of complexity. It suggests that at the point of all breakdown is the seed of the next breakthrough. In other words, in human systems, when something "bad" happens, information is present for those involved to *learn* what needs to occur to make something better occur next time. Life has at its essence a benevolent force (Spirit) that is continually evolving events in a positive direction. Any given event may seem bad to the minds and emotions of the people involved when it is occurring, but from a larger spiritual perspective, the event is exactly what is needed for them to improve themselves or the situation. There is a kind of "rightness" in all things, no matter how we might perceive them from our personal perspective.

For example, it is "right" that an organization goes out of business because it is not serving its customers adequately. This situation may seem bad to the people involved, but from a larger perspective, the marketplace is simply doing the necessary pruning of its dead wood so service to customers can naturally improve over time. Likewise, when an individual experiences personal crisis, the situation always offers the wake-up call and learning necessary for the person to make the positive changes required to build a better future. The key, of course, is remaining centered in yourself so you can discover the learning and integrate the growth offered.

Being in tune spiritually enables you to better see the lessons and positive direction offered in any challenging situation. With that capacity, it is much easier to "trust the process," because deep within yourself you know that it will ultimately move in a positive direction.

5. Increased Ability to Co-Create and Facilitate Optimal Solutions

When faced with challenges or complex change, people have a tendency to adopt an aggressive "gain power over and control of" behavioral style, especially when they are governed by their ego's self-interests, fears, or doubts. For OD practitioners, this spells doom. Seldom do optimal results come from attacking the organization with heavy-handed control interventions. Instead, OD practitioners need to work with (not against) the forces at play. Instead of resisting the "bad" things happening and attempting to control them, they must allow these forces to "speak and be heard," thus exerting their necessary influence on the system. Practitioners must not become blinded by their ego's automatic response to exert power over the "problems." Instead, they must *listen* for what intervention is called for. This level of listening and intervention skill can only occur when practitioners are centered, present, and tuned in spiritually to the benevolent opportunity at hand. Such an internal state allows them to trust the process so they can calm their power and control tendencies and operate co-creatively with the situation to deliver just the right intervention. This is why *doing* must follow *being*.

In Summary

By consciously turning your awareness inward, putting your *being* first, and developing yourself spiritually, you will develop OD mastery beyond simply applying the tools, methods, and practices of the trade. You will move beyond being a good technician to being an artist who has great technique. The best of luck to you in your inner and outer journeys. Mastery awaits you! ◀

Robert Tannenbaum, with the metaphor of The River, addresses some basic and timeless issues in the field of OD.

▶ OF TIME AND THE RIVER*

ROBERT TANNENBAUM

My intent this morning is not to keynote the conference theme of "Making OD Operational." I do not want to focus primarily on the day-in-day-out issues of operationalizing the theories and methodologies of OD. Rather, my desire is to go both more broadly and deeper. What I will do is to discuss some basic considerations affecting our profession—some factors that I think surround us as we attempt to operationalize OD on a continuing basis.

These themes are very important ones to me. Please minimally hear what I have to say as ideas that are coming from me personally—themes that deeply matter to me.

Each of you here can see the Columbia River, this magnificent river flowing past us. This river is over 1,200 miles in length. It originates in Columbia Lake up in British Columbia in the ice fields. It first flows northwest, and then reverses itself and comes south, going around the Selkirk Mountains, entering the State of Washington, then turning westward and forming the boundary between Washington and Oregon, and finally, not too far from here, it merges with the larger whole, the Pacific Ocean.

Stewart Holbrook (1956), over twenty years ago in a book called *The Columbia,* wrote as follows:

> "By the time I came to see the Columbia's headwaters, I had already lived thirty years on the lower Columbia. I had also seen long stretches of it over much of a thousand miles, but never seen its source or felt the magic of its headwaters. Standing at the source gives a man a sense that he has at least come to understand a river. On him descends the complete assurance of those ancients who composed the books of the Old Testament.

---

*Edited version of the keynote address presented before the OD Network conference, Portland, Oregon, October 8, 1978. Printed here with the author's permission.

They had no doubts as to where and how things had their beginnings. Here at the source, too, [I had] a satisfying sense of having followed a big stream from its outlet to its source. Only people who have done as much will understand."

The river and time have been widely used as metaphors. For example, in literature, mythology, religion, and personal fantasies, the river, time, life, stability, and change (development) are often closely interrelated. Thomas Wolfe (the writer the title of whose book I have chosen for the title of this session) has said that "Time is like a river." He has also said that "Life is like a river, and as fixed, unalterable in unceasing movement and in changeless change as the great river is, and time itself."

Holding this river (the Columbia) in our vision and in our souls, let's move toward some of the broad issues that are very central to us as we attempt to operationalize OD.

Planned Change

The first issue that I would like to deal with has to do with a concept that has been in our literature for a long number of years. It is labeled as "planned change" or "managed change." These phases bug the hell out of me. To me, they completely mislead us in terms of what OD is and should be about as we carry it forward in our practice. In order to say what I want to say about "planned change," I must briefly mention one of the bodies of theory that is so key to us in what we do, namely, systems theory. Recall that in systems theory we think of a bounded set of dynamic units; that these dynamic units are interrelated, interconnected, interdependent; and that the bounded units operate within a larger environment. And we are well aware, I think, that the larger environment is often a turbulent one, an environment that frequently is quite difficult to predict—often catching us by surprise. We frequently use the notion of open systems, recognizing that the boundary that defines each of these interdependent units is hopefully permeable in both directions—open to letting things in from the environment and also open to impact from the larger environment.

With these notions in mind, and coming back to "planned change," I submit that it is next to impossible for us to plan change. If by that phrase we mean (and I recognize different people mean different things by it) to plan, whether singly or in collaborative groups, a specific goal or outcome, sometimes lying six months or a year or five years hence, with the expectation that we can not only lay out the path for the achievement of that objective but also the steps that we will go through to get there, then such a notion is, in my judgment, sheer madness. We deal with complex human beings, with their interdependence with each other, and with the non-human aspects of the systems in which they function. We are painfully aware of the frequently turbulent environments that surround these people and their systems. Little wonder that we are so often faced with surprises. In fact, we constantly move step-by-step into the unknown.

Some of you may be familiar with a small paperback by Lewis Thomas (a well-known biologist) called *The Lives of a Cell* (1974). In the following quote, he contrasts applied science and basic science. When he is talking about applied science, he is talking about that process where the laws that are being dealt with are known and understood; one can reason from cause to effect, and with relatively high confidence move with a planning process. And by basic research he is *thinking* more of an open-minded, unpredictable process. He writes, "This is the element that distinguishes applied science from basic. Surprise is what makes the difference. When you are organized to apply knowledge, set up targets, and produce a usable product, you require a high degree of certainty from the outset. All the facts on which you base protocols must be reasonably hard facts with unambiguous meaning. The challenge is to plan the work and organize the workers so that it will come out precisely as predicted." (I suspect that very often in our deeper hopes, we wish that this is how it might be.) Thomas, going on, says: "In basic research, everything is just the opposite. What you need at the outset is a high degree of uncertainty; otherwise it isn't likely to be an important problem. You start with an incomplete roster of facts, characterized by their ambiguity; often the problem consists of discovering the connections between unrelated pieces of information. You must plan experiments on the basis of probability, even bare possibility, rather than certainty. If an experiment turns out precisely as predicted, this can be very nice, but it is only a great event if at the same time it is a surprise. You can measure the quality of the work by the intensity of the astonishment. The surprise can be because it did turn out as predicted."*

I submit that this second model is much closer to what we are involved in. We are involved in an unfolding process, faced with all kinds of ambiguity and uncertainty and unpredictability, and we are rarely, if ever, able to have very high confidence in what is going to appear at the next step. We have to live with that.

I mentioned a year ago at the San Diego conference some thoughts and feelings I had about the appearance of Sadat in Jerusalem, and the unfolding process that has followed is very much with me. I see it following this second model, with individuals and nations being faced with the necessity, almost day by day, to commit themselves to steps involving high uncertainty as to the outcome and yet having to have the courage and the strength to move in the face of an unknown future. We do, it seems to me, as OD practitioners, need to flow with the river. As individuals, most central is the personal characteristic of tolerance for ambiguity. There is a lot that differentiates us in this particular characteristic. But a person who has low tolerance for ambiguity, in my judgment, should not be in the OD field. It is essential somehow that we be able to live with the unknown, that we be able to function even though we have no certainty as to what is next to come.

There is an Hassidic tale that goes as follows: When the son of the Rabbi of Lentshno was a boy, he saw Rabbi Vitzhak praying. Full of amazement, he came running to his father and asked how it was possible for such a zaddick (a righteous or holy man) to pray quietly and simply, without giving any sign of ecstasy. His father answered, "A poor swimmer has to thrash around in order to stay up in the water. The perfect swimmer rests on the tide and it carries him." To me, the perfect swimmer, the ideal OD person with his or her keen sensitivity and flexibility, needs to be able to stay in continuing tune with the interacting and unfolding people, systems, and flow of events with which he or she is involved in order to be able to flow with the river.

---

*"The Planning of Science," from THE LIVES OF A CELL by Lewis Thomas, copyright © 1974 by Lewis Thomas; Copyright © 1971 by The Massachusetts Medical Society. Used by permission of Viking Penguin, a division of Penguin Putnam, Inc.

Patience

The second issue has to do with patience, which turns our attention to a perspective on time. It is my understanding as we again look at this wonderful river in front of us that the ancestral Columbia River established its present general course more than eleven million years ago and that its present course goes back to the ice age. We are now looking at it in the present. And yet, during millions of years this river has flowed from the mountains to the sea.

I recall one of my first deeply shaking peak experiences. I was in junior college and taking a course in astronomy in my freshman year. On a particular day our instructor presented to us the notion of the island universe. She illustrated it by what is called the Andromeda Nebula. Even though it is an island universe, it is the closest such universe to our own system. As she told us that it was 900,000 light years away, my mind exploded. I remember walking home from school that afternoon tingling all over and trying to internalize the meaning of 900,000 light years and looking at light from a source in the heavens that had been traveling at 186,000 miles a second for 900,000 years. Time as an extension can indeed seem endless.

In contrast with this, in our culture and many others there is a tremendous need for *now*—for certainly getting things done tomorrow, if today is not possible. We are under the constant pressure of time. At least we let ourselves experience things this way, so that our perspective is shrunk tremendously. But when one permits one's self to view a deadline that is even a month away against the time span of this river or of the universe, it can take on a quite different meaning.

As some of you know, a number of years ago I was involved in a community change project in Israel with the kibbutzim—the cooperative communities there. One of the principal interventions during the project took place over a nine-week period. It was aimed at helping a specific community better understand itself and its own directions. Now eight years later, I see that the river is still flowing—and in quite unpredictable ways. We had no notion at the time of the nature or direction of the processes that would unfold, involving, for just one example, the development of a major OD practitioner group in Israel that is now intervening in all kinds of ways in the kibbutzim and in the broader society of Israel itself. And it is hard to say where things will go from here. But I do know that when we in OD keep trying to evaluate what we do, we encounter the question of what to evaluate and against what criteria, since with a flow of time we have no way of knowing in advance what the ripples will bring.

Kenneth Clark, a psychologist who did research in the early 1950s in black schools, was quoted by Chief Justice Warren in the Brown versus Board of Education case in 1954, the civil rights case. Twenty-four years later, Clark faced the recent Bakke decision, and in the paper he was quoted as saying, "Once I thought we could get it done in my time. Now I know that my children and grandchildren are going to have to simply keep it going on. However, maybe that's what life is all about." I have spent much energy through the years, as many of you have, working on a counseling basis with individuals or in T-groups, and I think one of the things that I have learned most profoundly in that work has been the nature of patience and its importance. What happens that is significant rarely happens in a moment of time. It happens slowly, gradually, as the Grand Canyon itself was carved out by the Colorado River or the gorge to the east of us was carved out by the Columbia. Yes, Rome was not built in a day; it is important to make haste slowly. Yet there is deeply within us—those of us who have been raised in this culture—a tremendous need to make haste and to make it rapidly. Patience—patience needs to be with us.

In Ecclesiastes we are all familiar with the verse that begins, "To everything there is a season, and a time to every purpose under the heaven: A time to be born, and a time to die; a time to plant, and a time to pluck up that which is planted." We need, I think, to have within us the sense of time and its appropriateness—a deeply understood sense of the meaning of patience and its relevance to human affairs.

Techniques and Methods

My next theme is again one that troubles me considerably in our field, and that one involves the strong lure to us of OD techniques and methods. As the years have been passing, and particularly during the past few years, the trend has been in the direction of an increasing emphasis on techniques and methods in OD. I, in addition to a number of you, frequently work with interns—people who are new to the field. While doing so, I often find it difficult to deal with anything central in the field before I am confronted with the question, "Do you know a technique for implementing that? What method will work here?" Individuals are constantly reaching out for tool kits rather than for something more basic. Now tool kits are essential. I don't want to imply by what I say that a practitioner in our field should not know of and be skillful with a wide spectrum of techniques and methods. *To me the issue is when and how and with whom we choose to apply these techniques and methods.* The narrow adherence to the tool kit by many in our field does trouble me deeply, and it is dehumanizing our field. If I were to characterize OD presently, I would say that it is less humanistic than it was a few years ago, and I am concerned that the trend is in the direction of even less humanism. People are becoming less important to us, less central than issues such as, "Can I run this kind of an exercise?" or "What is the latest method being used?" We, as practitioners, are often so deeply afraid of being ourselves that we need techniques, methods, and a handy tool kit to fall back on to give us some security and support so that we don't have to face ourselves as professionals and as human beings.

A few months ago I received a questionnaire from a group of researchers who were looking at OD in a certain class of organization (for example, education, industry, or health). I'm going to be a bit ambiguous in talking about this in order to provide some anonymity. The research used the Delphi technique that involves a series of questionnaires through time where the data from one questionnaire is used in the second, and the data from the second in the third. For the first questionnaire, fifty respondents were chosen—twenty-five well-known OD specialists in the country and twenty-five well-known internal OD people in this particular class of organization. The people were asked to indicate from a long list of OD techniques and methods which ones they would use if they were do to an OD project in a unit in this particular field. I am told by the researchers— and I've had a couple phone conversations with one of them—that many of the twenty-five out of fifty who responded did indicate what techniques or methods they would use. And on the second round, where the questionnaire went to the twenty-five who first responded, a prioritized list of effective methods and techniques derived from responses to the first questionnaire asked, "Please prioritize the list of strategies based on the frequency with which you would use them." Twenty-three of the original respondents replied. Now tell me what sense does that make? To say in advance what technique or method you would use if you were going to do an OD project in a given setting where all you know in advance are some generalities of that particular area, say education, without being on the spot, sensing the people, sensing the organization, the unfolding issues, and so on. And yet twenty-five top consultants, internal and external, responded to this. What does that tell us about our field?

I have a quotation from a fellow who is not an OD practitioner, Phillip Lopate (1976), who has written a book, *Being with Children.* A number of years ago Lopate was assigned to a public school in New York City as an artist-in-residence, a writer, to bring a range of artistic inputs to the school system. He has written this book about his experience. He says in one part of the book, "Too often, it seems to me, studies about how to work with children in creative subjects concentrate exclusively on the exercises or techniques of stimulation, making the techniques appear an end in themselves, segregated from the local political, ethnic, and economic conditions in which the teaching will have to take place. It seems to me that the tasks which one sets for oneself and the children to accomplish, in poetry, drama, filmmaking, painting, or whatever, grow directly out of the unique local situation in which the teacher finds himself and out of the unique personalities of the children—as well as, of course, the national and global currents affecting the society at large. There is no such thing as a 'creative curriculum' divorced from personalities and social context. For me, this is especially so, because I see teaching as a sympathetic exchange which takes place through the medium of personal relationships."

To be able to be relevant in the here-and-now takes a person who is centered, who is sensitive, who is flexible, who has tolerance for ambiguity, and who can stay with the immediate situation and help those with whom he or she is working to again flow with the river.

OD and the Individual

Let me return once again to the conference theme, "making OD operational." I thought, originally, of dealing with the topic, "What is OD?" We all seem to have our own notions of what OD is, and I certainly have mine. I'm sure OD encompasses many different attributes, but to me it centrally includes the following:

First, *a body of humanistic values*—values that say something about human beings, about us as practitioners, and about the people with whom we work in ongoing systems. Second, *personal, interpersonal, organiza-*

tional, and inter-organizational processes deeply rooted in such values. And third, *the possibility of growth (development unfolding) of individuals and of all other social entities* toward ends widely and poignantly yearned for by the individuals within each entity. I think that we try, with our values and with our processes, to help those with whom we work to make explicit (to consciousness-raise) the objectives and purposes that are central to them and to work with them to help these unfold. As I think of words that are related to this conception of OD, the following come to mind, and they cut across the three central attitudes of OD that I have mentioned: common purpose, community, peace, hope, trust, compassion, caring, love, involvement, a sense of competence and of worth, development, fulfillment.

Out of the years of close work I've had with many of you and people like you, I deeply believe that most, if not all, of us have been primarily attracted to OD because of these attributes and because we have felt that our presence might make a difference with individuals, groups, and organizations and the purposes that they hold in common. If I were to ask you, "Why did you move into OD, and why do you stay in OD?," you might give some kind of off-the-cuff surface-level answer. But I think if I could watch you as you function and talk with you of your feeling as you face the agony that we often face in our work, the possibilities of burnout, the tiredness, and the discouragement, I would clearly sense that that which keeps you centered in this work is a real adherence to these aspects of OD and your deep belief that in some small way you can make a difference about things that really matter to you in this life. You are not alone. As each of us plays his or her own small role in this profession, I say once again—as I've said often in speaking and in writing—that the principal instrument that we have to use in this field is ourselves. We do have the tool kit, but the effective use of that tool kit depends on us—the sensitivity, the flexibility, the tolerance of ambiguity, the caring for the humanistic values, the setting of a model of what a human being can be. Very much depends on us and who we are.

Abe Maslow in his last public session, which was at UCLA in 1972, said the following:* "Helping in the first place is a very, very hard job and the helper can be a clumsy fool—the helper can be a hurter. Very frequently it would be best to be Taoistic about helping; to keep your damn hands off

---

*Reprinted with permission of the Maslow estate from *Abraham Maslow: A Memorial Volume*. Published by Brooks/Cole, Pacific Grove, CA 1972.

is frequently the best way to help. To know when to be available and when not is to think of the helper as being available, being a consultant, rather than being the manipulator, controller, interferer, giving orders and telling people what to do. The helper is very frequently just a plain god-damn nuisance—as, for instance, anybody in the ghettos can tell you. Why should it be that the social workers, who want to help, who devote their lives to helping, should be so frequently despised and hated? I've suggested that the Bodhisattvic kind of helping is a reliance on the self-choice of the person, with you the helper being available at the wish of the other, rather than you the helper taking control of the situation and telling people what to do. This implies a kind of humility, also, because in effect what I'm asking here is that the helper becomes a very perfect person. What is implied, therefore, is that one of the paths to being a helper is to become a better and better person in the sense of maturing, evolving, becoming more fully human. If you want to help other people be their best, improve yourself. Cure yourself." Perhaps the first step in making OD operational is to see that we are operational ourselves.

Now in closing I'd like to read to you from Hermann Hesse's (1951) *Siddhartha.* Hesse is a Swiss writer. Perhaps many of you know this story of his. It's a story of a soul's long quest in search of the ultimate answer to the enigma of man's role on earth. After meeting the Buddha, a decision to work out his own destiny and solve his own doubt, the sensuality of a love affair, the temptation of success and riches, the heartache of a struggle with his own son, Siddhartha moves toward self-knowledge. What follows is my editing of the last large number of pages of the book[*]:

> Siddhartha reached the long river in the wood, the same river across which a ferryman [Vasudeva] had once taken him when he was still a young man. He looked into the flowing river. Never had a river attracted him as much as this one. Never had he found the voice and appearance of flowing water so beautiful. It seemed to him as if the river had something special to tell him, something which he did not know, something which still awaited him.

---

[*]By Hermann Hesse, from SIDDHARTHA, copyright © 1951 by New Directions Publishing Corp. Reprinted by permission of New Directions Publishing Corp. Also reprinted by permission of Peter Owen Ltd. London.

Today he only saw one of the river's secrets, one that gripped his soul. He saw that the water continually flowed and flowed and yet it was also there; it was also the same and yet every moment it was new.

[At this point, Siddhartha again meets Vasudeva, the ferryman, who takes him across the river and who invites Siddhartha to stay with him.]

When the sun was beginning to set, [Siddhartha and Vasudeva] sat on a tree trunk by the river and Siddhartha told him about his origin and his life and how he had seen him today after [a terrible] hour of despair. The story lasted late into the night.

"I thank you, [Vasudeva]," said Siddhartha, "for listening so well. There are few people who know how to listen and I have not met anybody who can do so like you. I will also learn from you in this respect."

"You will learn it," said Vasudeva, "but not from me. The river has taught me to listen; you will learn from it, too."

[Siddhartha did learn] from [the river] continually. Above all, he learned from it how to listen, to listen with a still heart, with a waiting, open soul, without passion, desire, judgment, opinions. [Siddhartha] once asked [Vasudeva], "Have you also learned that secret from the river—that there is no such thing as time?"

"Yes, Siddhartha," [Vasudeva] said. "Is this what you mean? That the river is everywhere at the same time, at the source and at the mouth, at the waterfall, at the ferry, at the current, in the ocean, and in the mountains, everywhere, and that the present only exists for it, not the shadow of the past, nor the shadow of the future?"

"That is it," said Siddhartha, "and when I learned that, I reviewed my life and it was also a river."

[Vasudeva] took Siddhartha's hand, led him to the seat on the riverbank, sat down beside him and smiled at the river. "You have heard it laugh," he said, "but you have not heard everything. Let us listen; you will hear more."

They listened. Siddhartha looked into the river and saw many pictures in the flowing water. The river flowed on toward its goal. Siddhartha saw the river hasten, made up of himself and his relatives and all the people he had ever seen. All the waves and water hastened, suffering, toward goals, any goals, to the waterfall, to the sea, to the current, to the ocean and all goals were reached and each one was succeeded by another. The water changed to vapor and rose, became rain and came down again, became a spring, brook and river, changed anew, flowed anew.

Siddhartha had often heard all this before, all these numerous voices in the river, but today they sounded different. He could no longer distinguish the different voices—the merry voice from the weeping voice, the childish voice from the manly voice. They all belonged to each other: the lament of those who yearn, the laughter of the wise, the cry of indignation, and the groan of the dying. They were all interwoven and interlocked, entwined in a thousand ways. And all the voices, the goals, the yearnings, the sorrows, the pleasures, the good and evil, all of them together was the world. All of them together was the stream of events, the music of life.

[Vasudeva's] smile was radiant as he looked at his friend, and now the smile appeared on Siddhartha's face.

From that hour Siddhartha ceased to fight against his destiny. There shone in his face the serenity of knowledge, of one who is no longer confronted with conflict of desires, of one who is in harmony with the stream of events, with the stream of life, full of sympathy and compassion, surrendering himself to the stream, belonging to the unity of all things.

May our continuing awareness of this river as an ongoing symbol for us and of time lend perspective and depth to our important work and to each of us, both professionally and personally. ◄

Some contrasting informal comments on a deeply probing training approach focused on the self, by two participants in a "sensitivity training" program conducted in Ireland, conclude this chapter.

▶ RETURNING TO THE SELF: TWO VIEWS ON SENSITIVITY TRAINING

MR. X: A CONTRADICTION IN TERMS

Any resemblance that this report may bear to any normal report on a training course is purely coincidental. Even the heading "sensitivity training" is a contradiction in terms. Sensitivity is an emotional feeling, rather abstract, extremely difficult to define, and at times highly unpredictable. On the other hand, training conveys an orderly discipline, which controls predictable impulses. Perhaps I am confusing you, but should that be the case, then indeed I am conveying my true impressions of the sensitivity course.

Sensitivity is an emotional exchange between one personality and another personality or group of personalities. We, as individuals, project an image, which is quite a complex one, made up of sound, sight, and motion. We feel that if we use a certain combination of these then, in fact, we convey a certain image or impression to other people.

In reality, what happens? We intend to project a particular image but can we ever be really sure what, in fact, gets over to other people? Professor Massarik set out to guide the thoughts and feelings of the group attending the course into a state of awareness, whereby they might be able to interpret their feelings toward one another and to the group as a whole. This process involved a gentle, and at times, almost imperceptible progression of a group discussion from an exchange of ideas on to an exchange of feelings and emotions.

Then, once the group began to approach a state of sensitive awareness of their own and other people's feelings, it became possible to examine images projected by personalities and see how closely the intended image approached that received by others; altogether an enlightening, stimulating, and at times, somewhat perturbing experience.

Perhaps you are wondering what, in fact, was the advantage of this particular exercise. Well! Let us ponder on the gimmicks and slightly phony managerial approach of a few years back—the sort of managerial attitude based on a textbook approach to given situations and designed to get the boys on your side. What so often happened was that the image projected did not in fact ring true, and the whole exercise failed dismally. Everyone was trying so hard to improve human relationships in industry and yet making so little real progress in this field.

May one then conclude by saying that sensitivity training is a probe in the direction of trying to bring more genuine sincerity into everyday human relationships.

MR. Y: WAITING FOR MASSARIK

A sensitivity course is unlike any other management course. The participants are themselves the tutors and the professor's role is part bystander, part guide, philosopher, and friend. As I tumbled to this at an early stage, I reacted as I did on first seeing *Waiting for Godot,* "What's it all about? Is there going to be any action? Is this a hoax?" Yet, even at that stage, there was a sense of passionate involvement, of compulsive participation. Indeed, I might go on elaborating this comparison, but someone at the course, during his frank appraisal of me, said I was a literary bore. I must be more careful.

Yes! It was that kind of a course—no holds barred. But to begin at the beginning. . . . Professor Massarik opened the course—we called him Fred. He told us who he was, that sensitivity was the understanding of the impact that one person has on another, and that our personalities might be divided into four boxes, one of which we didn't know and that was what other people thought or knew about us. Then he stopped. Was he going to rebuke someone for not paying attention?

There was a silence of some four or five minutes. I looked around at the company and tried to label my companions—some were the bright young hopefuls; others, I surmised, were the lean, shrewd, couldn't-be-put-upon personnel officers, and one or two, looking like caricatures of capitalists in *Krokodil,* had the refulgent shine of having looked into many a balloon glass of expense account brandy. If they raised a hand, one knew instinctively that the index finger would be twitching—the effect of knocking the ash off too many cigars.

The silence grew oppressive. Then there was an explosion. An extrovert among us had grown tired of the silence: What was in it for him? He had come to learn something to enable him to function better. Was there anything to be learned sitting around?

Massarik's face smiled at a pitch between the Cheshire Cat and the Buddha; his shoulders shrugged. Another of us flashed a question at someone he had known for some time and asked if it was true that the other had found him irritating some years back? If so, why? He was answered. There was a rustle of mild irritation against the question—a chain reaction had been set up and we were with it.

From then on—broken only occasionally by short theory lessons from Massarik—we pursued one another. Group members even spoke of certain people being hurt. These were the extroverts among us—the irascible, sharply spoken man vainly trying to hide a heart of gold, the businessman to whom life appeared in shades of black and white.

Then the professor started to question one of us, and gradually the pitch of his voice grew softer. Were we on the verge of an emotional outpouring, a revelation of the depths out of which character is formed? We will never know. There was another outburst—more passionate this time—"I find this awfully embarrassing." The professor's face frowned—a cloud passed over the sunny features. There was, one felt, iron "in them thair hills," if one dug deep enough. "Why did he find it embarrassing?" We were off again. Another hare had been raised—the pack joined in pursuit. The hare twisted and turned, eventually to escape, but in the pursuit the wounds of self-knowledge had been bitten on his back.

For part of the object of this course is a development of the idea "know thyself." Self-knowledge is to most of us a most difficult branch of study. There are no guidebooks. The teachers who know most about us—our intimate friends and immediate relations—are mute of kindness, perhaps. Could one live with one's friends if they told you all they felt about you? Well, one lived with a group who were as frank as could be with one another, and respect and friendship grew during the week rather than diminished.

To return to the Godot image, the meaning of "Waiting for Godot" was what the individual took out of it. Each one of us is as complex and many-sided as Godot, projecting different images to people. The image that one man has of another may be very different from the image another man has—even contradictory. Yet both are true reflections, seen in different mirrors. ◀

Beyond the Horizon

We Cannot See . . . Only Imagine

—*Anonymous*

AS WE LOOK TO OD'S FUTURE, we recognize that uncertainty remains our inevitable leitmotif. Some time ago, a *Peanuts* cartoon cogently made this point. Standing at the pitcher's mound, Charlie Brown looks out on the sand-lot outfield. Lucy is standing there, glove poised for a potential catch; Charlie Brown shouts to her, "If a ball comes your way, don't yell 'I got it!' unless you're sure you've got it." Lucy yells, "I got it!" as a baseball flies in her direction. The ball goes "bonk"—and ineffectually drops three feet behind her. This does not shake Lucy's self-confidence, nor her aplomb. With conviction, she observes that, after all, *there are so many things in life that we can never be sure about* [emphasis added].

In our consideration of issues raised in this book, we surely must agree with Lucy. As consultants we often are expected to become prophets of certainty. The client has a problem; we are called on to "solve" it, and the solution is assumed to provide some measure of certainty. A quiet conspiracy ensues: Both consultant and client would like to see certainty in prospects ahead. Disclaimers and caveats, particularly as stated by the consultant, may prove to be low-key and quickly ignored. It's nice to believe that surely good things *will* happen; both consultant and client would like to think so.

A challenge comes from the financial markets: analysts, CEOs, CFOs, and their spokespersons, who often do a more thorough job in due diligence, explicitly identify future risks, in addition to and beyond hopeful and positive projections. Maybe OD can learn a lesson here. *Sometimes* managers and analysts are good role models, pointing to limitations, although illusion and misapprehension (and even deceit) obviously are by no means unknown in the turbulence of managerial and financial activity.

As we proceed to *imagine* conditions beyond the horizon (we cannot *see*), we will keep in mind the nine Cs and process and a special metaphor—"the Ox." We will conclude considering "The Right Speed" (Weber, 2001b), hard data, and intuition as OD faces an uncertain world. No, we will *not* predict "facts" about OD's future. But we will propose ways for thinking about OD's evolving functions, perhaps as an approach to wisdom management—in contrast to currently rampant information management—to help us cope with whatever it is that "we can never be sure about."

Re-Examining the Nine Cs

Numbers have a special magic. Every instructor is aware that when he or she utters the phrase, "I will now lecture on *five* principles . . ." all hands—with pens or keyboards—move into action, ready to record the expected immortal wisdoms about to be promulgated . . . 1, 2, 3, 4, and 5. (Perhaps because there is a good chance that the instructor will ask, probably on the next exam, "What are the *five* principles that we discussed in class?"—Heaven forbid . . . I can only remember four of them!)

It is evident that in this manner numbers constrain and invite rote recitation. As relates to the nine Cs we run this risk. As antidote, let us return for a moment to Figure 2.1, The Nine-C Field. Here the operative word is "field," and the nine Cs derive their meaning—and provide meaning—specifically *because* they exist within this field. In continuing flow, they interact and influence each other. And in their conceptual structure they are not independent or orthogonal.

To re-emphasize: By way of a visual mode, the nine Cs are *not* to be represented by separate "boxes." It is more difficult, however, to visualize an alternative model.

We need to think about multidimensional space with various Cs overlapping and coalescing, standing out or separating (Bubbles in a lava lamp? Ingredients in a cake mix? Those missionaries in a canoe navigating a stream, escaping from head-hunters? Even hitting a golf ball). Emphasis is placed on the *whole system* and on the interacting forces within this system at a given time. For rigorous considerations of the issues involved, we refer once more to the work of Kurt Lewin (1936, 1951) and to the basic field-theoretic conceptualization (Massarik, 2000).

What does this mean for OD? To recap, we believe that the nine Cs and their inherent overlaps, confluences, and complexities:

- Remind us to look at the *"big picture"* including aspects we have not thought about above and beyond any particular intervention or client relationship;

- Remind us to consider explicitly the *multiple systems* that may make a difference in a particular OD effort; and

- Call on us to focus on selected critical variables and on specific lines of influence that in a given instance form the basis for, let's hope, a successful planned change.

If used properly, the nine Cs constitute a template or *conceptual inventory* of items stored, not necessarily neatly, on the shelves of literature and in the chronicles of practice, to beckon review as a whole, from which we may draw grounding, perhaps wisdom, in each particular OD task.

Information Technology and Wisdom Management

It is old news to refer to "the information explosion" and to IT—information technology—as characteristics of the present era. Gigabytes and gigahertz, megabytes and megahertz are common parlance. The sheer immensity of amounts of information available is beyond human comprehension. For example, a year 2000 article on MSN, the Microsoft Network, recites statistics such as these: number of transactions per minute processed by Compaq's Proliant server running Windows 2000: 505,302; number of ad impressions sold by MSN (February 2001): 6,039,949,000 (Hill, 2001). After all, what's a billion or a trillion or two among friends?

The obvious question is, "So what?" To what end do we need or use all of this information? Money, of course, is one possible answer. Happiness is more elusive. Does OD as a profession look at human happiness, beyond the immediate client's satisfaction? In quick-fix mode or in long-term perspective? We've met few OD consultants who examine the concept and complexities of "happiness" explicitly as a basis for improving their work, even in face of an evident renascence of the topic. As a *New York Times* (Leonhardt, 2001) article points out, "*(in spite of material gains) . . . over the last thirty years, Americans have become somewhat less satisfied with their lives.*"

While this article cites some contemporaneous findings in "happiness research," even Aristotle had ideas that still have a current ring. To paraphrase a 20th Century recap of Aristotelian thought (Crowley, 1989):

> We will be able to get a better insight into human happiness if we first know something about the nature of human beings . . . We always desire happiness for its own sake and never as a means to something else . . . It appears . . . that happiness is something final and self-sufficient, being the end of all action.

A substantial systematic literature on the topic of happiness is available. For example, Freedman (1978), in *Happy People,* points to happiness as a relatively enduring state, but subject to gain and loss, and examines its (non-linear) relationship to factors such as marriage, love, faith, sickness and health, income, education, and work.

The neo-psychoanalyst Erich Fromm (1968) some years ago considered aspects of happiness in *The Revolution of Hope,* with particular focus on "humanized technology" and concerns with "dehumanization" associated with mechanical efficiencies. Notes Fromm, "Efficiency is desirable in any kind of purposeful activity. But it should be examined in terms of the larger systems, of which the system is part" (p. 35).

And in the *American Psychologist,* Sonja Lyubomirsky (2001) asks the eternal question, "Why are some people happier than others?" With focus on cognition and motivation, and upon review of considerable evidence, while noting the complexity of the relationships found, she concludes that, "Self-rated happy individuals appear to be less sensitive to social comparison information—especially unfavorable information—than unhappy ones" (p. 243).

It is our view that OD needs to broaden its horizon, beyond the proximate bounding of entry and contract on one side and intervention and end of engagement on the other, to include basic existential considerations such as happiness. Central among these is the impact of OD on *the happiness of real people in real time,* within and outside the particular organization in which an intervention or change program takes place. This kind of effort indeed calls for processing of information, but beyond that of purposeful wisdom. No one formula or algorithm suffices. Tradeoffs inevitably exist.

Will specified layoffs assure the survival of the company? If so, what is the balance in a "calculus of happiness"? Is it pain of separation, temporary or more extended unemployment, corporate charges taken, risk of bankruptcy of company and its potential impact on all sorts of people: top management, senior citizen investors relying on company's dividend to augment their Social Security, more employees to be "cut loose" (with what opportunities for re-employment)? If the company survives, what other social and economic hazards loom at the horizon? What time frame is our focus?

With conscious awareness of values, OD's role needs to include wisdom management. Here we consider with care the projected effects of interventions in context of other co-acting forces. These forces relate particularly to management decisions and to the nature of encompassing industry, social structure, and economy. We pay attention explicitly to the conditions of happiness, actual and aspired, as experienced and objectively defined by the widest possible spectrum of persons impacted.

As an agenda beyond the horizon, we take nothing for granted. We allot dedicated time to weighing the possible positive and negative consequences of OD's activities for human happiness in *various publics*—while reconsidering selectively the nine Cs. This calls for deeper knowledge and for wisdom beyond the conventional technology of OD intervention—a challenge to the development of the truly competent OD professional.

A Metaphor: The Search and the Ox

More and more, OD finds itself in the company of fields of inquiry beyond its initially defined boundaries. Ethnography and mythology are among these fields. Various authors have chosen to elaborate aspects of the mythic experience with direct focus on OD (Chan Allen, 2001; Marshak, 1994).

One recurring theme in otherwise distinct mythologies is that of "the search" or "the journey" (see Gries, 1984; Osborne, 1989; Pearson, 1989). Some schools of Zen present a metaphor of the search in terms of *ten ox-herding pictures*. We shall offer our version of these pictures in three stages: first, without interpretation (with minimal captions); second, we invite the reader to interpret; and third, we provide one co-author's interpretation[26].

The Ox Herding Pictures

1. I am looking for the ox.

2. I find the tracks.

3. I get my first look at the ox.

4. I catch the ox.

5. I tame the ox.

6. I ride the ox on my way home.

7. I am at home, alone . . . the ox is forgotten.

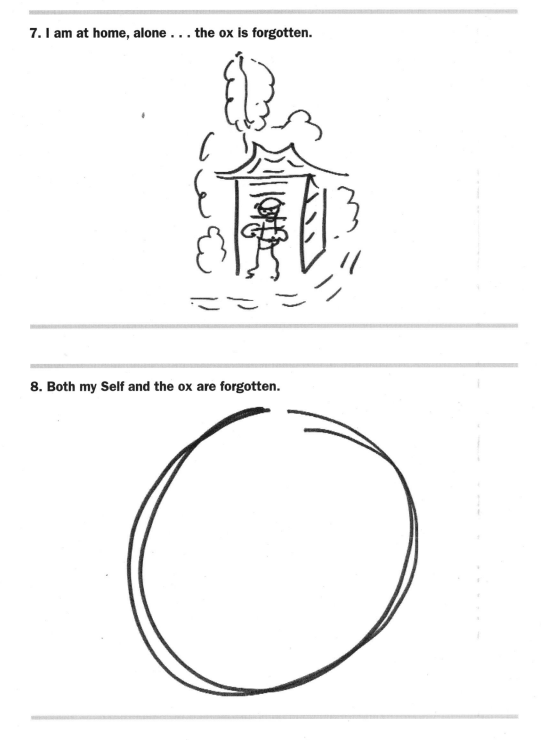

8. Both my Self and the ox are forgotten.

9. I return to the source.

10. With my hands in helpfulness I enter the marketplace.

There is no single meaning in these pictures; no right or wrong answers; no neat statement describing what is "really" happening. We suggest that, with this in mind, the reader now revisit this set of pictures as a whole, and then consider each of them one at a time. We suggest that the reader now review the pictures as a "blank slate" and *think* and *feel* what she or he experiences.

To more directly facilitate this process (some might suggest that here facilitation is altogether out of order), we believe that the reader might consider issues such as the following:

- *Who* is it? Who is doing the looking for the ox?
- What *is* the ox? Who is the ox?
- Can the ox ever be seen? Caught? Tamed? Ridden?
- Is there a "home" at all?
- How and what do we forget?
- Is there "a source"? What might it be?
- What about my "hands in helpfulness"?
- What am I doing? What can I do?
- What is "the marketplace"?
- What do these pictures have in common, if anything?
- Do we need an ox at all?
- Do I like the sequence of these images, or would I prefer some other sequence?
- Does it matter at all?

A co-author's ruminations on the ten ox-herding pictures follow:

I am in an abundant forest. I am not quite sure why I am here. I think I need to find some kind of creature. I see lots of greenery, but not much else. I am very uneasy and uncertain (Picture #1). Then I look down at the ground. There is a pile of brown crumpled leaves in front of me. It looks like some kind of animal has been rummaging through it. Somehow this makes me feel better. As I go a bit along the way, I see footprints . . . not sure what they are, an ox maybe, or an elephant? Does it matter? (Picture #2.)

OK, I think it's an ox. Now I decide I want to find that ox. I keep looking all around, right and left, up and down. Sure . . . there it is . . . I see the back parts of an animal; yes . . . it is an ox! (Picture #3.)

I'm not paying much attention to all that greenery now. I just want to catch that ox. I'm not sure how, but I've got a rope. Maybe I can trip him and then latch the rope about his neck. I'll do it. I hope the rope holds. Can I hold on to the rope? I hope the rope holds. I hope the ox doesn't get loose. What if he does? (Picture #4.)

We've become friends, the ox and I. We sort of talk to each other. Of course we use different "words," but somehow that's ok . . . it seems to work. Some people might say that I "tamed" the ox, but that isn't really so. As the ox and I ride home, we're just going in the same direction . . . both of us want to go to the same place (Pictures #5 and #6). Now I am spending more time at home; I've got to feed the ox twice a day.

Time goes by. And you know . . . I am not clear on whatever happened to the ox . . . haven't seen him for a while. Did he become invisible or something? I kind of miss him . . . it was fun to see him in the field behind the house. He was always nibbling at some sunflowers or on some petunias. Now I am by myself again. By my Self? I have to figure out what that means (Picture #7).

I think I am going around in circles. I see my Self going around in circles. I am with other people, and yet I feel like there is a big circular hole at my middle.

Maybe what I've got to do is empty my Self of all that old stuff. I've got to look at what I used to take for granted. It's all empty, but it's also full. Lots of possibilities.

I've really got to work on this. What about my old pal the ox? (Picture #8.)

I've really got to get back to basics. I used to look for tracks in the forest and ride home on the ox. Why was I doing all of that? There seemed to be good reasons at the time, but lately I'm not sure. Somewhere there are starting points . . . maybe a spring of bright water coming from behind those rocks . . . a seedling growing to be a stately elm . . . clouds becoming a thunderstorm? (Picture #9.)

I've got to get to work! I've got to do things because I *want* to be helpful. There are real people out there, and I've got to take them for what they are. I remember a cartoon in *The Wall Street Journal* a while back: a bearded white-robed "prophet" carries a large lettered sign to the effect "The World Will *Not* End Tomorrow! Deal with It!" I'll take that advice . . . ok, I'll deal with it! (Picture #10.)

OD and the Ox

Having presented some general thoughts and issues related to the ox pictures, I will now present my reflections on the ox as it applies to OD.

As I start a project (be it consulting, research, writing, or whatever), I feel somewhat overwhelmed by the possibilities. Let's consider OD consulting. I know that there is lots of stuff to be looked at. The client tells me something, and even before that I knew something about the client and the organization. There are also other, outside issues. I need some sort of focus. Am I really right for this job? I've got pressures on me. I've got to make a living (Picture #1).

After a while I get some ideas sorted out, like what I think the client wants and what I can contribute. It seems to me that I can trust my intuition. There are bits and pieces of information that I can see ahead of me like the bread crumbs that Hansel and Gretel follow in Grimms' fairy tale. I get some general idea what this engagement could be about, but I still have lots of unanswered questions. I'm finding the tracks (Picture #2).

By now I am getting a better handle. I think what these guys need for starters is some low-key "conflict resolution"—like I'm glimpsing an uninviting messy part of the ox (Picture #3). If we don't deal with these problems first, those covert and cynical battles between the CEO and the head of European operations, there is no way to work on a major change program for the European Division. And that's probably what is needed.

I'd better confront these guys. I arrange meetings separately with the CEO and with the head of European operations. I basically tell each of them (not exactly in these words): If we are going to go forward in this program (with a significant amount of people and resources at stake), we really have to get our house in order at the top. I get a bunch of static—each of the two explains at length why he's right. They don't even want to talk to each other; they just e-mail.

I reflect on my own mixed feelings about conflict. Maybe I would just as soon walk away from all this stuff? But I conclude that I can probably do some good things here. I know Europe well (especially Austria, Germany, and Switzerland), and I think that my style and values really would fit. And I have the needed OD skills, augmented by those of my staff colleagues.

I've got to get hold of my Self and of my doubts about myself. I don't really like to get into conflict, yet I manage to convince myself, the CEO, and the head of European operations that we probably can work it out. We all agree to meet and to discuss openly what's been bothering everybody. I think the ox has been caught, but I'm not sure (Picture #4).

The three of us do a lot of preliminary planning together. My associates and I propose a fairly articulate engagement plan with good flexibility. We then formulate a contract. The CEO decides to "run it by" Legal, but we all know that this is pretty much routine. We have built up mutual trust.

I think I'm really good at diagnosis, so I take the lead in this. We set up an intensive but time-limited diagnostic procedure involving several transcontinental trips. Europe is changing a lot; there is much more turbulence than there used to be. Even the corporate supervisory boards are waking up. And there are more and more mergers and acquisitions and, with mixed emotions, layoffs. The business inevitably is "global," with networked commerce transactions, particularly with former "East bloc" and Asian nations.

Relationships between the CEO, the head of European operations, and me, plus various work groups in the company, are good. We're pretty much "on the same page" as we get into the intervention program. This includes large-scale survey feedback and targeted conflict resolution sessions among European and U.S. managers; not all of them succeed! Growing out of these sessions, we get into all kinds of formal and informal coaching and counseling.

I'm pleased with the way things are going. I feel that we are riding toward a "home" of productive outcomes. "The world is a good place," we all agree (Pictures #5 and #6).

Eventually we wrap up the work we agreed to do. Things beyond our direct control are now happening. There is a sudden drop in demand for the company's principal product. The CEO decides to take early retirement; some say that he did this because an influential securities analyst laid the blame for the demand decline at his doorstep: "Poor strategic decisions," according to the analyst. I didn't agree with this interpretation, but I realized that, beyond the "hard numbers," many unknowns are involved.

I reduce my time load for OD "hands-on" consulting. I'm planning to do a book on OD basics and need to give priority to this task. Also, I really do want more family time. This never seems to be enough, as my wife sees it, and she's probably right.

After a while, I lose track of that company. Presumably the CEO is playing golf somewhere like Bermuda. I hear that the head of European operations has gone back to a brick-and-mortar food processor and distributor as executive VP, probably next in line for CEO.

I do feel out of it. I miss "being there" with these guys, and I miss (would you believe it?) even the battles we used to have. I would not have predicted this. I come around to the obvious query, "What am I all about?"

Yes, I like the place where I sit and scramble among papers, reprints, and books, working on that OD manuscript. I even connect with that greenery and with the forest where I started "seeking the ox." Now I'm in a different space: ox forgotten, self alone (Picture #7).

I am doing a lot of thinking. Causes and consequences? Was I responsible in some way for the CEO retiring early? I know that this question is unanswerable, and I don't believe in guilt. But just the same, I go "round and round" on this. I've got to empty my head of too much past mental debris. I need clarity. I've got to make a fresh start. Blank pages are not bad. An empty circle is not a bad symbol. It's time that I didn't worry all that much about my Self. Or about OD. It's one of those "been there, done that" situations. I know that what I do in my profession links up with all of my Self. I've worked on that; I'm not an automaton, but ok, enough is enough. I need to leave some things alone; I need to make more space: "Both ox and self" are forgotten. The circle is empty (Picture #8).

It's time to address some basic issues, outside my Self. Where did this OD profession actually come from? A post-WWII zeitgeist for democratic ways of managing? Lewin's experiments on group atmospheres? Spirituality in liberal churches? T-groups and sensitivity training? General systems theory? Humanistic values going back to ancient Greece? Studies in coal mines in Britain? All of the above? What did I leave out?

And as I reflect on clients . . . how much do I need to know about an organization's history and culture? About high-tech and low-tech if I'm going to deal with people steeped in their technologies?

I figure out that there is always a source behind the source that I look at. If I see a bubbling spring as the source of the creek, what about the water in the mountain behind the rock from which the spring emerges? What about the rainfall that got the water there in the first place? No end to this stuff, and it does seem important to "return to the source" (Picture #9).

I've come quite a way on this journey since I first tried to find this ox, saw his tracks, found him, tamed him, rode him home, forgot about him and about my Self, looked for ephemeral sources.

I need to go to work once more "doing OD." I'm not sure who made up the phrase "reality bites"; now it's bitten, even if the ox did not bite me. I pay attention to the helpfulness that I hope can flow from my hands: to what I can do for others, to the marketplace, to people, and to organizations in the world around me (Picture #10).

As I go to work, I know that there is no end to all this, no end to the journey. There are forests and mountains, creeks and streams, high points and low points, arrows and circles, happy clients and unhappy clients, old style interventions and new ones, good outcomes and poor ones. Lots of hurdles in between. Whatever happens, I've got to stay in the middle of it if I want to keep growing in what I know and in what I do, as I go beyond "the ox."

Beyond the Ox

In any journey, there is a question of how rapidly it moves along its course. How long does it take me to find the ox? How quickly do I confront the marketplace? Speed itself, as word and as value, is relative. Is it better to fly subsonically in planes that are more environment-friendly and less noisy, or is it better to fly supersonically, beat the sun across the continents, and deal with the boom through the sound barrier? Jonathan Weber (2001b), in *The Industry Standard,* takes the following position: "One of the lessons that many take from the dot-com implosion is that speed isn't so important after all . . . [at one point in time] it was a truism that big prizes went to the first mover. Even if you weren't in front you had better get a Net strategy, and fast. Today it sometimes seems that slow but steady really is the better way."

Yet elsewhere there is continuing emphasis on the need to respond promptly to rapidly changing conditions. In OD one may consider a simultaneous two-track approach: *First* there is the persistent requirement to thoroughly understand the underlying conditions that motivate human behavior and the conditions of mankind, individually and in large systems. *Second,* there is the urgency—in light of deep knowledge and rooted wisdom—to act quickly and with focus, when it really matters.

This dual stream of knowing and intervening affects all aspects of the OD process, from initial client contact to diagnosis and throughout any and all programs intended to bring about positive outcomes. Neat "packages" tend to fall apart if they do not respond in timely manner to forces embedded in the nine Cs.

We need new ways for addressing the dilemmas and solutions unleashed by the managerial and social environment of a new century. These challenges, we believe, call for continuing response at three principal levels:

- Formal education and training in the theory and practice of OD, for both consultants and academics[27];

- Skillful programming and dedicated design and presentation of special learning events and workshops in professional organizations, including national and regional OD Networks, NTL, the American Psychological Association, ASTD (American Society of Training Directors), Academy of Management, and others; and

- Purposeful use of the Internet and distance learning, while strengthening the "human touch" and genuine interaction among people, ever at the core of the OD vision.

The powerful pull of numbers also needs to be considered. Weber (2001a, p. 7) notes, "The challenge for managers in the age of data is twofold: to build sophisticated data collection and analysis into every piece of the business process; and to know when to ignore the numbers and go with the gut."

This lesson applies to OD: We need to build sophisticated modes of approach (quantitative and qualitative) into the OD process *and* we need to know when to ignore what has been preplanned. We rediscover the imperative "to go with the gut" as we seek to do something novel, different, and creative with purpose and with wisdom. Like Lucy, we never can be sure. But we can keep on trying to make things better in our work that for each of us beckons just beyond our horizon.

Endnotes

Preface

[1] The proposition that "there is nothing so practical as a good theory" is widely cited and is best understood by considering Lewin's work in broad perspective. In this vein, Alfred J. Marrow (1969) notes that this statement is frequently cited "without any idea of its source." It is, however, well exemplified by works such as Lewin's (1951) *Field Theory in Social Science: Selected Theoretical Papers*, which begins with a conceptual treatment of formulization and progress in psychology and then moves into applied fields such as learning, psychological ecology, including applications to the study of social trends and child development, and group dynamics, effectively linking theory and practice throughout.

[2] It is our present intent simply to draw attention to the complex nature of words, on paper and as spoken, as crucial aspects in organization development. The literature in this connection is substantial and expanding. As a reminder, we draw attention to selected classics: Brown (1958), Chase (1938), Chase & Chase (1954), Cherry (1966), Church (1961), Hayakawa (1949), Korzybski (1933), Morris (1950), and Sapir (1921).

[3] The issue as to what are "humanistic values" is pervasive. An exemplary statement appears in the *Journal of Humanistic Psychology* (Greening, 2001), which considers as well the topic of "positive psychology." OD activities honoring these postulates would be viewed as consistent with value positions implicit in these postulates. Concepts such as empowerment, involvement, participation in decision making, self-development, personal growth, goal commitment, seeking meaning and creativity in work, and positive change in Appreciative Inquiry are illustrative.

Chapter 1

[4] By its very nature, the term "systems" covers vast congeries of apparently distinct concepts and operations. Indeed, it is this breadth and encompassing quality that provides strengths and wide applicability to "systems." Yet these advantages can be vitiated by casual and imprecise use of the term, especially if a clear referent is lacking. While the literature is extensive, we point to a few classics as basis for thought and further exploration: Berrien (1968), Buckley (1968), Cleland & King (1972), Miller (1978), and von Bertalanffy (1968). Numerous texts in management and organization theory partake of the systems concept, particularly as relates to the open systems notion. To this end, see *Systems Research,* the official journal of the International Federation for Systems Research, and *General Systems,* the yearbook of the Society for General Systems Research.

[5] As Alfred J. Marrow (1969) points out, at early stages in the field's development, Gestalt theory took the position that "perception could and should be considered in terms of 'forms of organized wholes,' rather than in terms of 'aggregates of distinct parts'" (p. 13). Such wholes—as a whole system or an actual organization—constitute a previously unfathomed entity with their own emerging qualities that could not be fully understood simply by examining constituent parts, e.g., by looking at the characteristics of individual members of the system or organization. Following are some classic references: Ellis (1950), Koffka (1935), and Köohler (1947, 1969). For critical analysis and further review, see also Arnheim (1986) and Ash (1983).

Chapter 2

[6] An unpublished monograph relating to Lewin's work is *Lewin's Legacy/Lewin's Potential: A Source Book,* by Fred Massarik (ed.), based on NTL's fiftieth anniversary event, Bethel, ME, July 7–9, 1997. Included among the twenty-five contributions is Roger Evered's "An Exploration of the Origins of Lewinian Science," including

a complete list of Lewin's writings. (E-mail fred.massarik@anderson.ucla.edu for information.)

Chapter 3

[7] Considering fundamental philosophic perspectives, including the views of Kant, Calvin, and Luther, and the asserted "evils of selfishness," Fromm (1947) concludes, "not only others but we ourselves are the 'object' of our feelings and attitudes. . . . Love of others and love of ourselves are not alternatives. On the contrary, an attitude of love toward themselves will be found in all those who are capable of loving others" (p. 129).

[8] The literature on the self-concept is prodigious. To provide some indication of its scope and range, the following are varied examples: Friedman (1998), Jenkins (1996), Metzner (1986), Moustakas (1956), Pelham & Swann (1989), Rosenberg (1979), Suls (1993), and Wylie (1961).

[9] Entire courses and curricula are devoted to these topics. For perspective, the following provide starting points—classic and more recent—for further study. On the topic of classic psychoanalysis/Freud, see Holt & Peterfreund (1972), Lauzon (1962), Levitas (1965), and Sulloway (1979). On the topic of life history approaches, see Baltes & Schaie (1973), Erikson (1975), Sheehy (1995), and White (1964). On the topic of general personality theory, see Argyris (1974), Hall, Loehlin, Manosevitz, & Locke (1985), Pervin & John (2001), and Segal (1997).

[10] While research on "small groups" currently continues, much literature on T-groups (specifically with related variants and alternative nomenclature, e.g., sensitivity training, human relations laboratory methods, encounter groups, etc.) goes back to the 1960s and 1970s. For instance, see Bradford, Gibb, & Benne (1964), Dyer (1972), Golembiewski & Blumberg (1977), Lieberman, Yalom, & Miles (1973), Siroka, Siroka, & Schloss (1971), and Weschler & Reisel (1960). These methods are essentially experiential, involving important unstructured phases as well as focused interventions. In assessment of outcomes, it becomes clear that much depends on the deep and intuitive understanding of individuals and group process by the trainer/facilitator rather than the application of prescribed techniques.

Chapter 4

[11] In the diagram, the aspects of the self are represented as generally synonymous with Lewin's "innerpersonal regions" (see Leeper, 1943, pp. 209–210). For our

purposes, they represent tension systems and dimensions of the personality as relevant *at a given time.* Also see Massarik, 1972.

[12] We must remind ourselves that often "the" consultant is not singular either. Obviously in many engagements multiple consultants are involved. This generates a potentially complex set of relationships among consultants (not always a "team," sometimes with rivalries rampant) and between each specific consultant and the client system as a whole and with particular clients, one at a time and in coalitions. In different context but with helpful insights, see Roller and Nelson, 1991.

Chapter 5

[13] By way of example, one may examine most any organizational behavior text and find an array of citations and explications associated with change and related theoretic positions, for instance, contingency models, Force Field analysis, stages of group development, change-complexity environmental models, and many more.

[14] See Massarik, 1976. This paper's position also speaks to the matter of "change management versus OD," noting that as far back as the 1970s and before, OD and its emphasis on humanistic organization has been linked as well with the wholeness of the organization, "bottom line goals included." Throughout, tradeoffs in goal attainment must be kept in mind, as different populations are affected differently by a particular intervention or change effort.

Chapter 6

[15] For classic formulations in this context, see McGregor, 1985. For the traditional source on motivational factors associated with processes noted, see Maslow, 1987.

Chapter 7

[16] For a more detailed explanation, see Massarik, 1997, pages 235–258.

Chapter 8

[17] While there is little recent literature under the explicit heading of "sociometry," the method continues to be useful. For classic references, see Moreno, 1960, especially pages 153–180 and 221–226; and Fox, 1987, especially pages 102–112.

[18] For example, see Hook, 1943, especially chapters IX and XI; and Benson, 1974, especially pages 3–24 and 207–230.

[19] For sample diagnosis checklists focused on topics such as organization climate (including planning, decision making, conflict management, leadership configurations, communications, and control procedures), group processes (including teams, goals, unions, and supplier and customer relationships), and individual factors (including rewards and patterns of need satisfaction). For more information, e-mail fred.massarik@anderson.ucla.edu.

[20] For generic issues relating to experiential learning, see Torbert, 1972. For a brief but systematic view on case study, see Yin, 1984. There is, of course, the widely accessible literature on case study learning associated with Harvard University. For example, see Ewing, 1990, especially pages 219–233.

[21] A succinct classic statement on equifinality appears in von Bertalanffy, 1968, pages 132–134.

Chapter 9

[22] In the folklore of behavioral science, this is often talked about as "the law of the hammer," i.e., "give a kid a hammer and most everything looks like a nail."

[23] For technical detail on the survey, email: fred.massarik@anderson.ucla.edu.

Chapter 10

[24] Within a substantial literature, the following are illustrative: Crocker, Charney, & Chiu, 1984; Schmidt & Finnigan, 1992. For a conceptual and historical overview focused on the germinal work of W. Edwards Deming, see Gabor, 1990.

[25] Classic references in the "group" field's beginning are Lewin, Lippitt, & White, 1939; and Lewin, 1947, especially pages 19–28. Numerous versions have been reprinted in many forms, particularly in social psychology readings books.

Chapter 12

[26] Co-author Fred Massarik is indebted to the extensive work of Joseph Campbell and to Jonathan Young, particularly to the latter's interpretations in courses on mythic stories. Massarik's ox-herding interpretation, as follows, is his own.

[27] For instance, Warner Burke et al., Columbia Teachers College, Benedictine University, NTL-American University, Case Western Reserve, etc.

Bibliography

Adler, M.J. (1978). *Aristotle for everybody*. New York: Macmillan. (See especially Chapter 5.)

Ahmad, A. (1972). *Management and organization development: A behavioral science approach*. New Delhi, India: Rachna Prakashan.

Allaire, Y., & Firsirotu, M.E. (1989, Spring). Coping with strategic uncertainty. *Sloan Management Review, 10*(3), 7–16.

Argyris, C. (1957). *Personality and organization*. New York: Harper & Brothers.

Argyris, C. (1971). *Management and organizational development: The path from xa to yb*. New York: McGraw-Hill.

Argyris, C. (1974, Fall). Personality vs. organization. *Organizational Dynamics*, pp. 2–17.

Arnheim, R. (1986, July). The two faces of Gestalt psychology. *American Psychologist, 41*(7).

Ash, M.G. (1983). *The emergence of Gestalt theory: Experimental psychology in Germany, 1890–1920*. Ann Arbor, MI: UMI Dissertation Abstracts International, 43(9).

Baltes, P.B., & Schaie, K.W. (1973). *Life-span developmental psychology: Personality and socialization.* New York: Academic Press.

Beckhard, R., & Harris, R. (1987). *Organizational transitions.* Reading, MA: Addison-Wesley.

Beer, M. (1980). *Organization change and development: A systems view.* Santa Monica, CA: Goodyear.

Benson, L. (1974). *Images, heroes and self-perceptions.* Englewood Cliffs, NJ: Prentice Hall.

Berrien, F.K. (1968). *General and social systems.* New Brunswick, NJ: Rutgers University Press.

Blake, R., & Mouton, J.S. (1983). *Consultation* (2nd ed.). Reading, MA: Addison-Wesley.

Block, P. (2000). *Flawless consulting* (2nd ed.). San Francisco, CA: Jossey-Bass/Pfeiffer.

Bouglé, C. (1926). *The evolution of values.* New York: Henry Holt.

Bradford, L., Gibb, J.R., & Benne, K.D. (1964). *T-group theory and laboratory method.* New York: Wiley.

Brown, R. (1958). *Words and things.* Glencoe, IL: The Free Press.

Buckley, W. (Ed.). (1968). *Modern systems theory for the behavioral scientist: A sourcebook.* Chicago, IL: Aldine.

Bugental, J.F.T., & Zelen, S.L. (1950, June). Investigations into the "self-concept": I. The W-A-Y technique. *Journal of Personality, 18,* 483–498.

Burke, W.W. (1982). *Organization development: Principles and practices.* Boston, MA: Little, Brown.

Chan Allen, R. (2001). *Guiding change journeys.* San Francisco, CA: Jossey-Bass/Pfeiffer.

Chase, S. (1938). *The tyranny of words.* London: Methuen.

Chase, S., & Chase, M.T. (1954). *Power of words.* New York: Harcourt Brace.

Cherry, C. (1966). *On human communication.* Cambridge, MA: MIT Press.

Cheung-Judge, M.-Y. (2001). The self as an instrument: A cornerstone for the future of OD. *OD Practitioner, 33*(3), 11–16.

Chung, K.H., & Megginson, L.C. (1981). *Organizational behavior: Developing managerial skills.* New York: Harper & Row.

Church, J. (1961). *Language and the discovery of reality.* New York: Random House.

Clampitt, P.G. (2000). *Communicating for managerial effectiveness* (2nd ed.). Thousand Oaks, CA: Sage.

Cleland, D.I., & King, W.R. (1972). *Management: A systems approach.* New York: McGraw-Hill.

Crocker, O.L., Charney, S., & Chiu, J.S.L. (1984). *Quality circles.* New York: New American Library.

Crowley, J.F. (1989). *The changing world of philosophy.* Belmont, CA: Wadsworth. (See especially pages 60–61.)

Csikszentmihalyi, M. (1990). *Flow: The psychology of optimal experience.* New York: Harper & Row. (See especially chapters 4, 5, 6, and 7.)

Cummings, T.G., & Worley, C.G. (1975). *Organization development and change* (5th ed.). St. Paul, MN: West.

Dalton, L., & Greiner, L. (1970). *Organizational change and development.* Homewood, IL: Irwin/Dorsey.

Davis, M.K. (undated). *Change management: Not your father's OD.* Available: www.prodn.org/~handouts/notyourfathersod2.html [last accessed May 26, 2001]

Deal, T.E., & Kennedy, A.A. (1982). *Corporate cultures.* Reading, MA: Addison-Wesley.

Dones, L. (2001, May 14). Strategy can be deadly. *The Industry Standard,* pp. 74–75.

Duck, J.D. (2001). *The change monster.* New York: Crown.

Dyer, W.G. (Ed.). (1972). *Modern theory and method in group training.* New York: Van Nostrand Reinhold.

Eddy, W.B. (1981). *Public organization behavior and development.* Cambridge, MA: Winthrop.

Ellis, W.D. (1950). *A source book of Gestalt psychology.* New York: Humanities Press.

Emery, F., & Trist, E. (1975). *Toward a social ecology.* London: Plenum. (See especially page 38.)

Erikson, E.H. (1975). *Life history and the historical moment.* New York: W.W. Norton.

Evered, R. (1997). An exploration of the origins of Lewinian science. In F. Massarik (Ed.), *Lewin's legacy: A source book.* Unpublished monograph.

Ewing, D.W. (1990). *Inside the Harvard Business School.* New York: Random House.

Farias, G., & Johnson, H. (2000). Organizational development and change management: Setting the record straight. *Journal of Applied Behavioral Science, 36*(3), 376–379.

Feldman, S. (1959). *Mannerisms of speech and gesture.* New York: International Universities Press.

Fox, J. (Ed.). (1987). *The essential Moreno reader.* New York: Springer.

Freedman, J. (1978). *Happy people: What happiness is, who has it, and why.* New York: Harcourt Brace Jovanovich.

French, W.L., & Bell, C.H., Jr. (1999). *Organization development: Behavioral science interventions for organization improvement* (6th ed.) [originally published 1973]. Englewood Cliffs, NJ: Prentice Hall.

French, W.L., Bell, C.H., Jr., & Zawack, R.A. (1978). *Organization development: Theory, practice, and research.* Dallas, TX: Business Publications.

Friedman, J.A. (1998). *The origins of self and identity: Living and dying in Freud's psychoanalysis.* Northvale, NJ: Jason Aronson.

Fromm, E. (1947). *Man for himself.* New York: Rinehart.

Fromm, E. (1968). *The revolution of hope: Toward a humanized technology.* New York: Harper.

Gabor, A. (1990). *The man who discovered quality.* New York: Times/Random House.

Gellermann, W., Frankel, M.S., & Ladeson, R.F. (1990). *Values and ethics in organization & human systems development: Responding to dilemmas in professional life.* San Francisco, CA: Jossey-Bass.

Gillespie, R. (1991). *Manufacturing knowledge: A history of the Hawthorne experiments.* Cambridge, MA: Cambridge University Press.

Gleick, J. (1987). *Chaos: Making a new science.* New York: Viking.

Goldstein, J. (1993). Beyond Lewin's force field: A new model for organizational change interventions. In F. Massarik (Ed.), *Advances in organization development, vol. II* (pp. 72–88). Norwood, NJ: Ablex.

Golembiewski, R.T., & Blumberg, A. (1977). *Sensitivity training and the laboratory approach* (3rd ed.). Itasca, IL: F.E. Peacock.

Goodstein, L., & Burke, W.W. (1991, Spring). Creating successful organization change. *Organizational Dynamics*, pp. 9–13.

Gorer, G. (1955). *Exploring English character.* New York: Criterion.

Gray, J.L., & Starke, F.A. (1988). *Organizational behavior: Concepts and applications.* Columbus, OH: Merrill.

Greening, T. (2001, Winter). Five basic postulates of humanistic psychology. *Journal of Humanistic Psychology, 41*(1).

Gries, F. (1984). Knights of the first crusade. In *The knight in history* (pp. 21–46). New York: Harper & Row.

Gubrium, J.F., & Holstein, J.A. (Eds.). (2001). *Handbook of interview research.* Thousand Oaks, CA: Sage. (See especially Chapters 4 and 5.)

Hall, C.S., Loehlin, J.C., Manosevitz, M., & Locke, V.O. (1985). *Introduction to theories of personality* (3rd ed.). New York: Wiley.

Hamel, G. (2000, June 12). Reinvent your company. *Fortune*, p. 98.

Hayakawa, S.I. (1949). *Language in thought and action.* New York: Harcourt Brace.

Hersey, P., Blanchard, K., & Johnson, D.E. (1996). *Management of organizational behavior.* Englewood Cliffs, NJ: Prentice Hall.

Hesse, H. (1957). *Siddhartha.* New York: New Directions.

Hill, G.C. (2001, May). Slouching tiger, hidden dragon. *eCompany*, p. 60.

Holbrook. S. (1956). *The Columbia.* San Francisco, CA: Comstock.

Holt, R.R., & Peterfreund, E. (Eds.). (1972). *Psychoanalysis and contemporary science: An annual of integrative and interdisciplinary studies, vol. 1.* New York: Macmillan.

Hook, S. (1943). *The hero in history.* Boston, MA: Beacon Press.

Horney, K. (1937). *The collected works.* New York: W.W. Norton. (See especially Volume 1, pp. 13–78.)

Huey, J. (1993, April 5). Managing in the midst of chaos. *Fortune*, p. 38.

Huse, E.F. (1980). *Organization development and change* (2nd ed.). St. Paul, MN: West.

Jenkins, S.R. (1996, January). Self-definition in thought, action, and life path choices. *Personality and Social Psychology Bulletin, 22*(1), 99–111.

Joas, H. (2000). *The genesis of values.* Chicago, IL: University of Chicago Press.

Johnson, S., & Blanchard, K.H. (1998). *Who moved my cheese?* New York: Putnam.

Kanter, R.M. (1983). *The change masters.* New York: Touchstone.

Kaplan, A. (1998). *The conduct of inquiry.* New Brunswick, NJ: Transaction. (See especially pp. 3–12, 126–130, and 294–326.)

Kardiner, A. (1945). *The psychological frontiers of society.* New York: Columbia University Press. (See especially Chapter VIII.)

Kardiner, A. (1955). *The individual and his society.* New York: Columbia University Press. (See especially pages 5–12 and Chapter II.)

Koffka, K. (1935). *Principles of Gestalt psychology.* New York: Harcourt Brace.

Köohler, W. (1947). *Gestalt psychology.* New York: Mentor.

Köohler, W. (1969). *The task of Gestalt psychology.* Princeton, NJ: Princeton University Press.

Koolhas, J. (1982). *Organization dissonance and change.* New York: Wiley. (See especially page 69.)

Korzybski, A. (1933). *Science and sanity: An introduction to non-aristotelian systems and general semantics.* Lancaster, PA: Science Press.

Kroeber, A.L., & Kluckhohn, C. (1963). *Culture: A critical review of concepts and definitions.* New York: Vintage/Random House.

Kuriloff, A.H. (1972). *Organizational development for survival.* New York: American Management Association.

Lauzon, G. (1962). *Sigmund Freud: The man and his theories.* Greenwich, CT: Fawcett.

Leeper, R.W. (1943). *Lewin's topological and vector psychology.* Eugene, OR: University of Oregon Monographs.

Leiter, K. (1980). *A primer on ethnomethodology.* New York: Oxford University Press.

Leonhardt, D. (2001, May 19). If richer isn't happier what is? *New York Times.*

Levitas, G.B. (1965). *The world of psychoanalysis* (2 vols.). New York: George Braziller.

Lewin, K. (1935). *Dynamic theory of personality.* New York: McGraw-Hill. (See especially pages 206–211.)

Lewin, K. (1936). *Principles of topological psychology* (Fritz Heider and Grace Heider, Trans.). New York: McGraw-Hill.

Lewin, K. (1938). *The conceptual representation and the measurement of psychological forces.* Durham, NC: Duke University Press.

Lewin, K. (1947). Frontiers in group dyanamics: Concept, method and reality in social science, social equilibria and social change. *Human Relations,1*(1).

Lewin, K. (1951). *Field theory in social science: Selected theoretical papers.* New York: Harper & Brothers.

Lewin, K. (1963). *Field theory in social science.* London: Tavistock.

Lewin, K., Lippitt, R., & White, R.K. (1939). Patterns of aggressive behavior in experimentally created social climates. *Journal of Social Psychology, X,* 271–299.

Lieberman, M.A., Yalom, I.D., & Miles, M.B. (1973). *Encounter groups: First facts.* New York: Basic.

Lopate, P. (1976). *Being with children.* New York: Bantam.

Luft, J. (1984). *Group process: An introduction to group dynamics* (3rd ed.). Mountain View, CA: Mayfield.

Luthan, F. (2002). *Organizational behavior.* New York: McGraw-Hill/Irwin.

Lyubomirsky, S. (2001, March). Why are some people happier than others? *American Psychologist, 56*(3).

MacLeod, R.B. (1964). Phenomenology: A challenge to experimental psychology. In T.W. Wann (Ed.), *Behaviorism and phenomenology.* Chicago, IL: University of Chicago Press.

March, J.G., & Simon, H.A. (1958). *Organizations.* New York: Wiley. (See especially pages 140–141 and 169.)

Margulies, N., & Raia, A.P. (1972). *Organizational development: Values, process, and technology.* New York: McGraw-Hill.

Margulies, N., & Raia, A.P. (1978). *Conceptual foundations of organizational development.* New York: McGraw-Hill.

Marrow, A.J. (1969). *The practical theorist: The life and work of Kurt Lewin.* New York: Basic.

Marshak, R.J. (1994, Summer). The tao of change. *OD Practitioner, 26*(2).

Marshall, I., & Zohar, D. (1997). *Who's afraid of Schrödinger's cat?* New York: Quill/William Morrow.

Maslow, A. (1972). *Abraham Maslow: A memorial volume.* Pacific Group, CA: Brooks/Cole.

Maslow, A. (1987). *Motivation and personality* (3rd ed.). Reading, MA: Addison-Wesley.

Massarik, F. (1968). *Functional ambiguity and the cushioning of organizational stress.* Los Angeles, CA: University of California at Los Angeles, School of Management.

Massarik, F. (1972). The "natural" trainer: A systematic-normative view. In W.G. Dyer (Ed.), *Modern theory and method in group training* (NTL Learning Resources Series). New York: Van Nostrand Reinhold.

Massarik, F. (1976). The humanistic organization: From soft-soap to reality. In H. Meltzer & F.R. Wickert (Eds.), *Humanizing organizational behavior* (pp. 231–249). Springfield, IL: Charles C. Thomas.

Massarik, F. (1981). The interviewing process re-examined. In P. Reason & J. Rowan (Eds.), *Human inquiry* (pp. 201–206). New York: Wiley.

Massarik, F. (1983). Seeking essence in executive mind. In S. Srivastva (Ed.), *The functioning of the executive mind.* San Francisco, CA: Jossey-Bass.

Massarik, F. (1993). *Advances in organization development, vol. II.* Norwood, NJ: Ablex.

Massarik, F. (Ed.). (1997). *Lewin's legacy/Lewin's potential: A source book.* Proceedings from the NTL 50th Anniversary Event, Bethel, ME.

Massarik, F. (2000). Field theory. In A.E. Kazdin (Ed.), *Encyclopedia of psychology.* New York: American Psychological Association and Oxford University Press.

McGregor, D. (1960). *The human side of enterprise.* New York: McGraw-Hill.

McGregor, D. (1985). *The human side of enterprise: 25th anniversary printing.* New York: McGraw-Hill.

McLean, A., Sims, D., Mangham, I., & Tuffield, D. (1982). *Organization development in transition: Evidence of an evolving profession.* New York: Wiley.

Meltzer, H., & Wickert, F.R. (Eds.), *Humanizing organizational behavior.* Springfield, IL: Charles C. Thomas.

Merton, R.K., et al. (1981, May). Qualitative and quantitative social research: Papers in honor of Paul F. Lazarsfeld. *Contemporary Sociology, 10*(3).

Metzner, R. (1986). *The unfolding self: Varieties of transformative experience.* Novato, CA: Origin Press.

Middlemist, R.D., & Hitt, M.A. (1981). *Organizational behavior: Applied concepts.* Chicago, IL: Science Research Assoc.

Miller, J.G. (1978). *Living systems.* New York: McGraw-Hill.

Miner, J.B. (1980). *Theories of organizational behavior.* Hinsdale, IL: Dryden.

Moreno, J.L. (Ed.). (1960). *The sociometry reader.* Glencoe, IL: The Free Press.

Morris, C. (1950). *Signs, language and behavior.* New York: Prentice Hall.

Moustakas, C.E. (Ed.) (1956). *The self: Explorations in personal growth.* New York: Harper & Brothers.

Naisbitt, J., & Aburdene, P. (1985). *Re-inventing the corporation.* New York: Warner.

Nichols, M.P. (1995). *The lost art of listening.* New York: Guilford.

Olson, E., & Eoyang, G. (2001). *Facilitating organization change: Lessons from complexity science.* San Francisco, CA: Jossey-Bass/Pfeiffer.

Osborne, M.P. (1989). Journey to the underworld. In *Favorite Greek myths* (pp. 45–50). New York: Scholastic.

Pearson, C.S. (1989). The hero's journey. In *The hero within: Six archetypes we live by.* New York: Harper & Row. (See especially pages 1–24.)

Pei, M. (1998, Dec.) Whole Systems HRIS training. *IHRIM Journal* 2(4), 33–45.

Pelham, B.W., & Swann, W.B., Jr. (1989, October). From self-conceptions to self-worth: On the sources and structure of global self-esteem. *Journal of Personality and Social Psychology, 57*(4), 672–680.

Pepper, S.C. (1958). *The sources of value.* Berkeley, CA: University of California Press.

Pervin, L.A., & John, O.P. (Eds.). (2001). *Handbook of personality* (2nd ed.). New York: Guilford.

Plounick, M.S., Fry, R.E., & Burke, W.W. (1982). *Organization development: Exercises, cases, and readings.* Boston, MA: Little, Brown.

Prigogine, I., & Stengers, I. (1984). *Order out of chaos: Man's new dialogue with nature.* New York: Bantam.

Reinventing America. (1993, January 19). *Business Week.*

Roethlisberger, F.J., & Dickson, W.J. (1946). *Management and the worker: An account of a research program conducted at the Western Electric Company, Hawthorne Works, Chicago.* Cambridge, MA: Harvard University Press.

Rokeach, M. (1973). *The nature of human values.* New York: The Free Press.

Roller, B., & Nelson, V. (1991). *The art of co-therapy: How therapists work together.* London: Guilford. (See especially pages 11–28, 75–87.)

Rosenberg, M. (1979). *Conceiving the self.* New York: Basic.

Rosenthal, P. (1984). *Words and values.* New York: Oxford University Press.

Rothwell, W.J., Sullivan, R., & McLean, G. (Eds.) (1995). *Practicing organization development: A guide for consultants.* San Francisco, CA: Jossey-Bass/Pfeiffer.

Sadler, P.J., & Barry, B.A. (1970). *Organisational development.* London: Longmans, Green.

Sanjek, R. (Ed.). (1990). *Fieldnotes.* Ithaca, NY: Cornell University Press.

Sapir, E. (1921). *Language: An introduction to the study of speech.* New York: Harcourt Brace.

Schaffer, R.H. (1988). *The breakthrough strategy.* Cambridge, MA: Ballinger.

Schein, E.H. (1985). *Organizational culture and leadership.* San Francisco, CA: Jossey-Bass.

Schein, E.H. (1997). *Organizational culture and leadership* (2nd ed.). San Francisco, CA: Jossey-Bass.

Schmidt, W.H., & Finnigan, J.P. (1992). *The race without a finish line.* San Francisco, CA: Jossey-Bass.

Schmuck, R.A., & Miles, M.B. (1976). *Organization development in schools.* San Francisco, CA: Jossey-Bass/Pfeiffer.

Segal, M. (1997). *Points of influence: A guide to using personality theory at work.* San Francisco, CA: Jossey-Bass.

Senge, P. (1990). *The fifth discipline: The art and practice of the learning organization.* New York: Currency/Doubleday.

Sheehy, G. (1995). *New passages: Mapping your life across time.* New York: Random House.

Sikes, W., Drexler, A.B., & Grant, J. (1989). *The emerging practice of organization development.* Alexandria, VA: NTL/San Francisco, CA: Jossey-Bass/Pfeiffer.

Siroka, R.W., Siroka, E.K., & Schloss, G.A. (Eds.). (1971). *Sensitivity training and group encounter.* New York: Grosset & Dunlop.

Smith, H. (1992). *Forgotten truth: The common vision of the world's religions.* San Francisco: Harper Collins.

Snyder, C.R., & Ingram, R.E. (Eds.) (2000). *Handbook of psychological change: Psychotherapy processes and practices for the 21st century.* New York: Wiley. (See especially Chapter 1.)

Spradley, J.P. (1979). *The ethnographic interview.* New York: Holt, Rinehart & Winston.

Strasser, S. (1963). *Phenomenology and the human sciences.* Pittsburgh, PA: Dusquene University Press.

Steers, R.M. (1984). *Introduction to organizational behavior.* Glenview, IL: Scott Foresman.

Sulloway, F.J. (1979). *Freud, biologist of the mind.* New York: Basic.

Suls, J. (Ed.). (1993). *Psychological perspectives on the self, volume 4: The self in social perspective.* Hillsdale, NJ: Erlbaum.

Tannenbaum, R., Margulies, N., & Massarik, F. (Eds.) (1985). *Human systems development.* San Francisco, CA: Jossey-Bass.

Thomas, L. (1974). *The lives of a cell.* New York: Penguin.

Torbert, W.R. (1972). *Learning from experience.* New York: Columbia University Press.

Varney, G.H. (1977). *Organization development for managers.* Reading, MA: Addison-Wesley.

von Bertalanffy, L. (1968). *General system theory: Foundations, development, applications.* New York: George Braziller.

Von Clausewitz, K. (1965). *War, politics and power* (E.M. Collins, Trans.) Washington, DC: Regnery. (See especially pages 115–118.)

Weber, J. (2001a, March 26). The numbers game. *The Industry Standard,* p. 7.

Weber, J. (2001b, April 30). The right speed. *The Industry Standard,* p. 5.

Weschler, I.R., & Reisel, J. (1960). *Inside a sensitivity training group.* Los Angeles, CA: University of California at Los Angeles, Institute of Industrial Relations.

White, R.W. (Ed.). (1964). *The study of lives.* New York: Atherton.

Worren, N.A.M., Ruddle, K., & Moore, K. (1999). From organizational development to change management: The emergence of a new profession. *Journal of Applied Behavioral Science, 35,* 273–286.

Wylie, R.C. (1961). *The self concept: A critical survey of pertinent research literature.* Lincoln, NE: University of Nebraska Press.

Yin, R.K. (1984). *Case study research.* Thousand Oaks, CA: Sage.

About the Authors

ⓕred Massarik, Ph.D., professor emeritus at UCLA's Anderson School of Management, is a behavioral scientist with roots in a wide range of disciplines: psychology, anthropology, sociology, applied social research, and group dynamics. His ongoing interests include the direct study of human experience (with focus on phenomenology and the work of Edmund Husserl), pedagogy and teaching, group process, and examination of the historical roots of the applied behavioral sciences (with special interest in the germinal work of Kurt Lewin), seeking significant positive change in the human condition.

Dr. Massarik has been a member of the Academy of Certified Social Workers; a past president and treasurer of the American Psychological Association, Division 32; a past president of the Association for Humanistic Psychology; a past director of the Division of Applied Behavioral Science at the University Extension of UCLA; and is active in both the NTL Institute and the Organization Development Network.

He has published extensively on topics such as leadership and organization, human systems, group process, and on various social work and community planning specialties. He is managing editor of *Self-Help and Self-Care* (Baywood Publishing) and has previously edited the journals *Small Group Behavior* (Sage) and *Interpersonal Development* (Karger).

He has served as an external consultant to firms such as McKinsey and Andersen and teaches and consults worldwide to corporate and family businesses with assignments in Switzerland, Germany, Austria, Hungary, the UK, Ireland, Japan, India, Nepal, and the United States.

Dr. Massarik received both his Ph.D. (in psychology) and his master's degree (in sociology) from UCLA. He has also undertaken advanced studies at the Bureau of Applied Social Research at Columbia University and at the Institute of Social Research at the University of Michigan.

ⓜarissa Pei-Carpenter, Ph.D., has spent the last sixteen years consulting to a myriad of organizations on both coasts of the United States and in Western Europe. Her satisfied client list includes companies like AT&T, Toyota, Exxon Chemical, Allied Signal, Rockwell International, Unocal, Orange County Transportation Authority, Amgen, and the American Heart Association.

She uses her Ph.D. in organizational psychology to help individuals, groups, and companies help themselves—in areas like strategic planning/management decision making, quality and continuous improvement, cross-functional and self-directed teamwork, information systems implementation, and cross-cultural diversity.

In addition to consulting, Dr. Pei-Carpenter has also taken her experience into the academic world, teaching as a graduate school professor at Boston University Brussels, European Business School, Claremont College, Antioch University, California School of Professional Psychology, and, most recently, at the Anderson Graduate School of Management at UCLA. Her course repertoire includes managerial interpersonal communication, organization development, systems thinking, environment and ethics, negotiation and conflict resolution, diversity in organizations, and group theory and teamwork.

Dr. Pei-Carpenter can also be seen on several ABC, Fox, and Discovery channel TV specials, including "Out of Control People," "Surveillance in the Workplace" and "Busted on the Job." She has also been a featured speaker for the Management Centre Europe, the Institute of International Research, the Deming Group, and the American Society of Quality. Her keynote speeches include:

- Diversity at Work. . .Why We Just Can't Get Along?
- Is It Still a Man's World in Business. . .The Implications of Women Working With Men At Work

- Balance. . .The Difference Between Wanting It All and Having It All
- Finding Ways to Motivate People at Work. . .A Futile Exercise?
- Leadership and Management—Joy and Ecstasy
- Why Do People Do Stupid Things at Work?

About the Editors

William J. Rothwell, Ph.D., is president of Rothwell and Associates, a private consulting firm, as well as professor of human resource development on the University Park Campus of The Pennsylvania State University. Before arriving at Penn State in 1993, he was an assistant vice president and management development director for a major insurance company and a training director in a state government agency. He has worked full-time in human resource management and employee training and development from 1979 to the present. He thus combines real-world experience with academic and consulting experience. As a consultant, Dr. Rothwell's client list includes over thirty-five companies from the *Fortune 500.*

Dr. Rothwell received his Ph.D. with a specialization in employee training from the University of Illinois at Urbana-Champaign, his M.B.A. with a specialization in human resource management from Sangamon State University (now called the University of Illinois at Springfield), his M.A. from the University of Illinois at Urbana-Champaign, and his B.A. from Illinois State University. He holds lifetime accreditation as a Senior Professional in Human Resources (SPHR), has been accredited as a Registered Organization Development Consultant (RODC), and holds the industry designation as Fellow of the Life Management Institute (FLMI).

Dr. Rothwell's latest publications include *The Manager and Change Leader* (ASTD, 2001); *The Role of Intervention Selector, Designer and Developer, and Implementor* (ASTD, 2000); *ASTD Models for Human Performance* (2nd ed.) (ASTD, 2000); *The Analyst* (ASTD, 2000); *The Evaluator* (ASTD, 2000); *The ASTD Reference Guide to Workplace Learning and Performance* (3rd ed.), with H. Sredl (HRD Press, 2000); *The Complete Guide to Training Delivery: A Competency-Based Approach*, with S. King and M. King (Amacom, 2000); *Human Performance Improvement: Building Practitioner Competence*, with C. Hohne and S. King (Butterworth-Heinemann, 2000); *Effective Succession Planning: Ensuring Leadership Continuity and Building Talent from Within* (2nd ed.) (Amacom, 2000); and *The Competency Toolkit*, with D. Dubois (HRD Press, 2000).

Roland Sullivan, RODC, has worked as an organization development (OD) pioneer with nearly eight hundred systems in eleven countries and virtually every major industry. Richard Beckhard has recognized him as one of the world's first one hundred change agents.

Mr. Sullivan specializes in the science and art of systematic and systemic change, executive team building, and facilitating Whole System Transformation Conferences—large interactive meetings with 300 to 1,500 people. Over 25,000 people have participated in his conferences worldwide; one co-facilitated with Kristine Quade held for the Amalgamated Bank of South Africa was named runner-up for the title of outstanding change project of the world by the OD Institute.

With William Rothwell and Gary McLean, he is revising one of the field's seminal books, *Practicing OD: A Consultant's Guide* (Jossey-Bass/Pfeiffer, 1995). The first edition is now translated into Chinese.

He did his graduate work in organization development at Pepperdine University and Loyola University.

Mr. Sullivan's current interests include the following: Whole system transformation, balancing economic and human realities; discovering and collaborating with cutting-edge change focused authors who are documenting the perpetual renewal of the OD profession; and applied phenomenology: developing higher states of consciousness and self-awareness in the consulting of interdependent organizations.

Mr. Sullivan's current professional learning is available at www.rolandsullivan.com.

Kristine Quade is an independent consultant who combines her background as an attorney with a master's degree in organization development from Pepperdine University, and years of experience as both an internal and external OD consultant.

Ms. Quade draws from experiences in guiding teams from divergent areas within corporations and across many levels of executives and employees. She has facilitated leadership alignment, culture change, support system alignment, quality process improvements, organizational redesign, and the creation of clear strategic intent that results in significant bottom-line results. A believer in whole systems change, she has developed the expertise to facilitate groups ranging in size from eight to two thousand in the same room for a three-day change process.

Recognized as the 1996 Minnesota Organization Development Practitioner of the Year, Ms. Quade teaches in the master's programs at Pepperdine University and the University of Minnesota at Mankato and the master's and doctoral programs at the University of St. Thomas in Minneapolis. She is a frequent presenter at the Organization Development National Conference and also at the International OD Congress and the International Association of Facilitators.

Index

A

Aburdene, P., 81

Accountability issue, 54

Adler, M. J., 60

Alderfer, C. P., 162

Allaire, Y., 39

American Psychological Association, 32

American Psychologist (Lyubomirsky), 198

Anderson, N. J., 167

Appreciative Inquiry: (Watkins and Mohr), 128

Argyris, C., 164

Aristotle, 11

Aristotle for Everybody (Adler), 60

Arrow communication approach, 155–156

The art and science of 360 degree feedback (Lepsinger and Lucia), 158

Awareness Model (Johari), 30–33, 31*fig*

Axelrod, R., 135

B

Backup method model, 117

Bakke decision, 184

Bartee, E. M., 162

Be (Anderson), 168, 169

Beckhard, R., 147

Behavioral science: defining, 5–6; Johari Model of Awareness, 30–33, 31*fig*; positioning, 7*fig*

Being with Children (Lopate), 186

Bell, C. H., Jr., 89, 162

Benne, K. D., 114, 164

Bennis, W., 164

"Beyond Lewin's Force Field: A New Model for Organizational Change Interventions" (Goldstein), 65

Bigframe company, 15–16

Billable time period agreement, 88

Blake, R., 115, 122, 164

Blanchard, K. H., 59

Block, P., 137

BouglÈ, C., 10

Bradburn, N. M., 133

Bradford, L., 114

Brewer, B., 36

British Airways story, 65–66

239